641.59715
WAT

Simple Pleasures

from our

Maritime Kitchens

→ *Anecdotes, History & Recipes* ←

JULIE V. WATSON

RAINCOAST BOOKS

Vancouver

Raincoast Books is a member of CANCOPY (Canadian Copyright Licensing Agency). No part of this publication may be reproduced, stored in a retrieval system or transmitted in any form or by any means without prior written permission from the publisher, or, in case of photocopying or other reprographic copying, a license from CANCOPY, One Yonge Street, Toronto, Ontario, M5E 1E5.

Raincoast Books acknowledges the ongoing financial support of the Government of Canada through The Canada Council for the Arts and the Book Publishing Industry Development Program (BPIDP); and the Government of British Columbia through the BC Arts Council.

Cover and text design by Gabi Proctor/DesignGeist
Author photo by John Watson

National Library of Canada Cataloguing in Publication Data

Watson, Julie V., 1943-
    Simple pleasures from our Maritime kitchens

    Includes index.
    ISBN 1-55192-461-7

    1. Cookery, Canadian—Maritime style. I. Title.
TX715.6.W37 2002   641.59715   C2002-910548-X

Library of Congress Catalogue Number: 2002091848

Raincoast Books
9050 Shaughnessy Street
Vancouver, British Columbia
Canada   V6P 6E5
www.raincoast.com

In the United States:
Publishers Group West
1700 Fourth Street
Berkeley, California
94710

At Raincoast Books we are committed to protecting the environment and to the responsible use of natural resources. We are acting on this commitment by working with suppliers and printers to phase out our use of paper produced from ancient forests. This book is one step towards that goal. It is printed on 100% ancient-forest-free paper (100% post-consumer recycled), free of processed chlorine and acid, and supplied by Rolland; it is printed with vegetable-based inks by Transcontinental. For further information, visit our website at www.raincoast.com. We are working with Markets Initiative (www.oldgrowthfree.com) on this project.

Printed and bound in Canada.

1 2 3 4 5 6 7 8 9 10

Table of Contents

Dedication

*The passing of several good friends and mentors
caused me to pause and reflect on the many
supporters who have helped me along the path
to a successful writing career:*

*Hartwell Daley — night school teacher who
taught me the importance of "The Plan."*

*Evie Davidson — whose spin on storytelling
and faith in me brought joy.*

*Gerry Auld — entrepreneur who made it
possible for me to take advantage of
opportunities.*

*Larry Jackson — who encouraged, helped
and welcomed me as one of a special group
of creators.*

*I will always remember them for their belief
in my abilities and willingness to verbalize it.
Thanks, guys. Hope you are enjoying the
new world you have gone to.*

Introduction

Researching Canadian history I find myself a tad annoyed. It is as if women did not exist. Their contributions had no value unless, like Cap'n Molly Kool (who in 1939 became the first registered female sea captain in North America; second in the world), they took on "man's work." How did society fall into a pattern of failing to recognize all contributors, acknowledging only a select few?

Reading through the histories it often seems women were worked to death, bearing numerous children and then feeding, clothing, nurturing, educating and making a home for them. Many men, particularly those deemed "successful," went through more than one wife as they pursued success.

The books tell us of men at war, on the water, in the field, minding the business, practising the "professions" or posturing in the political arena, but rarely do they mention the women of the Maritimes who stood behind them and looked after hearth and home, who with little recognition nourished and nurtured. The women's base of operations was the kitchen — the heart of the home. As well as putting three squares on the table each day, here the wives, mothers and housekeepers fashioned clothing, knitted gloves, hooked mats, made candles, oversaw lessons, balanced household accounts, earned pin money, hosted neighbours to plan "good works" and, most important of all, provided a warm, welcoming haven for kith and kin.

All of these activities and many more are the base of treasured memories captured between these covers. Not an academic journal, this is a collection of simple things, small moments in time that I have attempted to bring to life.

As well, I have written about the cooks and the food and its preparation that are our heritage. The culinary mix that finds its way into Maritime kitchens is influenced by many migrations: the Native peoples were first, followed by the French, English, Scottish, Dutch, Irish, German, Danish, Chinese, Japanese, Lebanese and, as time went by, others of more nationalities than can be named here. United Empire Loyalists fled the American Revolution, just as other refugees have left their homelands to seek a better life for their families in the years since. Thus the kitchens of the Maritimes have long been a treasure trove of skill and understanding of foods and cooking.

…

Basic skills of the past are often lost, and indeed are not needed today. However, by going back to old cookbooks, talking to cooks and listening to memories we learn to appreciate the valuable contributions women made and the level of their skill and dedication.

But we cannot just take a recipe from the 1700s or even the 1800s and whip it up for dinner. Ingredients have changed, become more refined. Flour was more coarsely ground. Yeast has undergone many changes. Sugar, too, was not as dried and refined; in fact, it often tasted like molasses. Bread did not last long. It would sour or mould — thus the need to make bread frequently and use up leftovers in puddings and such.

As long as chickens laid eggs they were kept; those that went to the kitchen could be old and scrawny. Milk was not homogenized, or pasteurized, for that matter. Animal feed was more natural, so the taste was very different.

Early Maritimers were true scratch cooks. Until the mid-1800s almost everything had to be made at home. Need bread? Start by gathering hops and making yeast. Planning a turkey or chicken meal? Start by killing and plucking the bird. Spices, dried fruits, and fresh fruits such as lemons, oranges and bananas were a luxury, even for the wealthy. Other ingredients we take for granted, such as baking soda and baking powder, are relatively modern inventions.

Changes happened a lot more slowly than in the 20th century. Open-hearth fireplaces were replaced with inserts that burned wood or coal, then with stoves, but it took decades for change and a long while before electricity became the norm.

Running water must have seemed a miracle. Just imagine how homemakers in Charlottetown might have felt when the law that required two water-filled wooden buckets to be hung by the front door of every home to fight fires, common due to the wooden construction and open-hearth cooking and heating, was no longer policed.

In the early days there was no refrigeration. Meat and fish had to be salted or dried to preserve them. Vegetables and fruits had to be eaten quickly, dried or stored in cold cellars.

It is no wonder that pickles and jams were such an important part of life. Peas and beans, dried in attics or spare rooms, were highly valued as they could cook for a long time and replace or stretch meats. The climate had a direct effect on the role of the family cook and the running of the household. Not only did she have to feed the family, she had to put things by to ensure survival through the long, cold winter.

Summer was a time of incredibly hard work. Contrary to many opinions, women did not limit their work to the home. They were involved in all aspects of running the family farm, fishing boat or business. At harvest time, be it on land or sea, every hand was required. Whether clearing land, bringing in crops, preparing fish for drying or to market, or working in the canning factories to preserve the lobster, the women were needed.

On top of these demands, they preserved foods as they were harvested or caught and they fed families often extended by an influx of workers or visitors. This constant drain on their time brought a need to simplify meal preparation. Boiled dinners and stews that could be left for hours at a time became the norm. Food that was convenient to transport was vital. Whether the menfolk were out in the fields or bobbing up and down on the ocean, they needed a nourishing "lunch" to sustain them. Breads, double-crusted pies and substantial sweets like solid cakes, cookies and such were staples. Sugars and other sweeteners were expensive and used very carefully. Thus, the food had a tarter, different taste.

The demand for ways to preserve food led to the use of ice. Cut from local bays and rivers, it was used in root cellars and later in iceboxes. As refrigeration became common practice it brought about tremendous change. Imagine the satisfaction of having a glass of lemonade chilled with ice chips or a dish of homemade ice cream on a hot summer Sunday afternoon.

Refrigeration also brought a change in basic meals served at home. Salted, smoked or pickled meats had dominated for generations. Now people were able to enjoy lighter, fresh meat more often. Society moved away from the heavy basics: breads, suet puddings, dumplings, fried and baked goods. "Made dishes," the forerunner of the casserole, joined the family menu.

Throughout history a bountiful table symbolized success. For the middle class this meant dinners that would literally put many of us today under the table, in pain from overeating. Dinner could mean a soup or two, a "made dish," roast meat and some fish, with hot bread on the side, followed by dessert of pie or pudding and rich cakes. This was the era of the stay-at-home wife dedicated to her home and family.

As society changed, many women began working outside the home and "cooking" evolved into fast preparation — fried, heavy foods were quick and tasted good. Ingredients became more refined, packaged and quicker and easy to use. The advent of food science brought us baking soda and baking powder, which along with finely milled flour and refined sugar forever changed the product of the art of cake making from the solid and firm to the light and delicate. These changes led to a whole industry that created new cooking utensils, pans and such. Tea biscuits and muffins displaced crumpets and fried cakes. While the changes were not bad, they did lead to a less healthy mode of eating that we are combatting today. We are recognizing that basic foods such as fresh fruit and vegetables, whole grains and less-processed or refined ingredients are better for us and, frankly, more satisfying.

…

The focus of this book is, in part, on ingredients produced here in the Maritimes, but it's not limited to them. After all, even back in the days of sailing ships we had access to ingredients from around the world. Oranges and lemons came in the same ships as rum.

If I quote from an old cookbook, book or magazine, it is one that either originated in the Maritimes or was used in a Maritime home. The anecdotes and stories all have that same Maritime link.

That alone ensures a vast array of material. Just as the ocean currents and weather patterns mix it up, creating extreme conditions that can vary vastly within a relatively small area, diverse immigration patterns create many cultural differences.

Recipes are often family heirlooms, representing the family history and tradition. In many cases the owner is fully acknowledged, but in others anonymity was requested and granted. As one proud lady said, "If the cousins ever know I gave out that pickle recipe, when I wouldn't give it to them over the years, I would be drummed out of the family!"

A great source of inspiration and material has been handwritten personal journals, diaries and scrapbooks. Oral tradition is a vital part of kitchen life. Many recipes were learned by rote at the side of mother or grand-mother. Even today in our modern, high-tech era, pen and paper appear at a gathering as recipes are exchanged.

In the past, recipes were written for the basic ingredients available. In the early days that was wild game and scant store-bought supplies. Today we have fantastic availability of exotic ingredients.

Many early cookbooks contained hints on such things as how to put out a petticoat fire — after all, women cooked before open fires in huge fireplaces and their clothes were prone to catching fire. Our concerns are safe water and the growing use of additives and pesti-cides that compromise the safety of some food products.

The growing popularity of organic foods is testimony to a return to an appreciation of the basics — good food, well-prepared and served with love. If I have one wish for readers it is that they visit their local markets, try organic foods and get back to basics. Make a nourishing soup or stew, get your kids making cookies, haul out some of those tried-and-true recipes and put them back into your reper-toire. Most importantly, work to create a kitchen that is the heart of the home — you can give your family and friends no greater gift than that of kinship, warmth and caring: simple pleasures from *your* kitchen.

January

— Always an exciting time of new beginnings.

Here woman's empire is within, and here she shines the household star of the poor man's hearth; not in idleness, for in [North] America, of all countries in the world, prosperity depends on female industry.

— Emily Beavan (1845), New Brunswick pioneer and author who, with a wild-goose quill and maple bark ink, wrote a handbook for prospective settlers. She is considered New Brunswick's answer to Ontario's Susanna Moodie and gives the best and liveliest account of life in New Brunswick in the first half of the 19th century, although her writings were never as widely distributed.

I make the same resolution almost every year: to be grateful for the small things that enrich my life, to enrich the lives of those around me and to take pride in myself and the things I do. Entertaining special folks kicks the year off to a good start and gives me the sense of living that resolution!

…

JANUARY 1 — New Year's Day brunch is a casual way to wrap up a hectic holiday season. A midday meal has the double advantage of being not too early after a night of celebrating and sending folks on their way midafternoon, so that we can get into our comfies for a relaxing evening before heading back to the reality of work. There is something wonderfully decadent about donning one's jammies before rustling up leftovers for supper.

The brunch came into being as a meal served after an early-morning hunt. Those 18th-century folk knew what they were doing. The hunt pretty well died out in the Maritimes by the late 1800s but the midday feasting carried on. Perfect for entertaining.

One or two extra-special dishes make for a festive affair to start the year right. Lobster, for instance, blends perfectly with breakfast ingredients to create unique omelettes that are quick and easy to fix. Add a few more regional specialties and you have a perfect Maritime repast. Complete the menu with warm muffins or biscuits, assorted cheeses and a variety of fruits and favourite teas or coffees. A sparkling Maritime wine is perfect to toast the incoming year.

BAKED LOBSTER OMELETTE

Serves 8

My friend Kasey Wilson shared this while we were giving cooking classes at Stanhope Beach Lodge on Prince Edward Island. Easy to expand for up to a dozen by preparing half the recipe again in an 8 x 8-inch baking dish. Have the smaller omelette ready to go into the oven when you take out the first and you will be able to offer piping hot "seconds" on the whistle.

½ cup	flour	125 mL
1 tsp	baking powder	5 mL
1 dozen	eggs	1 dozen
5 drops	Tabasco sauce	5 drops
1 lb	lobster meat, cut into bite-size pieces (if using frozen lobster meat, thaw and drain well)	450 g
1 lb	Monterey Jack cheese, grated	450 g
2 cups	creamed cottage cheese	500 mL
½ cup	melted butter	125 mL
	salt and freshly ground pepper	

Preheat oven to 400°F. Butter a 9 x 13-inch baking dish. Sift flour with baking powder. Beat eggs and add Tabasco. Stir in flour, lobster, cheeses and butter, season with salt and pepper. Pour mixture into baking dish, bake for 15 minutes. Reduce heat to 350°F, bake for 15 minutes longer or until omelette is puffed and light golden brown on top. Cut into 12 squares, serve at once.

SMOKED OYSTER OR MUSSEL PÂTÉ

Whip up hours ahead, ready to grab from the fridge when guests arrive. Place in a bowl in the centre of a plate and surround with crackers. Add a spreading knife for a delicious munchie.

4 oz	cream cheese, room temperature	100 g
4 oz	smoked oysters or smoked mussels, chopped	100 g
1 tbsp	mayonnaise	15 mL
1 tbsp	milk	15 mL
1 tbsp	minced green onion	15 mL
	pepper	
	squeeze of lemon juice	

Blend all together. Chill at least 4 hours.

Tip

Set a definite time when guests are to arrive so that you can plan when the food is to be served, AND an ending time so that they don't linger into dinner! "Please come to brunch 11 a.m. to 2 p.m." should do the trick.

Around the Kitchen Table

Before we go to bed on New Year's Day our family gathers around the kitchen table and toasts our New Year's resolutions — just for the fun of it. Not everyone has such a positive take on the resolution concept. A good friend, Evie Davidson, brought laughter and tears to thousands of people through her weekly CBC Radio commentary, *Life's Like That*, a glimpse into the wacky life she shared with her large Prince Edward Island family. We spent hours expounding over our shared love of the written word. When not delighting in her wit face to face, I would time my breakfast so that I enjoyed her broadcast take on life at my kitchen table.

JANUARY 1, 1993 — I've made New Year's resolutions for at least 45 years. As much as I hate to admit it, I've never followed through on any of them. So this year I've decided to face it: for me, making New Year's resolutions is a waste of time, so I'm not making any. I hope Gordon has the same idea, because often his resolutions get to be my nightmare!

Take last year. Gordon resolved that he wouldn't bring any more work home from the office, so we could spend our evenings together.

I was all for it — until Gordon discovered the world of board games, and instead of coming through the door hefting his briefcase every night he came through the door hefting a new board game. The TV was off and Gordon had the latest game set up before we finished supper, let alone the dishes. Scrabble, Trivial Pursuit, Pictionary, Scruples, Balderdash — believe me, we went through them all.

After a couple of weeks the entire family had board game burn-out. Except Gordon. Finally, when he could no longer convince anyone to play with him, he gave up board games and discovered another world. The world of cooking.

I was all for that, too. Every day Gordon would call me from the office and tell me not to make supper. He had a special recipe he was going to try. I loved the food he cooked. I

A convenient way to purchase lobster is as frozen meat in cans or vacuum packs. The price may seem high, but this is pure meat, already cooked, so there is no shrinkage or waste. Check the label carefully to find out exactly what is enclosed. Tail, knuckle and claw meat are ideal when you want to see the meat, have chunks or flaunt the showiness of lovely white flesh with its sensuous red trim. Cheaper packs, with leg meat or broken pieces, are fine for sandwiches or recipes where you would be cutting the lobster into small pieces.

Immerse the unopened can in cold water to thaw. It takes a couple of hours. Before assembling your dish, open the can and drain meat well.

loved relaxing with a book while he cooked the food. But after a few weeks, I got fed up with spending hours in the kitchen cleaning the mess he left.

The night Gordon made a marble cake, "Like the kind mother used to make," as he put it, was the last straw. At 2 a.m., while I was scrubbing splattered batter off the walls, I told "Gourmet Gordon" his cooking days were over unless his mother came to clean up the mess, which wasn't likely.

So the next night Gordon found another pastime. He came through the door all smiles, with a new set of strings for his old fiddle. "Guess what!" he said. "I'm going to restring that old fiddle of mine, brush up on my technique and you and I are going to work up a repertoire. You on the piano, me on the fiddle. It'll be fun."

That seemed innocent enough, and I went along with it. I thought it would be nice, both of us playing "Minute Waltz" and "The Flight of the Bumble-bee." Romantic. But "The Flight of the Bumble-bee" became "The Rage of the Killer Hornet." Night after night, Gordon stood over me, shaking his fiddle bow and screaming like a conductor gone mad whenever I hit a wrong note, until I was ready to give Maestro Gordon a do-re-mi right on the chin.

You can't imagine how happy I was the night Gordon came home hefting his briefcase and set up shop on the dining room table. He had work to do from the office, I was in the kitchen making supper, and all was right with the world.

So don't tell me about New Year's resolutions. I've seen it all, heard it all, been through it all. In fact, when I get home I think I'll hide Gordon's fiddle.

— Evie Davidson

An Apple a Day ...

Wartime shipping difficulties have cut off, or seriously cut down, Canada's export of apples, so we must find our markets at home. The government is trying to help with the sale of the crop by a campaign of education — distributing apple recipes, pointing out that the old adage about "an apple a day" is founded on scientific truth. So on the farm, whether we have apples of our own or must buy what we use, we could possibly increase our consumption with definite benefit to the family's health."

— *Farmer's Magazine*, January 1940

APPLE SALADS

WALDORF SALAD:

Mix 1 cup tart apples and 1 cup celery, both cut into small dice. Moisten with salad dressing. Add 1/2 cup broken walnut meats just before serving.

GREEN PEPPER AND APPLE SALAD:

Combine 1 cup diced apples, 1 cup cut celery and 1/2 cup shredded green pepper. Moisten with salad dressing.

APPLE AND DATE SALAD:

Use 4 parts diced apple to 1 part dates cut in similar-size pieces (chopped walnuts may be added). Mix and moisten with salad dressing.

APPLE-PEANUT SALAD:

Mix diced apple with half as much cut celery. Make a dressing of 5 tablespoons lemon juice mixed with 1 tablespoon peanut butter. Mix dressing through apples and celery and serve on lettuce garnished with chopped peanuts.

Tip

Need to crush peppercorns? Place them in a resealable bag and roll with a rolling pin.

Old Wooden Spoon

Old wooden spoon
nipped, gauged, a hairline crack on the
uppermost right
your left side
worn down, worn out

I detect a spot of char
remnants of an old flame
possibly the price of too much heat

How many mistresses have held you tight
and what kind of pots have you been privy to?

Perchance you have pleasured
in the sweet smells of pickling
not to mention
heated memories of winter stews

You if anyone would understand
how a meal cooked with love sustains
us forever, while
a smidgeon of hard-heartedness
can sour molasses
forging a bitter flavor in our souls

You've likely lost count of the tears shed
as you mixed and blended them into
the daily offerings
or the number of times you fell
or were thrown to the floor

Were you replaced by something new and shiny
or were you treasured for being just as you are?

Oh wooden spoon
I wish you could talk and tell the world

the stirrings of a woman's heart.

— Sandra Phinney

From My Kitchen Window

On a cold winter night, after the storm, the view from my back-of-the-house kitchen sink is magnificent as snow-laden trees and fields take on an ethereal glow in the moonlight. In winter, I turn off the lights and open the drapes so that we will be greeted by as much morning light as possible when the alarm goes at 6 a.m. On this night, the street light at the front of the house draws my attention to its yellow glow. Snow, gently falling, glistens like sparkling diamonds floating down from the night sky. Better plan a hearty breakfast for the snow-moving crew; it's sure to drift in by morning.

Nana Farrell's Old-Fashioned Biscuits

One of my earliest and most vivid memories is visiting my Great-Aunt Milly and Great-Uncle Larry's place. They lived in a simple farmhouse that had seaweed piled around the foundation for winter insulation, in Donaldston, P.E.I. Walking in the door, you were usually greeted by the delightful aroma of hot biscuits, baked in a wood-fired Enterprise range. Unlike my seven siblings, I didn't slather butter on each half of the golden mounds, but simply drizzled them with lots of rich, dark molasses. The mouth-watering treats literally melted in your mouth and, even today, biscuits and molasses are my special comfort food.

As a preteen I learned to make tea biscuits under the tutelage of my maternal grandmother, Nana Farrell. Originally from Antigonish, Nova Scotia, she later moved to Waltham, Massachusetts, but would often come to the Island for extended visits.

Nana Farrell's biscuits were unrivalled for their succulent texture and taste. I can still see her stooped, slight figure as she sifted the flour, salt and baking powder, cut in the shortening and made a well in the middle before adding the milk. She never measured the ingredients — she knew the portions by heart. Dusting her work-roughened hands with flour, she'd knead the sticky dough, adding more flour or milk as needed. She'd sprinkle flour onto the bread board, set the clump of firm dough on top, fold it a couple of times, then deftly flatten the mound with the red-handled rolling pin. Nana Farrell would use an old baby-food tin, dipped in flour, to cut the biscuits and I'd place them on the pan and gently pierce the tops with a fork — in a cross pattern. (My nine-year-old daughter now performs this task when I make biscuits with her.)

After 10 to 12 minutes of anxiously peering in the oven window, Nana Farrell would see that her biscuits had risen to double their original height and turned a light brown. She'd remove them from the oven and, when they were barely cool enough to handle, I'd cradle a crusty biscuit in my hand and break it open. A steamy fragrance would waft forth and soft layers of pillowy perfection would be

Back from their honeymoon, Virginia and Bill invited Mother and Dad to their first Sunday dinner in the new home. Driving out to the old place that night, Dad remarked reflectively: "They're better off than we were, Mother, when we set up house-keeping."

And indeed, Virginia and Bill are better off! Thirty years ago, Mother and Dad drove straight from the church to their first home — in Dad's horse and buggy. Virginia and Bill have a smart car. There was no radio in the parlor of that home ... no glistening white electric refriger-ator in the kitchen ... no auto-matic water-pump ... no electric iron ... no washing machine. One of Mother's first purchases was a broom. Virginia had bought one too. But she also has something Mother never heard of as a bride — an electric vacuum cleaner that saves elbow grease and keeps the house brighter.

— *Farmer's Magazine,*
January 1940

revealed. After drizzling the requisite molasses, I didn't take much time to savour the taste-tempting treat, but would guzzle it down and ask for more!

Now, when my mother, Anne, and her sisters — Isabel, Laura or Mary — come to visit me, I often make the biscuits as a special treat, serve them with molasses and we all savour the tasty morsels. For the ultimate Maritime taste experience, serve with tea (or coffee).

— Susanne MacDonald

...

Born and raised in Prince Edward Island, Susanne MacDonald writes for Harlequin Temptations as Meredith March. She wrote this recipe while residing in Moncton, New Brunswick.

4 cups	white flour	1 L
½ cup	shortening	125 mL
8 tsp	baking powder	40 mL
1 ⅔ cups	milk	400 mL
1 tsp	salt	5 mL

Preheat oven to 475°F. Sift flour, baking powder and salt into large bowl. Add shortening and cut into the flour mixture until texture is mealy. Make a well in the centre and pour in milk. Combine the mixture with a fork, then dust your hands with flour and work into a firm dough, adding milk or flour as necessary. Do not overknead. Turn onto floured surface and roll out to ½-inch thick-ness. Dip a round cutter or small glass into flour before cutting each biscuit. Arrange biscuits on an ungreased cookie sheet and lightly pierce tops with the tines of a fork. Bake for approximately 10–12 minutes, until golden brown. Break open and spread with butter and/or molasses or jam.

Enjoy!

Molasses

The table was not considered set for any meal until the molasses was there. Both blackstrap and golden types came in from the West Indies and in the days of sailing ships you got what come into your home port — thus tastes for one or t'other were formed. Why was it on the table? Spread on bread, biscuits, bannock, pancakes and Acadian dishes like poutine, it also was used as an ingredient in bread, cookies, taffy, fruitcake and baked beans, and it was even added to animal feed during the harsh, long winters.

The Good Old Cookbooks

One of my favourite activities when away from home is to explore the local library. Since I have a passion for food history and what was termed "household management" in days past, I gravitate to the archival cookbook collections.

While in Vancouver's magnificent main library edifice, I found a copy of a delightful book published in 1877. Its cover browned and worn, pages brittle with age, *The Canadian Home Cook Book Compiled by Ladies of Toronto and Chief Cities and Towns in Canada* was delivered with gloved hands and encased in a sturdy wooden box. What a treasure! I spent hours with it, enthralled with learning how those women ran their households. Months later, exploring a used book store in Halifax, I

found a copy of the same book in remarkably good condition, its cover still wrapped in brown paper bearing a George Washington stamp and postmarked from New York. Presumably the paper wrapping was left on to protect it, as inside, the book is marked as being the property of "Alice W. Thompson, Jan. 11th, 1906" and sold by "E. P. Meagher Bookseller, Barrington Street Halifax." Notes found between the pages indicated that it had been used and treasured by its owner. Buying it was such a treat!

Within its pages lies not only a wonderful collection of recipes but also narrative about life as lived by the contributors, and "Medicinal Receipts" for everything from "Fig Paste for Constipation" to "An Indian Remedy for a Caked Breast or Swollen Glands." Read on for a sampling of the work that went into maintaining the families' good health:

Grandmother's Salve For Everything

Two pounds of resin and half a teacup of mutton tallow after it is hard, half as much beeswax, and half an ounce of camphor gum; put all together into an old kettle, and let it dissolve and just come to a boil, stirring with a stick; then take half a pail of warm water, just the chill off, pour it in and stir carefully until you can get your hands around it. Two persons must each take half and pull like candy until quite white and brittle; put a little grease on your hands to prevent sticking, and keep them wet all the time. Wet the table, roll out the salve, and cut it with a knife. Keep in a cool place.

— Mrs. Gardner

*Frozen strawberries for dessert?
Reserve the juice and mix with
cream cheese in a food processor
(with a metal blade). Use just
enough to make a spreadable
mixture. Delicious on bagels.
Add a few strawberries and …
Wow!*

Tip

*Adding a spoon of salt to your
last rinse water will keep your
laundry from freezing as stiff as
a board on the clothesline.
Applying heavily salted water
around the edges of doors or
windows that are frozen shut
helps loosen them; try using a
long-necked plant-watering can
to keep the water going where
you need it without making a
big mess.*

As the dark days of January slow life down, why not relax and putter by treating your plants to a nice shower? Set them in the kitchen sink, then shower with a warm, fine spray. It's the fastest way to clean their leaves and gives them a good watering. Don't forget to drain well before returning them to their regular spots. I move my African violets to my kitchen window this month. The sun is strongest there.

…

Funny how things stick in your head. I once read a newspaper headline that said, "Winter vegetables come out of the dark." Every time I shop at this time of year and find trusty root veggies in such abundance, I think of past generations venturing into the dark root cellar to get the ingredients for dinner. Potatoes, rutabagas, carrots, parsnips, onions, beets and, of course, ever-popular onions have long been a mainstay in Maritime kitchens simply because they keep so well. The fact that they also have distinctive tastes and are nutritious, economical and versatile helps maintain their popularity.

Root veggies and the winter squashes can be boiled and mashed, stewed, braised and in some cases pickled. Foil-bake, grill on a barbecue or even an open fire … well, the list just goes on! In days past, when meat was scarce these vegetables would form the meal — a tradition we could well emulate. In our house we love winter veggies, particularly braised or oven-roasted.

Braised Veggies

Braising, a method of slow cooking in a small amount of liquid in a tightly covered pot, develops flavours and tenderizes foods by gently breaking down fibres. It's a wonderful way to cook tougher cuts of meat, or you can do veggies on their own. Brown meat in a little oil in the same pan, add veggies, a little stock, wine, tomato juice or water and cook in a slow (325ºF) oven for the afternoon. Be sure the lid is tight. Add herbs or spices if you wish, or a sprinkle of seasoning. If necessary add a little liquid, but not much — you are not making stew! Turn once or twice and voila, you have a great dinner. If we have company coming in the cold winter months, we often serve braised veggies. Visitors ALWAYS rave over the parsnips. Always.

ROASTED WINTER VEGGIES

Serves 8

Choose a variety from beets, celery, carrots, fennel, onions, parsnips, potatoes, rutabagas, sweet potatoes, turnips, winter squashes; peel and cut into equal-size chunks or slices. If desired, peel and add garlic cloves, left whole, or shallots. Wipe a baking dish with oil, ensuring that it is large enough to hold all of your vegetables without crowding. Combine olive oil and balsamic vinegar (2 teaspoons oil to 1 teaspoon vinegar for each pound of veggies). Pour over vegetables and stir or turn till all are lightly coated with oil. Sprinkle with herbs of your choice — we keep it simple because of the flavour of the vinegar, using lemon pepper and sometimes garlic. I know others choose savory or thyme. Also good without the balsamic vinegar. Bake at 425°F for 45 minutes, or longer at a lower temperature. Gently turn at least once.

These tender browned vegetables go well with any meat. One of our favourites is to buy the tubes of ground lamb that come frozen. Cook as you would a meat loaf, then slice into medallions.

PARSNIP CHOWDER

1/8 pound	salt pork	60 g
1	small onion, sliced	1
3 cups	parsnips, cut in cubes	750 mL
1 cup	potatoes, cut in cubes	250 mL
2 cups	boiling water	500 mL
1 qt	rich milk	950 mL
4 tbsp	butter	60 mL
	rolled cracker crumbs (optional)	
	salt and pepper	
	minced parsley (optional)	

Fry out salt pork; remove cracklings. Add onion and sauté gently; add parsnips and potatoes; add water and cook about 30 minutes or until parsnips and potatoes are done. Add milk and butter. Season to taste. Some recipes call for the addition of 1/2 cup rolled cracker crumbs; others thicken chowder slightly with 2 tablespoons flour mixed with 2 tablespoons cold water. Top with minced parsley.

Living History

One place where we can experience food preparation similar to that of long ago is at national historic sites and museums that have preserved or recreated kitchens of the past. Such kitchens are at Fortress Louisbourg in Cape Breton. Visitors can partake of "period" meals on-site. What better place to sample the cuisine enjoyed by our French ancestors, back when Canada was being colonized? Do drop in to the bakehouse.

I have a great appreciation for those who put energy into preserving our culinary past. A number of years ago, Hope Dunston turned her fascination with history into a delightful book that offers insight into 18th-century dishes and the complexities of cooking way back then. *From the Hearth: Recipes from the World of 18th-Century Louisbourg* is a wonderful work filled with recipes more than 200 years old that have stood the test of time. Hope's enthusiasm spawned a "living history" treasure:

"Everyone at the Fortress of Louisbourg was enthusiastic about recreating the past; I was particularly intrigued by the idea of cooking as the original inhabitants had, two centuries earlier. Little did I know then how much I had to learn!

"The first challenge was the fireplace. Nobody on staff had ever cooked with one before and no experienced teacher could be found. But we had to start somewhere. So we began, simply enough, with toast. It took a while but at long last we were able to make it without dropping or burning it. We gradually added to our repertoire and slowly began to feel smug about our mastery of fireplace cookery. Then we received our come-uppance. The occasion was a day-long class in fireside cooking. All went well until a television crew arrived to film the finishing touches of the meal. The table was set, lights up, cameras ready, mikes on, interviews begun — when suddenly the room began to fill with smoke. Within minutes everyone was obliged to run outside, where we concluded the interview. We later discovered the damper (which had not been invented by the 1740s) had accidentally fallen shut, just as the interview began.

"As we were learning about fireplaces, we were also going through the period cookbooks in the Fortress's rare book collection. We selected recipes that called for ingredients we knew to have been in the original town. That was relatively easy. The hard part was trying to carry out the 18th-century instructions and put a finished meal on the table. Quantities and cooking times were only vaguely hinted at, with references being made to an amount the size of an egg or a nut, or a fist or a head. Some directions called for doing a cooking step for the length of time it takes to say a specific prayer or sing a particular hymn. Not surprisingly, a few ingredients were completely unknown to us. With experience, however, it all began to make sense. At last, we were able to prepare authentic, traditional fare."

Simply Pioneering

When you are on a bare-bones budget, take a tip from the early pioneers who put bare bones to good use — Okay, we confess this is more than "bare bones" …

PIONEER BEEF STEW WITH DUMPLINGS

Serves 6–8

	flour, sufficient for dredging meat	
1 tbsp	bacon drippings or oil	15 mL
1 1/2–2 lb	beef chuck, bottom round or short ribs, cut into 2-inch pieces	700–900 g
3	medium onions, chopped	3
1	clove garlic, crushed	1
1/2 cup	green pepper, diced	125 mL
1/2 tsp	crumbled leaf sage	2.5 mL
1/4 tsp	crumbled leaf thyme	1 mL
1/4 tsp	pepper	1 mL
1 tbsp	chili powder	15 mL
1 tbsp	salt	15 mL
2	large tomatoes, peeled, cored and chopped, and their juice	2
1 qt	water	950 mL
1	celery stalk, diced	1
1	small acorn squash, peeled, seeded and cut into 3/4-inch cubes	1
2 cups	diced potatoes	500 mL
2	carrots, diced	2
1/2 cup	diced parsnips (optional)	125 mL
	dumplings (optional — see following recipe)	

Heat oil or drippings in a large heavy kettle. Dredge meat in flour then brown in fat. Remove meat. Sauté onions, garlic and green pepper in same pot. Add sage, thyme, pepper, chili and salt. Return beef to kettle. Add tomatoes and water. Bring to boil, cover and simmer gently for 2 hours. Taste for salt, add more if needed. Add remaining ingredients, making sure broth covers vegetables. Cover and simmer for 10 minutes.

PARSLEY DUMPLINGS

Makes 8–10 dumplings

Sift together 2 cups flour, 3 teaspoons baking powder and 1 teaspoon salt. Add 1/4 cup finely chopped parsley or a little less chopped chives. Cut in 1/4 cup shortening until it looks like coarse cornmeal. Use fork to mix in 1 cup milk, stirring as little as possible, to make a soft dough. Drop by spoonfuls into stew, then simmer for about 10 minutes uncovered; cover and simmer 10 minutes longer. Serve at once.

Haggis

JANUARY 25th — Those with Scottish heritage, those who wish they had it and those who just plain love a good time gather in banquet rooms, community halls and even church basements this day to celebrate the birth of the great Scottish bard Robbie Burns. It's a long celebration. Burns was born in 1759.

The centre of many of these celebrations will be steaming haggis, a pudding of sheep organs, oatmeal and savoury spices, ceremoniously piped in and addressed with a rendition of the poet's audacious "Ode to a Haggis," which begins:

> *Fair fa your honest sonsie face*
> *great chieftain of the puddin' race!*
> *Weel are ye wordy of a grace*
> *as lang's my arm.*

The ode praises the most famous of Scotland's dishes, reputedly named after a mythical Highland beastie with two long legs and two short legs — all the better to run around hillsides. Great, as long as they didn't want to change direction!

Although not to our tastes today, some folks make haggis for the celebration. Just in case you do have the yen, here is an authentic recipe from the Scots North British Society in Halifax. Frankly, I suggest you tipple a few before tackling this one. Here's what you need: 1 sheep's pluck (heart, lungs, liver) and bag; 2 teacups toasted oatmeal; 1 teaspoon salt; 8 oz shredded suet; 2 small onions; 1/2 teaspoon black pepper.

Scrape and clean bag in cold and then warm water. Soak in salt water overnight. Wash, pluck, then boil 2 hours with windpipe draining over side of pot. Retain 1 pint of the stock. Cut off windpipe, remove surplus gristle, chop or mince heart and lungs, grate best part of liver (about 1/2). Parboil and chop onions, mix suet, salt, pepper and stock to moisten. Any mix of savoury spices can be added to the haggis during preparation. Pack mixture into the bag, allow for swelling. Boil for 3 hours, pricking regularly all over.

The haggis is placed on a platter, decorated in fine style and served with pomp and ceremony. Traditionally dinner consists of haggis, neeps (mashed turnip), tatties (creamed potatoes) and a variety of mutton pastries, washed down with copious quantities of whisky used for the various toasts that are a mandatory part of Burns celebrations — as are Scottish music, dancing and readings of poetry.

Herbs and Vegetables Used in Soups

Of vegetables the principal ones are carrots, tomatoes, asparagus, green peas, okra, macaroni, green corn, beans, rice, vermicelli, Scotch barley, pearl barley, wheat flour, mushroom or mushroom catsup, parsnips, beet-root, turnips, leeks, garlic, shallots, and onions; sliced onions fried with butter and flour until they are browned, then rubbed through a sieve, are excellent to heighten the color and flavor of brown sauces and soups. The herbs usually used in soups are parsley, common thyme, summer savory, knotted marjoram, and other seasonings such as bay-leaves, tarragon, allspice, cinnamon, nutmeg, cloves, mace, black and white pepper, red pepper, lemon-peel and juice, orange-peel and juice. The latter imparts a finer flavor and the acid is much milder. These materials, with wine, and the various catsups, combined in various proportions, are, with other ingredients, made into almost an endless variety of excellent soups and gravies.

Soups that are intended for the principal part of a meal certainly ought not to be flavored like sauces, which are only intended to give relish to some particular dish.

— The New Cook Book (1905)

Flights of Fancy

One of our stress busters operates at full efficiency this month. It was New Brunswick naturalist, veterinarian and newspaper columnist Nelson Poirier who put the label "stress buster" on feeding and observing birds. He really hit the nail on the head.

Chickadees, woodpeckers, juncos, finches, blue jays, starlings, crows, mourning doves, pigeons and various feathered cousins visit our backyard in shifts throughout the day. Observed from the comfort of our kitchen window, they bring hours of pleasure as they flit back and forth. We can always tell when bad weather is imminent — the traffic increases, the pecking order disappearing as our winged family feeds with gusto.

Extra seed is the order of the day as the bad weather increases in intensity. It amazes me that I will find myself hardly able to fight the wind to the feeder, only to have chickadees come flying in to supervise what I'm doing. How do they do that?

January

Many a scrapbook is lovingly created at the kitchen table. Collections are a long-established source of entertainment; a hobby where people detail all manner of things: recipes, records of achievement by family members, pets, communities, heroes or heroines. Old scrapbooks, often containing clippings from periodicals, have become valuable historic documents and collectibles. They should never be thrown away. I dream of finding my Elvis scrapbook with signed letters and cards from the great one. Avid collectors are well advised to will old books, journals, scrapbooks and recipes to an archive or museum. Today's records are tomorrow's history.

Creating scrapbooks is a wonderful winter activity for children — or yourself, for that matter. Spreading papers about, wielding scissors and glue and chatting across the kitchen table about discoveries made hold a magic that a computer and scanner can't equal. Modern technology does have one plus, though. Don't cut or destroy old publications, papers or documents. Keep the originals intact by photocopying or scanning bits and pieces needed.

I fill all feeders and scatter lots of seed on the ground when it's cold or stormy. A little grit is added to the mix if a real blizzard sets in. We know that the "huns" (Hungarian partridges) will venture in from the fields to hunker down under our pine trees until it's over. They seem to know that every time I go to my kitchen window and see that the snow has covered the seed, the dog and I will break trail from the storage shed to the feeders to keep them all safe. This month a flock of lovely little redpolls joined our backyard community, obviously fans of niger seed.

February

— *Let the winds blow and
the snows fall; it's
snuggle-into-home time.*

When I visited Dr. Stuart Macdonald in the years before his death in 1982, he often spoke of a pie that his mother used to make. It was called a mock cherry pie. I puzzled over the frequency with which these pies came into his memory. It pointed to the role that food plays in a family — a mother provides food to give sustenance. She also provides it to show love. The recipe had come from Prince Edward Island, just as she had, and connected her past, her son, his friend, and her, in a web of caring and pleasure — pleasure in Island delicacies, pleasure in sharing them with others.

— Mary Henley Rubio, professor of English at Guelph University in Ontario, writing about Lucy Maud Montgomery, author of *Anne of Green Gables*, for *Aunt Maud's Recipe Book* by Elaine Crawford and Kelly Crawford

It was cold. Cold as the Antarctic in a blizzard. Seriously. The wind chill factor was something ludicrous like minus 60 degrees. Cars were tough to start, snow squeaked, houses creaked in the cold and everyone was wearing those masks with eyeholes. This was the time we had chosen for a cross-country ski weekend at The Doctor's Inn in Tyne Valley, P.E.I. Owned and operated by Paul and Jean Offer, the inn is surrounded by the fruits of these organic market gardeners' labours — in the summer. Now, in the dead of winter, nothing but snow lay in the gardens.

Our visit was like stepping back in time. Wood stoves, the primary heat and cooking source, beckoned. There is little as appealing as being snugly warm as the winds howl outside, basking in slightly smoky heat and scents of good things simmering on the stove. When the power went out we spent hours around those stoves, toasting our feet and fronts and then turning to do our backs, chatting and forming the bonds of a friendship treasured today.

Constantly simmering kettles were used to fill hot water bottles so that our chilly rush into jammies was rewarded by diving into a cozy warm nest lined with flannelette sheets. The next morning our tingling noses, the only part not tucked under the covers, confirmed that the power was not back on. A quick dash to the bathroom and instant … warmth. Ahhhhhhhhh.

Located above the kitchen, the floor was warmed from below. It was a reminder of my husband Jack's youth, when he had lucked into the most coveted bedroom — the one above the kitchen. Warm air, rising through a hole in the floor, took the chill off. Even so, he remembered waking to water frozen in his glass.

The Offers' wood stove was hummin'. The fire crackled, the kettle sang and the coffee pot "perkled," all incredibly comfortingly. Toast was made by dropping slices of homemade bread directly on the stovetop.

"The only things I cook for breakfast are eggs … of all kinds," says Jean, whose simple approach earns her many fans. Of course, homegrown free-range eggs don't hurt.

Jean Offer's Omelette "Recipe"

Slice mushrooms and sauté them in butter ("I imagine any kind would do, but I use regular ones"). Beat 2 eggs well, pour into a buttered frying pan. Cook until almost firm, cover the top half of the omelette with sliced cheddar cheese and place the mushrooms on top. Sprinkle on fresh chopped chives and fold the omelette in half. Let cook a few minutes more. There are no set amounts for the cheese or mushrooms, it depends what you like. Everyone seems to like this.

…

A most curious aspect of Canadian gastronomy is the number of "mock" dishes featured in books, leaflets, notebooks and almanacs from the very earliest times. Obviously some provided a meal when supplies were low, but others were to make food appealing. They run the gamut from the mock cherry pie mentioned by Stuart Macdonald, to mock duck and mock goose.

MOCK CHERRY PIE

"One large cup cranberries, 1/2 cup raisins chopped together. Cook with 1 cup boiling water and 1 cup sugar. Add 1 tablespoon cornstarch, wet with cold water. Boil, stirring frequently until cooked. When used add 1 teaspoon vanilla. Bake with 2 crusts."

— Mabel MacLean, *Recipes from Cape Breton*

Or use this more detailed version:

1 cup	cranberries	250 mL
1/2 cup	raisins	125 mL
1 cup	sugar	250 mL
1/2 cup	water	125 mL
2 tbsp	flour	30 mL
1 tsp	vanilla flavouring	5 mL
1 tsp	almond extract	5 mL

Cook together in double boiler 10 minutes. Put in shell and bake in hot oven (400°F) for 10 minutes. Reduce heat to 350°F and continue cooking 45 minutes.

— Women's Institute of Prince Edward Island, *Popular Recipes*

Mock Duck

"Remove the large bone from a shoulder of mutton, fill the space with toasted pine nuts or seasoned bread crumbs and tie in the shape of a duck. Make the leg and knuckle bone form the neck and bill, and fasten in the blade to represent the tail. Cover with oiled paper, brown in a quick oven for fifteen minutes, and then bake at a moderate temperature for an hour. Dish on a bed of cress. Serve with brown sauce and sweet potatoes, croquettes or rice."

— M.A.S., Sussex, The Modern Cookbook for New Brunswick (1920)

This recipe reminded me of an amusing incident in our own farm kitchen one day when we disguised mutton. New friends invited for dinner walked in sniffing the air, remarking how good something smelled. Jack said, "That's good. We're having something a little different today." "Just as long as it's not mutton," they replied. "We hate eating sheep."

Oh, heavens. We looked at each other. Mutton was simmering away in my Crock-Pot. Now what? Jack shrugged and said, "Oh, I think you'll like this beef. We've cooked it with some special touches." An hour later we looked at each other and burst out laughing. The roast we had thought would provide leftovers for a couple of meals was gone. Both guests had "seconds" — more than once. Now they leaned back in their chairs, stuffed, complimenting us on just how good that beef was.

We confessed. They relented, saying taste was obviously in the cooking. We agreed. Our secret was to remove all visible fat, then lay the meat on a bed of onions and carrots, sprinkle liberally with mint sauce and a splash of beer and slow-cook for five to six hours. Since this was old, strongly flavoured mutton, the vinegar and mint cut the fatty mutton taste. We served it with new potatoes, cooked with sprigs of mint, and rich gravy.

Mock Goose

"Pare and cut in two lengthwise a good sized vegetable marrow and remove the seeds. Rub this over inside and out with salt, and leave for an hour to drain. Have ready some onions boiled and chopped, with a little sage, add to them pepper, salt and a little butter, and fill up the halves of the marrow with the mixture. Close up and tie over with tape. Butter a pie dish, place the 'goose' upon it, and bake in a moderate oven till it is browned and tender. Serve warm with a little white sauce."

— Una Abrahamson, *God Bless Our Home: Domestic Life in Nineteenth Century Canada*
...

This put me in mind of the "impossible" dishes we used to whip up when I was a "just-married" with a tiny grocery budget. We loved this, especially when served with crushed strawberries. A great starter for kids to cook.

IMPOSSIBLE COCONUT PIE

4	eggs	4
2 cups	milk	500 mL
1/2 cup	margarine	125 mL
1/4 tsp	nutmeg	1 mL
1 cup	flour	250 mL
1 cup	sugar	250 mL
1 cup	coconut	250 mL
2 tsp	vanilla	10 mL

Mix thoroughly in blender or by hand. Pour into greased 10-inch pie plate. Bake at 350°F for 50 minutes or until centre tests firm. Makes its own crust.

Pioneer Homemaking

Although pioneer life seems romantic today, in fact it was darn hard, especially for homemakers. Cooking was labour-intensive and time-consuming. During cold weather, life revolved around the heat source. First an open fireplace, later a wood- or coal-burning stove, depending on where you lived. Carrying fuel from outside or a cellar was back-breaking work. I know! Ashes had to be removed and carted off to the garden or driveway.

Last to bed banked the fire to ensure live coals for morning. First up stirred the ashes to build it again. Hot water for bathing, washing, cleaning or cooking was dependent on it.

Even going to church entailed forethought and preparation. Churches were not heated and sermons were long, tedious affairs. Foot warmers (iron boxes filled with burning charcoal or wooden boxes containing heated bricks) had to be prepared and transported; warm clothing, including fur coats, was found for every family member, and even the family dog was rounded up to take to the service — not to absorb the good Word, but to provide warmth.

Early settlers' homes contained a cooking hearth where an iron chaudière, or soup kettle, hung suspended over the fire from a movable "crane" or stood on a three-legged stand placed over hot embers, which could be raked forward or back to keep the right cooking temperature.

Living History

The Ross-Thompson House in Shelburne, Nova Scotia, circa 1785, is typical of buildings constructed by the United Empire Loyalists. The only original store building remaining in Shelburne, the house is in the custody of the Nova Scotia Museum and operated by the Shelburne Historical Society. The family had a "servant girl" who worked for them in the kitchen, which was in the cellar. The floor was dirt and cooking was done in the open fireplace. A large table would have been pulled up to the brick hearth, for ease of working.

Cooking in the cellar was actually a pretty decent place to work, for it was warm in winter and cool in summer. One very real danger was the fire. A swirl of a long skirt or a step too close and those long, natural-fibre dresses would burst into flames.

Perogie Perfection

"Remember to pinch them together completely," Grandma Koldesk used to say as we were making perogies. "That way they will stay together when we cook them." "Grandma, can you tell me a story about when you were growing up?" I often asked.

That was typical of many afternoons we spent together in the kitchen when I was a child. My grandma came to Canada from Poland when she was 10. Although by today's standards she had a hard life, she never complained. Instead, she told wonderful stories about coming to this new land and the adventures it had brought her. I heard stories about how she arrived at Pier 21 in Halifax after spending several weeks seasick, and then riding the train to Saskatchewan. "The trip," she said, "took forever and there was nothing but flat land …" And another story about how her father sent her out to work as a live-in housemaid for $10 a month. He then took her earnings to buy a wagon for the farm. "We all pitched in to make a new home for ourselves. It wasn't all hard work and I was able to learn English as I worked."

Grandma's stories somehow made the time-consuming job of making perogies go by quickly. Grandma is gone now, but her memories live on inside those she touched. It's my turn to pass this recipe on to my daughter, along with many of the stories I learned from a very remarkable woman.

— Michelle Breker-Klassen, Bedford, Nova Scotia

GRANDMA KOLDESK'S PEROGIES

DOUGH:	4 cups	white flour	1 L
	1/2 cup	vegetable oil	125 mL
	1 1/2 tsp	salt	7.5 mL
	1 1/2 cups	water	375 mL
FILLING:	2 cups	mashed white potatoes	500 mL
	2 cups	dry curd cottage cheese	500 mL
		(may substitute well-drained cottage cheese)	
	1	egg	1
	1/2 tsp	onion powder	2.5 mL
		salt and pepper to taste	

Stir dough ingredients to make a soft mixture, gently squeezing it together when the dough gets dry. Take care not to knead or the perogies will be tough. Roll out dough to 1/8-inch thick. Using a floured glass, cut into circles, usually about 3 1/2–4 inches in diameter. Place a teaspoon of the filling on dough, fold it in half and pinch edges together. Place perogies on floured cookie sheet and freeze until cooking time (once frozen, they can be packed into plastic bags). To cook: Drop 12–15 perogies in large pot of rapidly boiling, salted water. Stir occasionally with wooden spoon (be gentle!). When they rise to top of pot, cook them an additional 2 minutes and drain. Toss with melted butter, softly fried diced bacon and sautéed onions. Serve with sour cream.

…

As an additional treat, Grandma would save the scraps from rolling out the dough, reroll them and put chunks of apple inside. She would cook them up and serve them tossed with butter, sugar and cinnamon. To this day, I'm not sure which kind is my favourite!

From My Kitchen Window

FEBRUARY 20 — Although it's Sunday my body clock got me up at 6:30 just in time to enjoy the sun rising. Filling the kettle, I gaze out into the backyard and am awestruck. Mother Nature left a hoar frost last night — a beautiful sight as the rising sun casts a pink glow over the world. Enchanted, I enjoy my first cup of brew at the window. As the day brightens, the lacy frost seems to grow before my eyes. I have to be on the other side of that window! After days of severe cold it is pleasant to step out with Tipsy, our mini schnauzer. I top up the suet holder, fill the feeders, empty the compost pot, take a wee walk and finally, still putting off going in to tackle the dishes, get my camera. I photograph the frost on trees, against the sun! Tipsy chasing a cranberry. There probably won't be a decent picture on the whole film, but I'm having a wonderful time so it doesn't matter. If there is, it's a bonus, perhaps next year's Christmas card.

After extending what is usually half an hour feeding the birds and letting the dog do her "ablutions" to 1½ hours, I must say a second cup of hazelnut coffee, crumpets and an orange are a very welcome second breakfast. On this morning I feast on what is outside and thank the big fella upstairs for sharing it with me.

Portable or Pocket Soup

Years ago, heading away from home required vast amounts of preparations in the kitchen. Think about it: Your man is heading off to trap furs, work the lumber camps, transport goods or go to sea, or perhaps you are responsible for feeding troops of soldiers or sailors heading off to do battle. There are no fast-food outlets or grocery stores along the way. These travellers must be nourished, and can't spend all of their time hunting or foraging for food. Therefore they have to take much of it with them. Portable or "pocket soup" is, like jerky, easy to carry and prepare.

Next time you pop one of those instant soups into a pack for your lunch, or use a bouillon cube, be grateful …

Boil one or two knuckles of veal, one or two shins of beef, in as much water only as will cover them. Take the marrow out of the bones, put any sort of spice you like, and three large onions. When the meat is done to rags, strain it off, and put it into a very cold place. When cold, take off the cake of fat (which will make crusts for servants' pies), put the soup into a double bottomed tin sauce-pan, and set it on a pretty quick fire, but don't let it burn. It must boil fast and uncovered and be stirred constantly for eight hours. Put it into a pan, and let it stand in a cold place a day; then pour it into a round soup china-dish, and set the dish into a stew-pan of boiling water on a stove, and let it boil, and be now and then stirred, till the soup is thick and ropy; then it is enough. Pour it into the little round part at the bottom of cups or basins turned upside down to form cakes; and when cold, turn them out on flannel to dry. Keep them in canisters. When they are to be used melt them in boiling water; and if you wish the flavour of herbs, or anything else, boil it first, strain off the water, and melt the soup in it.

This is very convenient in the country, or at sea, where fresh meat is not always at hand; as by this means a basin of soup may be made in five minutes.

— *A New System of Domestic Cookery*, undated

A Resurrected Green

When we moved to rural Prince Edward Island I learned many things: what it was like to have no money for groceries, how to think ahead and put things by and how to be innovative about putting food on the table. In a self-sufficiency stage I decided sprouts are healthy, replace lettuce and are cheap. I was pretty successful at having a jar ready and developed a real taste for sprouts.

Now just in case you think I was in a hippie stage or something, just remember that the Chinese mention sprouts in writings dated around 2939 BC, and a surgeon in the British Royal Navy wrote of their benefits in the 18th century.

A half cup of nutrient-filled seeds can turn into 3 1/2 cups of sprouts in just four or five days. This is a good thing.

You can sprout darn near anything: just make sure the seeds and foliage are edible. Don't sprout potatoes, tomatoes, peppers or eggplants; nor should you use seed that has been treated with a chemical fungicide. Buy sprouting seeds at a health food store.

Use a wide-mouth jar bigger than the amount of sprouts you want to grow. You need cheesecloth or screen (nylon is best) to cover the end of the jar, something to hold it on — a rubber band works — and a fine strainer (coffee filters are great). Experiment for different tastes.

To make approximately a quart: Soak 1/4 cup of seed in several inches of filtered or spring water for 5–8 hours in a low-light area. Pour off the water, rinse well under a running tap, then turn the jar upside down and place on a 45-degree angle to drain (a dish drying rack works great). Put jar into a medium-light location. Each day, rinse 2–3 times and drain, always keeping the jar at the same upside-down angle. Sprouts will be ready in 5 days. Before eating, swish them in a bowl or sink of water to remove husks; drain well. Some seeds, such as alfalfa, mustard, radish and red clover, are best if returned to the jars to green up a little by exposing them to bright light (not direct sunlight) for 6–8 hours after that final rinse. Use immediately, or store in refrigerator for a day or two max.

Sprouts are great in sandwiches, salads, stir-fries and soups, and make a great garnish. Being able to put on the table a veggie I have grown myself in midwinter makes me feel smug.

Around the Kitchen Table

A friend born in Czechoslovakia vividly remembered arriving in Canada. Her family had fled their native country and ended up in a refugee camp in Germany, where they spent many years before finally setting sail for Canada. Almost 50 years later we shared experiences of our postwar arrivals in our new land.

All of her family's worldly goods were packed in wooden boxes, including her mother's treasured porcelain tableware, which had been carried through the turmoil. On arrival railway workers who saw German markers on the crates threw them to the ground. All of her mother's porcelain was shattered. Because the children spoke German they, too, were treated very badly. "People would take our food and throw it on the ground. Our good clothes were stomped in the mud, then rehung on the clothesline." It was terrible for a youngster who had anticipated a life much improved from that in the refugee camps.

My own introduction to Canada had its unpleasant side. As the child of English immigrants who many felt were taking scarce jobs I was, for a time, a target. Walking to and from school was a nightmare of torment. I was regularly "mustarded," smeared with the yellow stuff — in my hair, eyes, mouth … can't abide it to this day. I was saved from the bullies by a bad-ass, Fonz-type young man who set himself up as my protector in Grade 4. I eventually married him. We'll soon be celebrating our 40th.

Not all newcomers had bad experiences; Brigette's was vastly different. She and her fiancé survived the war in Holland. They applied to come to Canada and were accepted more quickly than expected. Hurriedly, they married and honeymooned aboard ship.

Brigette thought she had found heaven and it wasn't all from marital bliss — she was overjoyed with the food aboard the ship. It was the first time in years that she had enough to eat. She recalled being "full" as a wonderful feeling. The fact that everything tasted good was a bonus. So intense was the experience that she gazed upon the shores of Halifax with dread. She could not believe that these riches would continue. She even considered hiding — to simply stay on-board to eat her way back and forth across the Atlantic. Of course, she and her husband did disembark, at

Pier 21, now a museum commemorating thousands of immigrants who arrived there. Passing through customs, they were shunted onto trains that chuffed away — destination unknown. Happily for the newlyweds they were taken to Prince Edward Island, where they became potato farmers.

I often think of these experiences. Just imagine: sailing away from friends and family with no idea where you would end up, what your future held. Such faith immigrants had that a better life waited in Canada. So many Maritime women's heritage involves seeking a better life in a new land. Even though those born and bred here had to be thrifty to keep families nourished and cared for, few had to face the direct hardships of war in their backyard. Adversaries were weather, shortage of jobs and such. Their challenge was to make the best of what they had. Fortunate!

Fools

Talk desserts, or "afters" to anyone from "the Old Country," and they are sure to mention "fools." Not silly people, but the sweet dish made with almost any kind of fresh fruit. Although the most popular in this region were made with blueberries, plums, rhubarb and gooseberries, they were also made with apricots, blackberries and raspberries and still are. These traditional desserts take on a uniqueness with each cook. Some combine fruit with cream only, others use a rich egg custard.

The creation war brides would have brought with them was likely a cold, sweet dish made with whipped cream or custard, or both, and fruit purée, although one lady referred to it as "a dish of crushed fruit with whipped cream." You can make it with canned or preserved fruit. If you are in the mood for experimenting, try this shortcut. Buy canned or preserved gooseberries and a can of custard. Drain the fruit and purée by rubbing through a sieve, or use a blender or food processor. Chill the purée and the custard until quite cold, then fold together. Some folks also fold in an equal amount of whipped cream; we prefer a dollop on top. I like to serve our fool in individual tall glasses, topped with whipped cream and a little of the fruit or purée, with a cookie or ladyfinger.

Valentine Memory

Hilda King Robinson, referred to as Grammy Robin by her grandchildren, was born in 1901 in St. John's, Newfoundland. The youngest of 10, she moved to Charlottetown, P.E.I., with her mother and siblings when she was 11 or 12. Hilda married Poppy (Nelson) Robinson on Valentine's Day.

Every Saturday her grandchildren had music lessons in town, so they would go to Grammy's until Father picked them up after work. Hilda was a fabulous storyteller and each grandchild had its own story: "Debbie the Duck," "Gail the Whale," "Peter the Penguin" and so on. Grammy loved to play games. During family birthday parties she would be outside playing with the grandkids while the other adults were inside.

"She was one of those people who was never old. She had dark hair, very little grey. She always worried that people would think she dyed it. Only loose women dyed their hair!" recalls her granddaughter, Debbie Gamble-Arsenault.

"She started to teach me to cook when I was four. One of my favourite things when I was a kid was that when Poppy came home she would say, 'Oh, your grandfather's home—you'd better go hide.' I would hide behind the big flour barrel set under a counter.

"One of my favourite things she made was beef barley stew. Maybe I'm dreaming, but it seems to me that she never served her beef barley stew the day she made it. As I recall it, she always held it over till the next day." The recipe is very similar to our Earth Stew, which follows. Debbie has a treasured collection of her Grammy's recipes, which she has generously shared. The puddings show how every bit of food was utilized by cooks of years past.

GRAMMY'S PARTRIDGEBERRY BATTER PUDDING

Serves 6–9

This honours her Newfoundland heritage. If you don't have partridgeberries, use cranberries, choosing the largest.

1 1/2 cups	all-purpose flour	375 mL
3 tsp	baking powder	15 mL
1/2 cup	sugar	125 mL
1/2 tsp	salt	2 mL
1/2 cup	milk	125 mL
1	egg	1
1/4 cup	shortening	50 mL
2 cups	partridgeberries	500 mL
1/2 cup	sugar	125 mL

Place berries mixed with 1/2 cup sugar in bottom of greased 8 x 8-inch baking dish. For the pudding batter, sift together flour and baking powder. Cream shortening, beat in sugar gradually, then salt and egg, beating until soft and fluffy. Add milk and flour alternately, folding flour into mixture until just moistened. Spread batter over berries and bake in moderate oven (375°F) for 30 to 35 minutes. This pudding can also be steamed. Berries may be added to the batter if desired. Serve with your favourite sauce (optional).

CRUMB AND CUSTARD PUDDING

1 cup	milk	250 mL
1	egg	1
1/3–1/2 cup	crumbs	80–125 mL
2 1/2 tbsp	sugar	40 mL
	flavouring (vanilla or other extract)	

Pour boiling water over bread crumbs (cracker or cake crumbs may be used), drain, then press out and rub bread through coarse sieve. Add sugar to hot bread. Mix milk, beaten egg (or yolk) and flavouring, beat into bread. Bake in moderate oven until set like custard. If using cake crumbs, just soak them in milk. Candied cherries, dates, raisins, etc., may be added.

Jam may be spread on top and heaped with stiffly beaten egg white, sweetened with powdered sugar and flavoured. Brown delicately in oven.

Lazy Pudding

I remember my own English grandmother making this. I loved it. Cooks would have used homemade bread and their own preserves. Here's all you need: white bread; one jar of preserved raspberries or cherries; stiffly whipped sweetened cream.

Cut bread in inch-thick slices; trim off crusts; line pudding mould with bread, fitting the slices nicely. Turn preserved raspberries or cherries into saucepan and bring to boil. Pour fruit into mould (If there is not enough syrup to fill it to the brim, add some extra water and sugar to fruit while heating). Trim more of the thick bread to make a cover for the mould; put it in place, put a plate on it and press down with a weight. There must be so much syrup that it will run out a little, or the bread will not be completely soaked. Let stand overnight; chill. To serve, turn out on flat dish, cover all over with cream. Garnish with some of the fruit, held out for the purpose.

EARTH STEW

Serves 4–6

We call this our Earth Stew because of the earthy flavours of mushrooms and barley combined with beef, stock and tomatoes. Serving with roasted red chieftain potatoes and parsnips makes full use of the oven. An in-the-oven dessert rounds out a perfect meal. Barley really absorbs liquid, so check the fluids and top up as needed.

2 ½ lbs	fat-free stew or stir-fry beef	1.25 kg
2 tbsp	olive oil	30 mL
2	medium onions, chopped	2
3	garlic cloves, minced	3
2	medium to large carrots, cut into chunks	2
1	stalk of celery, chopped	1
2-3	broccoli stems, peeled and cut into chunks	2–3
½ tsp	dried rosemary, crumbled	2.5 mL
½ tsp	dried thyme	2.5 mL
¼ tsp	freshly ground black pepper	1 mL
1	bay leaf	1
¼ cup	chopped fresh parsley	50 mL
¼ cup	pearl barley, rinsed well and drained	125 mL
2 cups	beef stock	500 mL
¼ cup	Bovril beef cordial	50 mL
2 cups	water	500 mL
½ cup	tomato sauce or dry red wine	125 mL
28–oz	can diced tomatoes (optional)	796 mL
1 lb	mushrooms, quartered or halved (depending on size)	450 g
	salt to taste	

or
in

In a pot or Dutch oven that can go from element to oven, heat oil over medium-high heat. Add meat; sear until browned on all sides. Add onions and garlic; cook about 5 minutes. Add carrots, celery, broccoli, rosemary, thyme, pepper, bay leaf, parsley, barley, stock, sauce or wine, and tomatoes with juice; stir well to mix. Bake covered at 350°F (180°C) for 1 ½ hours. Taste to see if it needs seasoning. Check fluid: you may need to add stock. Stir in mushrooms, cover and bake for an additional 60 minutes or until meat is tender.

If stir-fry beef is not available, buy boneless inside round steak, trim excess fat, cut into 1-inch (2.5 cm) pieces.

FEBRUARY 26 — Temperatures are milder today, luring us out to dig channels for water runoff and walk the dog. Outdoor efforts make us hungry so it's nice to smell earthy flavours cooking in the oven.

Medicinal Receipts

Cookbooks are popular Maritimes fundraisers. Folks contribute favourite recipes, then buy the book so that they can get those of their friends and neighbours. These that follow are from High Crest Enterprises Ltd.'s 10th Anniversary Cookbook. *The company operates nursing homes in Springhill, New Glasgow, Antigonish and Sherbrooke, Nova Scotia.*

Tee's Sore Throat Remedy

3 tbsp	strong black tea	45 mL
1 tbsp	vinegar	15 mL
1/2 tsp	salt	2.5 mL

*Gargle with this 3 times a day.
It really works.* — Honey Smith

Jell-O Popsicles

Another way to soothe a sore throat, especially for the younger set, is by eating a popsicle. Make your own by freezing juice or try this one, which won't drip as easily.

1	6-g package Kool-Aid	1
1	85-g package Jello-O	1
1 cup	boiling water	250 mL
2 cups	cold water	500 mL
	sugar to taste	

Mix together. Pour into moulds, or small paper cups, with a coffee stir stick as a handle. Freeze.

Cape Breton

*Cape Breton is a tasty dish,
Full of tang and savour;
For garnishing, its lakes and trees,
And for its fine folk, the flavour.*

*Full measure of good Highland Scot,
Irish, to give it spice,
Add French to lend it piquancy,
The palate to entice,*

*A generous dash of English
To make it taste just right,
So, come, and try this food supreme,
An epicure's delight.*

— Ellah Liscombe

MELTING MOMENTS

This treat is from *Recipes from Cape Breton Island,* a delightful little book put out by the First United Church Afternoon Guild in Sydney, Nova Scotia, back in the days when telephone numbers had just four digits. My dog-eared copy is full of handwritten notes: "Mrs. Calver's Cookies — Good," "Add salt to Muriel's gingerbread," and so on. Melting Moments is a perfect example of cooking with staples in the cupboard.

1 cup	butter	250 mL
1 3/4 cups	flour	425 mL
3/4 cup	brown sugar	175 mL

1	egg (unbeaten)	1
½ tsp	cream of tartar	2.5 mL
½ tsp	soda	2.5 mL
1 tsp	vanilla	5 mL
1 tsp	salt	5 mL

Cream butter and sugar together, add egg. Beat well. Add sifted dry ingredients together, mix with other portion. Form into balls size of walnut. Press out with fork dipped in flour. Bake 4 or 5 minutes in moderate oven.

— Mrs. MacLean of Airlie,
Recipes from Cape Breton Island

Glacé Paste for Tender Sweet Ham

This is one of those wonderful old-fashioned masterpieces that should be taken to the table to show off before the ham is sliced. I remove the skin and all but a thin layer of fat, being careful to keep a smooth surface for appearance.

"This is a favourite recipe with most homemakers for keeping juices in ham."

— Mrs. A. F. MacKinnon,
Recipes from Cape Breton Island

For one half ham, use 1 cup brown sugar, 2 tsp dry mustard, 3 tbsp flour moistened with 3 tbsp vinegar. Pat this paste on top of ham, basting occasionally with the fat from the bottom of the pan to give a shiny glacé. Dot with cloves if desired.

Bake in oven 425°F for about 25 minutes. Serve on platter garnished with peach halves or pineapple rings stuffed with red and green cherries.

Seafood Smarts

In the early 1960s Charlie and Clara Harris took over an eatery down Yarmouth way. Harris' Quick-N-Tasty became "the" place to go if you wanted good down-home-style food. The Harrises have retired and Paul and Debbie Swette have taken the helm, but the diner-style restaurant continues to foster the same talented food preparation. It's traditional and delicious.

I asked a few patrons and staff for their favourites. The list reads like a Maritime buffet: hot lobster sandwich, fish cakes, ham or turkey casserole, "mile-high meringue on their pies" and rice-and-raisin-bread pudding — simple foods, well prepared.

The folks at Quick-N-Tasty generously shared a few secrets about what makes their offerings special:

HOT LOBSTER SANDWICH

"Luscious lobster in a cream sauce served on toast, open-faced or closed."

Pan-fry lobster (precooked) over low heat in butter, when warm add cream and heat. DO NOT BOIL. To serve, "put a piece of toast, smother it with lobster, another piece of toast, more lobster."

So dedicated to seafood are the folks down Digby and Yarmouth way, they have their own variation on the burger. Here you are likely to find a clamburger or a quahogburger, for clams are king.

Flights of Fancy 🌾

Raisins are delicious treats for birds that eat fruit. They won't visit a bird feeder, so try scattering raisins on the ground or placing them in a shrub to simulate fruit of the bush. To be totally fair, you should try for organic raisins.

Once a year I purge the cupboards. Things like old nuts, cornmeal, petrified raisins or dried fruit are all fodder for the birds. Add old molasses or syrup, even suet. Mix together and pat into a loaf to place on a tray feeder.

SEAFOOD CHOWDER

Quick-N-Tasty makes a thinner chowder than most, but it's rich in fish. Potatoes are cut into small pieces, tiny compared with the bigger chunks of haddock. A little lobster, pan-fried in butter, is stirred in and the chowder is topped with a piece of orange roughy, pinky red in colour from being pan-fried in the same butter as the lobster.

FISH CAKES

Made in the traditional way but with fresh haddock, they are thick (1 3/4 to 2 inches). What makes them extra special? A dollop of butter is popped on the top of each one before they are served, with green tomato chow on the side.

MARITIME 'BREW'

A truly decadent end to any meal combines hot coffee, dark rum, brown sugar and whipped cream. Experiment to find the measurements that suit you — after all, the testing is part of the fun!

March

— *Winter-weary, we welcome a kitchen scented by savoury soup and sweet maple treats.*

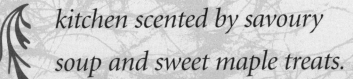

The enduring influences on today's East Coast cooking are those of the Acadians, the British and the Loyalists. It was these early settlers who combined the food traditions of their home countries with the ingredients available to them in their new land and, in doing so, established what we consider today to be down-home cooking. Our cooking heritage is as wide and varied as the country itself.

— Marie Nightingale, writing about East Coast cooking in
Northern Bounty I: A Celebration of Canadian Cuisine

What better sign that spring is near than folks heading for the sugar bush? And what better place to enjoy the experience than Kings Landing Historical Settlement in Prince William, N.B.? Each year it opens so that people can experience how maple syrup was produced 150 years ago by settlers using horse-drawn collectors and iron cauldrons to boil down sap. This chance to enjoy candy-on-the-snow or a pancake breakfast is one of many such events around the region. Go on, get out your winter duds and enjoy a sugar bush weekend. Oh, do bring home some maple syrup, it's a great staple for the kitchen.

Maple Syrup

Of course, there are many more things to do with maple syrup. Years ago it was one of the few accessible sweeteners, enjoyed with blueberry pudding, johnnycake, hot biscuits or ploye. Introduced to settlers by the Native peoples, maple syrup was often preserved in cake form as maple sugar because it was easier to store.

OVEN-BAKED FRENCH TOAST WITH MAPLE SYRUP

While pancakes are the traditional way to enjoy maple syrup, many Maritimers prefer French toast. Great for lazy Sundays, overnight company or holidays, because you can make ahead and freeze. We're always looking for an excuse to enjoy maple syrup as soon as it comes in — this way we can be ready! Once the egg is absorbed, place slices on a tray and freeze, uncovered. Once frozen, store in plastic bags. To cook, place frozen slices on a greased baking sheet and proceed as in the recipe.

— CBM, Nova Scotia

Serves 4

4	eggs	4
1 cup	milk	250 mL
1 tbsp	sugar	15 mL
1 tsp	vanilla	5 mL
$^1\!/_4$ tsp	nutmeg (optional)	1 mL
8	slices day-old French bread, cut $^3\!/_4$ inches thick	8
	butter or margarine, melted	
	maple syrup	

Preheat oven to 500°F. Beat together eggs, milk, sugar, vanilla and nutmeg. Place bread slices on rimmed baking sheet. Pour egg mixture over bread and let stand a few minutes. Turn slices over and let stand until all egg mixture is absorbed. Place slices on greased baking sheet. Brush each with melted butter, bake 8 minutes. Turn, brush again, bake 10 minutes longer. Serve with maple syrup. Note: can also be fried in a medium-hot, well-buttered pan.

Maple Sugar on Snow

Boil maple sap until it forms a soft gummy puddle when dropped upon clean, freshly fallen snow. Ladle a small, bite-size portion at a time, then give it a moment to cool. Enjoy. It forms a delicious, hot lump that can be savoured as is or enjoyed with a plain "old-fashioned" doughnut (the closest we come today to the fry cake eaten with this years ago) and a hot drink. Nova Scotian writer Florence M. Hilchey once wrote that "served with plain doughnuts, hot coffee and sour pickles, there is little to compare with its taste simplicity."

Cinnamon Maple Toast

Always wonder what to do with maple sugar, other than eating it like candy? A "pioneer" at Kings Landing explained that it was shaved for use as a sweetener. Her family favourite was enjoyed in the evenings as a "bed lunch" made with Mom's homemade bread. All you need is maple sugar, butter, cinnamon and bread for toasting. Cream together enough butter and shaved maple sugar to allow mixture to spread easily on hot toast. Sprinkle with cinnamon. Serve at once.

Drying fish is a method of preservation that dates back to prehistoric times when it was air-dried on racks located close to the shore. Maritimes settlers did the same. Later, salting fish became feasible on a large scale and faster methods, not as dependent on the weather, gradually replaced outdoor drying. Fish are salted, then dried until their water content is reduced to about 15 percent. Resembling weathered boards, fish prepared this way are superior for storage.

MAPLE PARFAIT

"I remember my old aunt in Truro, she would never tell you a recipe straight. She always left out an ingredient," reminisced my friend Karen Murray of Charlottetown. But she did figure out the how-to of one of her aunt's specialties. "It's important to do all of the blending before heating, or it will get lumpy. The original recipe said to beat three eggs in a dipper," she recalled. "My aunt made it in those old-style ice cube trays, the ones with the removable dividers. I use a Pyrex cake pan." Cut into squares to serve. "It's delicious."

3	eggs, well-beaten	3
1 $^1/_2$ cups	maple syrup	325 mL
1 tsp	gelatin	5 mL
1 tbsp	cold water	15 mL
2 cups	whipping cream	500 mL

Mix eggs and maple syrup until smooth. Bring to medium heat in a double boiler. Dissolve gelatin in cold water and add to egg mixture. Stir occasionally until it thickens. Cool. Whip cream until stiff. Beat maple syrup mixture again to smooth it out, then blend well into whipped cream. Pour into Pyrex cake pans ($^1/_{12}$–inch–thick mixture) and freeze.

SALT COD AND SCRUNCHIONS

Serves 4

Any collection of old Nova Scotia recipes includes ingredients that could be stored over the long winter. Many kitchens had a supply of dried salt codfish, potatoes and fat salt pork. Variously known as fish-and-scrunchies (for "scrunchions," salt pork scraps traditionally used as a topping for main dishes), Dutch mess, house bankin and hugger-in-the-buff, salt cod and pork scraps still make a popular dish. You may have seen salt cod looking like dried-up pieces of gnarled old shingle off the back barn; it's hard to believe it can be as delicious as it is.

1 lb	salt cod	450 g
4	medium potatoes, cut in eighths	4
¼ cup	diced salt pork	50 mL
2	medium onions, sliced	2
2 tbsp	vinegar	30 mL
¼ cup	milk	60 mL

Soak cod in water overnight, then cut into serving portions. Place in saucepan with potatoes, cover with boiling water. Simmer 30 minutes or until potatoes are tender. Drain, place on warm platter. While fish and potatoes are cooking, fry salt pork until crisp. Remove and set aside. Add onions to fat, cook until tender. Return pork scraps to pan, stir in vinegar and milk. Bring to boil and pour over fish and potatoes.

Note: Any leftovers would be added to a white sauce, along with a few peas, and when hot poured over toast for a noon meal.

Scottish Fare

"Aahck now, we canna talk about the food wi'out a mention of the sheep and lambs brought in by the Scots. A bonnie animal that kept us warm wi' its wool, multiplied itself to serve us and finally gave us meat for the larder." Words like these would surely have been spoken by some of the Scottish immigrants who settled our countryside. It is a certainty they would not have used lamb in stews such as this from Cape Breton; it would have been mutton that found its way into the stewpot. The fact that we can easily get lamb and rarely see mutton is a sign of how things have changed.

It isn't easy to get stewing lamb, and roasts or chops are expensive to use in a stew, so I have turned to the ground lamb that comes in a tube, like sausage meat. Thaw in the package, then carefully slice.

SCOTCH LAMB STEW

Serves 4–6: a dish for company!

½ cup	oil	125 mL
3 lbs	lamb stew meat, cut into 1-inch cubes	1.5 kg
1	clove garlic, mashed	1
1	large onion, diced	1
2	carrots, sliced	2

2	stalks celery, diced	2
4	sprigs parsley, chopped	4
	salt and black pepper to taste	
1 cup	pearl barley	250 mL
2 cups	beef bouillon	500 mL
1 cup	dry white wine	250 mL
1	bay leaf	1

Heat $^1/4$ cup oil in large skillet, add lamb, brown on all sides, remove to slow-cooker. Place garlic, onion, carrots, celery and parsley in skillet and sauté lightly; add to lamb and sprinkle with salt and pepper. Add remaining oil to skillet and sauté barley, stirring constantly, until barley turns a golden colour — be very careful not to burn it. Add barley and remaining ingredients to slow-cooker. Cover, turn on low and cook for 8–10 hours or until lamb is tender.

Nellie McGowan

Nellie McGowan was born in Tynemouth Creek, New Brunswick, on July 6, 1876. In 1878 her father moved his family to Partridge Island at the mouth of Saint John Harbour, established as a quarantine station in 1785 to protect the inhabitants of the port of Saint John from diseases that often ran rampant through the crowded quarters of ships packed with immigrants. Her father took the position of assistant lightkeeper, continuing to work for the marine and quarantine departments until he died in 1902. Nellie saw much tragedy in her life as immigrants succumbed to disease. She was, however, a young woman who did her utmost to make the best of any situation, as shown in her diary. "The sick men are very sick indeed," she wrote. "Bessie's birthday (March 14) passed without much celebration of any kind only I made a nut cake with all the ring, thimble, button and cent combination. Fred got the button and Bessie a cent, sure sign that she will be married first. The rest of us didn't count.

— *The Diary of Nellie McGowan, Partridge Island Quarantine Station* (1902) by Harold E. Wright, Fredericton Public Library Historic Collection

MARCH 14, 2000 — Enjoying my lunch while watching the noon news, I was saddened to see the demolition of the old Red Rose Tea building in Saint John, N.B. Pity.

From My Kitchen Window

In the 1970s we lived in Riverdale, a half-hour drive from Charlottetown in the summer and a lot longer in winter. Our house was on the far side of a small valley, a couple of miles from the highway. The big farm kitchen, at the front, was the perfect place to sit sipping a coffee while watching for the snowplow, often in vain. Our road caught snow. Drifts could get almost up to the wires on the telephone poles. It took special equipment to get through that.

We had a Kemac stove that burned wood or gravity-fed oil. Oil was handy for night warmth, especially when the power went out, but was dangerous. When home we burned wood, turning off the oil with a "turny thing" on the pipe from the tank outside. One day I didn't get that turny thing turned all of the way. Oil dripped into the ash catcher, eventually overflowing and seeping out the front. When I lit the stove the oil created a ribbon of fire across the kitchen. Thankfully Jack was home and quick-thinking. He opened the back door, pulled the ash-pan out, threw it into the snow, dashed back in and smothered the flames. If I had been alone we would have lost the house, because all I could think of was getting everyone out.

Another never-to-be-forgotten memory arises from a blizzard that lasted for more than a week. Jack was heading for Kentucky for a two-month farrier course; he had always wanted to shoe horses so was eager to go. After days of high winds and continuous snow, the weather abated. Our road was drifted in and the power was out, but the airport was reopening. Nothing would do but the man had to go. Friends agreed to pick him up on the Trans-Canada Highway if he walked out.

Our son John and I stood at the kitchen window for hours, watching him climb up and over drifts, down the steep hill, up the other side, sliding his luggage along, until he was out of sight. Seeping cold warned us the stove was nearly out so we took turns with the telescope, one watching and praying, the other feeding the fire. Hours later our friends called; they had him.

The warm, cozy kitchen was a welcome place for doing the farm bookkeeping during the winter months. "Like many others we used to start out the year with a brand new account book and lots of pep. It was a grand hobby for stormy evenings, but always our zest for bookkeeping gradually waned, until, along about syrup making time, our account book lay unopened for days at a time," wrote one woman who kept two calendars on the wall, one specifically to record the daily egg count, the gas bill and the cream cheque. She maintained that by summarizing at the end of the year they realized that 85 well-cared-for hens laid more eggs than 125 kept the year they were short of grain, and that they should always keep well stocked with feed because running out in stormy weather cut production. Her other calendar was for "a radio program we may forget, birthdays, or a reminder of a promise to provide a contest prize for the church social." Smart lady!

March

43

Two days later he called — he had finally made it to Kentucky.

Meanwhile, our power was still out. It would be another few days before it came back on. Not to worry, we had the power-out-snowed-in thing down pat.

Blankets were hung over doors to partition off parts of the house we didn't need to heat, keeping the warmth in the kitchen and the bathroom above it — thanks to a hole and grate in the floor — thus protecting the pipes from freezing.

Firewood was brought up from the cellar and stacked to dry for at least a day before we used it in the stove. Dry wood burns best, lasting longer. We always used seasoned wood for best heat value.

As country dwellers we had many jugs of water stored away. However, in power outages of this length we collected buckets full of snow to melt for flushing the toilet. We also had an ample supply of food, canned and frozen. After two days of no power we started seriously cooking frozen food. Canned goods keep, thawed food won't.

Since we had horses to care for we had no trouble filling the daylight hours. Water for several animals had to be melted, then carried up and over a drift that was almost up to our second-floor bedroom windows. There was no sense trying to dig. Snow drifed in almost as fast as we shovelled. The only way over that ground drift was to slide out the kitchen door, then crawl spread-eagled so that we didn't sink, sliding the buckets ahead.

Darkness came early, but John and I were tired. We spread our sleeping bags in front of the stove and talked ourselves to sleep. Those eight days, and many other power outages and winter storms, provided wonderful, magical memories for our family. Inconvenient times, but the best. Working together to survive the elements is a great bonding experience if you have the right attitude.

Turnips

There is a common belief that potatoes were the most important vegetable for the first European pioneers to homestead our shores. Not so, said one historian. The turnip deserves credit it doesn't get.

Early accountings tell of its importance. Easy to store, rich in vitamin C, turnips were valued by sailors and settlers alike. Apparently Jacques Cartier wrote that he planted "seeds of our country," which included turnip, on his third voyage to Canada in 1541. Early Acadians recorded being heartily fed up with turnip in late winter; served boiled, in a stew or soup for the main course, then served up again as a second course.

The yellow table turnip we eat today is said to be a descendant of a later Swedish variety called "rotabagge," meaning "round root," which made its way to Scotland and then Canada in the 1880s. The turnip, or rutabaga, we eat today is tastier and more tender.

RUTABAGA AND POTATO SOUP

1	small rutabaga, peeled and cut into small pieces	1
1 1/2 cups	water	375 mL
1 tsp	salt	5 mL
2	medium potatoes, thinly sliced	2
2 cups	milk	500 mL
3/4 tsp	sugar	3 mL
2 tbsp	butter	30 mL
	salt and pepper to taste	
	parsley	

Place rutabaga, salt and water in saucepan, bring to boil and cook 15–20 minutes. Add potatoes and continuing cooking 10 minutes. Do not drain. Mash thoroughly; add milk, sugar, butter and additional salt if needed, and a dash of pepper. Reheat and serve piping hot garnished with chopped parsley, or croutons and paprika; serve with bread sticks and dark rye bread.

MASHED TURNIP-POTATO SUPREME

Serves 6

6 cups	diced turnip	1.5 L
2 cups	diced potatoes	500 mL
2 cups	boiling water	500 mL
1	chicken bouillon cube	1
2 tsp	salt	10 mL
1 tbsp	sugar	15 mL
3/4 tsp	black pepper	3 mL
1 cup	grated cheddar cheese	250 mL
2 tbsp	minced onion	30 mL

Dissolve chicken bouillon cube in boiling water. Add turnip, potatoes, salt and sugar. Bring to a boil, cook until turnips are tender. Drain, mash; add pepper, cheese and onion. Beat until fluffy.

There is another chapter to the turnip tale. In 1901 *The New Household Manual* published in New Brunswick suggested the turnip was an important decorating device for the home: "Produce a large-sized turnip or carrot; trim off a portion of the root end, and scrape out the inside, leaving a pretty thick rind all around; fill the inside with earth, and plant therein a morning glory or some other clinging vine. Suspend the vegetable with cords, stalk downward, and in a short time the vines will twine around the cords, and the turnip or carrot sprouting from below, will put forth leaves and stems that will turn upwards and curl gracefully around the base."

All I can say about these hanging planters is that they must have had some of the biggest carrots…

BEEF IN GUINNESS

In celebration of the St. Paddy's Day storm, which seems to be pretty nearly a sure thing, we bring you this Irish recipe to honour our friends at the Olde Dublin Pub in Charlottetown. They say a narrow neck keeps the bottle from being emptied in one swig.

2 1/2	beef briskets	2 1/2
2	large onions	2
6	medium carrots	6
2 tbsp	seasoned flour	30 mL
1 cup	Guinness stout and water, mixed	250 mL
	fat or beef drippings	

Cut beef into chunks. Peel and slice onions and carrots. Toss beef in flour and brown quickly in hot fat. Remove beef, fry onions gently. Return beef, add carrots and liquid. Bring to boil, reduce heat and simmer. Cover tightly and cook for 1–2 hours. Check that it doesn't dry out, adding liquid if necessary.

VERSATILE MEAT SAUCE

This recipe card has been in my box so long it's all dog-eared and torn. That's okay because I have made it so many times I almost know it by heart. I cool it and measure it out into freezer bags.

Measure sauce into amounts appropriate for a layer in lasagne, a topping for spaghetti, over cooked rice, for sloppy joes, or to combine with a tin of red kidney beans and touch of chili powder for chili; freeze. Excellent combined with cooked macaroni and veggies for a casserole.

— VJM, Pictou, N.S.

TIP

Try putting slices of onion in the bottom of a pan in which you roast meat. It will caramelize, making nice colour for your sauce or gravy. I often add carrots and parsnips, making a bed for braising ribs. Drain off the fat, mash or purée vegetables and add to the gravy. Delicious.

3 lbs	lean hamburger	1.35 kg
	cooking spray or oil	
2 cups	chopped green pepper	500 mL
3	cloves garlic, peeled and minced	3
1 tbsp	salt	15 mL
1 tbsp	curry powder	15 mL
1 tbsp	chili powder	15 mL
1 tsp	mustard (dry)	5 mL
5–6	drops Tabasco sauce	5–6
1 tbsp	Worcestershire sauce	15 mL
½ tsp	ground black pepper	2.5 mL
2	onions, chopped	2
1	13-oz can tomato paste	1
2 ½ cups	water	625 mL

In a large, heavy-bottomed pot brown meat, garlic, onion and green pepper until all redness is gone from the meat (if necessary use a spray or brush of cooking oil to coat the skillet before starting). Add remaining ingredients and simmer over low heat for 45 minutes: if you like milder garlic flavour, leave the cloves whole and remove after simmering. Allow to cook, then divide and use or freeze.

DOUGH FOR CHILDREN'S PLAY

1 cup	flour	250 mL
1/2 cup	salt	125 mL
1/4 tsp	cream of tartar	1 mL
1 cup	water	250 mL
2 tbsp	vegetable oil	30 mL
	a few drops of food colouring	

Add food colouring to water and mix all ingredients together. Cook on low heat until solid. After cooling, store in fridge in airtight container or bag.

CHICKEN POT PIE

Although I have an English heritage and grew up loving meat pies, I bow to those who credit our German ancestors with contributing the chicken pot pie to our culinary mix. Chicken pies were, according to folks more knowledgeable than I, famous in Nova Scotia — anywhere there were German settlers.

Serves 6

1	stewing fowl (5–6 lb/2.25–2.75 kg)	1
1	onion, whole	1
2 tsp	salt	10 mL
	dash of pepper	
2 cups	milk	500 mL
1 1/2 tbsp	chicken fat	20 mL
1 1/2 tbsp	flour	20 mL
	dash of paprika	
1/2 tsp	salt	2.5 mL
1 cup	chicken stock	250 mL

Cut chicken in pieces; place in kettle with whole onion. Add seasonings; add hot water to cover. Simmer gently until tender; remove fat; strain stock. Remove meat from bones. Blend chicken fat and flour together; add paprika and salt. Let bubble 3 minutes. Add milk; cook and stir until smooth; add chicken stock.

Birdfeeders

Niger seed can be fed in a pantyhose feeder — a handy thing to know when high winds threaten to smash the plastic tube kind. If they have a few runs it's easier to get the seed out, so use old ones. Cut off one leg, pour seed in and tie a knot to close it. You can slip the knot into a "V" in the branches, or use string to hang. Goldfinches (wild canaries, in layman's lingo) and redpolls will love you.

Combine with chicken; place in 2-quart greased casserole. Cover with tea biscuit topping, rolled ¹/2-inch thick; cut a 2-inch round from centre to allow escape of steam during baking. Alternatively, biscuit mixture may be cut in small rounds and placed close together to cover pie, but leave the vent. Bake in hot oven, 425°F, for 20 minutes.

Prune Pie

Carefully wash 1 cup of prunes and soak for several hours in enough cold water to cover. Add ¹/2 lemon, thinly sliced, and the juice of 1 ¹/2 lemons. Cook until tender in water in which prunes were soaked. Remove stones from prunes and stir into juice; pulp ¹/2 cup sugar and 1 tablespoonful flour mixed together. Line a pie plate with pastry, pour in prune mixture. Cover with an upper crust, bake in moderate oven.

Fig Relish

Relishes, much favoured in the Victorian era, were usually made at home. This one used the dried fruits that came in on sailing ships:

"Take equal parts of figs and dried apricots. Cover with water and cook until slightly tender. Add one-half as much sugar as fruit, one-half as much water as sugar. Cook until mixture is the consistency of jam. Nuts chopped fine, raisins and orange may be added if desired. This is a delicious relish for meats or jam to be eaten with bread and butter."

One of the few times the boys lined up to wash dishes was when we went winter camping. The camp kitchen was always protected and the dishwater a nice, warm place to put your hands for a while.

RUBY SCONES

Makes 8

At this time of year early cooks were forced to use ingredients stored in cans and jars: unlike modern cooks they couldn't just pop out to the grocery store. Many wonderful tastes and flavours have been forgotten as a result of our growing dependence on the convenience of store-bought foods. Taking time to do some scratch cooking is a good thing and will bring back old satisfactions. This modern recipe duplicates an old favourite prepared from what was in the pantry. Delicious served warm on a chilly day.

³/₄ cup	maraschino cherries	175 mL
2 cups	all-purpose flour	500 mL
¹/₄ cup	granulated sugar	60 mL
¹/₂ tsp	salt	2.5 mL
2 tsp	baking powder	10 mL
¹/₂ tsp	baking soda	2.5 mL
¹/₃ cup	butter or margarine	75 mL
1	egg	1
¹/₂ cup	flaked coconut	125 mL
1 tsp	crystallized ginger, finely chopped	5 mL
1 cup	confectioner's sugar	250 mL

Drain cherries, reserving 2 tablespoons juice. Cut cherries into quarters; set aside.

In large mixing bowl combine flour, granulated sugar, salt, baking powder and soda. Using pastry blender, cut in butter until mixture resembles coarse crumbs. Beat together egg and buttermilk. Add egg mixture, coconut, ginger and drained cherries to flour mixture, stirring with fork only until combined.

Lightly knead on floured surface 12 times. Pat or lightly roll dough to ¹/2-inch thickness. Cut into 8 pieces, using floured, 4-inch round biscuit cutter. Place on ungreased baking sheet. Using sharp, floured knife, cut each scone into 4 wedges, but do not separate.

Bake in a preheated 400°F oven 10–12 minutes, or until light golden brown. In a small bowl, combine confectioner's sugar and reserved maraschino cherry juice; mix well. Drizzle glaze over hot scones. Serve warm.

POOR MAN'S PUDDING

Serves 6–8

"I don't have a lot to tell about this recipe except that the reason it's called Poor Man's Pudding is that it's cheap to make. Mom, who lives in the Annapolis Valley, told me they couldn't afford a lot so it was a 'poor man's' dessert. It's best served hot straight from the oven, so we always had it in the wintertime. It always seemed to warm you up on a cold winter's day. I still make it for my family."

— Deborah Ann Smeltzer

Mix a batter in a large bowl, using the following ingredients:

1 cup	white sugar	250 mL
4 tsp	baking powder	20 mL
1 cup	milk	250 mL
2 cups	flour	500 mL
1 tsp	salt	5 mL
4 cups	apples, chopped fine	1 L
	(optional; they make the pudding moist)	

Make a sauce:

1 cup	brown sugar	250 mL
1 tbsp	butter	15 mL
2 ½ cups	boiling water	625 mL

Place batter into a deep round baking dish. Pour hot sauce over it. Bake for approximately 30 minutes at 375°F until nicely brown. When done, the batter will be on top and sauce on the bottom. Serve hot.

Kitchen Organization

We moved into our current home in March in the midst of a Prince Edward Island winter. It was, according to friends, a sign of true insanity. Mother Nature sucked us in, then zapped us with storm after storm, so the final move became a true test of fortitude.

The kitchen contents were among the last to go. We had everything in baskets and boxes, fully intending to put it away and go back for another load. That was when I realized that we had half the cupboard space and much of it was too high, too deep, and out of reach. At five feet one-half inch I could reach only the bottom shelf of the cupboards.

In desperation I tossed spices into a drawer. They had to lie down, but the drawer was big and long so I got them all in. It functioned so well that they reside there to this day. It is dark, handy, and everything is easy to find. If your drawer is deep, stand the bottles up, buy round stickers to fit and put the names on top.

I love my drawer system so much that I took another drawer to house my tea, coffee and such. I always have a good variety of herbal teas, hot chocolates and coffees on hand to suit various friends' tastes. In the drawer they are in plain sight and easy to access. Once coffee is open it goes in the freezer.

Tancook Cabbage

The Island of Tancook, seven miles out from Chester in Mahone Bay, is famous for its cabbages and the sauerkraut residents make from them. Prolific crops of oversize cabbages weighing up to 25 pounds were shipped abroad, but it is the sauerkraut produced by generations of Tancookers that has placed it on Canada's culinary map. Sauerkraut as a favoured dish spread to Lunenburg and indeed throughout the south shore of Nova Scotia. Its giant cabbages have made Tancook unique among the offshore islands, for here farming is as important as fishing.

PORK, KRAUT AND POTATO DINNER

Serves 6–8

In times when dinner could simmer on the wood stove all day long, stews and one-pot dinners were very popular. Few of us have a wood stove today, and if we do we don't usually cook on it. We do, however, have slow-cookers that work almost as well. This recipe would have been made with a family's own pork and sauerkraut. We have adapted to store-bought.

2–3 lbs	smoked pork shoulder roll	900 g– 1.35 kg
4	potatoes, peeled and quartered	4
2	onions, diced	2
27-oz	can sauerkraut, drained	796 mL
2 cups	chicken broth or other stock	500 mL
	salt and black pepper to taste	

Place pork and potatoes in cooker. Combine all other ingredients, pour over all. Cover, cook on low heat for 6–8 hours, or until pork is tender and potatoes cooked.

…

Sauerkraut put down in the fall is ready to eat. A mainstay of those with German heritage, it is excellent with sausages on a bun. Or try these German pork chops, today's adaptation of yesterday's casserole:

March

51

GERMAN CHOPS

Serves 4

Any kraut lover will tell you these smell good, look good and taste great! This recipe from Tatamagouche, N.S., was originally made using individual-serving covered dishes.

27–oz	cans sauerkraut, drained and rinsed well in cold water	796 mL
2 tsp	caraway seeds	10 mL
3	pork chops, about $\frac{1}{2}$-inch thick	3
2	cooking apples, peeled, cored and sliced	2
2 tbsp	raisins	30 mL
4 tsp	brown sugar, packed firm	20 mL
4 tbsp	apple juice or water pepper to taste	60 mL

Preheat oven to 375°F. Grease or oil shiny side of 4 sheets of foil (heavy-duty). Press excess liquid out of sauerkraut. Divide between sheets of foil. Sprinkle with caraway seeds, place chop on each and give a shake of pepper. Top with apple slices and raisins. Add brown sugar and apple juice. Seal in foil, with a double fold to seal. Place on cookie sheet and bake 1 hour. Open carefully when ready to serve.

Around the Kitchen Table: Seed Catalogues

As we anticipate winter winding down, one sure addition to the kitchen table is a proliferation of seed and garden catalogues. Even nongardeners take heart from these indicators that spring is just ahead.

We decided to create a garden that features plants and trees

TIP

Now is a good time to start saving those empty spice bottles with the holes in the top. They are great for planting tiny seeds. Just sprinkle or, if very fine, mix the seeds with unflavoured, powdered gelatin. It breaks down in the soil, releasing just a little nitrogen, and the colour helps you see where you have sowed seeds.

native to our home province, Prince Edward Island. To learn about what works where, we turned to Macphail Woods Tree & Shrub Nursery in Orwell, P.E.I. Managed by the Sir Andrew Macphail Foundation to preserve the homestead and surrounding property, it is a wonderful place that offers opportunities to enjoy meals served in the old style and to learn about trees and plants. Great place to take kids.

The nursery's message is that native species are reliable and hardy, adapted to local climatic conditions. Valuable to wildlife for food and cover, natives are also a great indicator of how early pioneers used plants to enhance their lifestyle. At Macphail they sell "collections" — plants that work well together to serve special needs: shade, birds, windbreak, big tree and Acadian forest collections. They also sell Jam Lover's Mix with common elder, wild rose, serviceberry, chokecherry, mountain ash and apple. Okay, that one is ticked in my order.

And I added highbush cranberry! The berries are edible and were once commonly used with other fruits in pies and jams. I like the idea of ruby red berries gracing the bushes during the winter — at least until the birds gobble them up. They are a favourite with ruffed grouse and cedar waxwing, and are eaten by more than 20 other species. Fruits hang on throughout the winter, serving as critical emergency food when other sources are not available.

I like to think I'm creating a natural kitchen out there in my garden, stocked by me and enjoyed with my feathered friends.

Another thing to consider when poring over seed catalogues is planting flowers that can be used in the kitchen. Edible flowers greatly enhance salads, make plates look wonderful for special occasions and have uses as both household and beauty aids. Cosmetics, nice smellies and such had their origins in home kitchens. Today there is a growing trend to duplicate the skills of our great-grans by mixing our own concoctions for everything from skin care to sleep enhancement.

April

— Anticipation of spring is tempered
by late storms, lingering snow,
chilly days and acres of mud.

I consider it downright impertinence for a man on a farm to talk about supporting his wife. When she cooks his meals and sews and mends for him and his children from dawn until dusk, what is she doing if she is not supporting herself?

— Francis Marion Beynon, Canadian writer

Breakfast — or "break one's fast," if you can honestly say the hours between evening snacks and the first meal of the day a fast make — is one of the most enjoyable parts of the day for those of us fortunate enough to work at home. I rise early. Jack gets up at 6 a.m. to get to work on time. Since I love early morning, when the air is fresh and the world is still at peace with itself, I join him. Besides, Tipsy decided early in life that she HAS to go as dawn breaks and the ONLY person who knows how to take her is yours truly. On good days I get to plug in the coffee maker before we head outside. On bad days it's blowing snow or freezing rain and she will hardly let me in the bathroom to do my own … well, you know … before we hit the world outside. No matter what, breakfast with a good cup of coffee is surely enjoyed when you've had a crisp winter wake-up while coaxing a dog to hurry up. She's wise enough to know that when she finishes we head indoors, so she takes her time.

During the week I partake of fruit and toast made with a nice satisfying grain- and seed-filled bread. Weekends and company days tend to be a little more luxurious.

MARMALADE FROM SCRATCH

Makes about 4 cups

In our family, something to spread on toast or a scone is a mandatory part of breakfast, tea and even a bedtime snack. One did not always have the money for store-bought jam or marmalade. They were so easy to make and fruit was plentiful enough that it was simply habit to cook up what was needed. A tart marmalade made with your own hands brings a sunshiny feeling to chilly mornings. Traditionally made with citrus, marmalade benefits from other fruit such as cranberries. Making marmalade was a skill I'd forgotten until visiting

April

cousins in England. Jennifer took up her basket and "popped off to the greengrocer" for a grapefruit and two oranges to make marmalade for tea.

I love lemons and cranberries, so came up with this favourite, but you have to use it up within three weeks or so. Choose large, good-quality fruit.

2	oranges, sliced very thin, any thick skin or seeds removed	2
2	lemons, sliced very thin, any thick skin or seeds removed	2
1 cup	cranberries	250 mL
1 ½ cups	sugar	375 mL
1 cup	water	250 mL

You should have 5–6 cups of citrus. Place in large, heavy kettle with water. Bring to full boil. Reduce heat so that mixture comes down to slow boil and cook for 20 minutes, or until fruit is tender. The key to success is the stirring — don't neglect it. Stir often, all through the process! Add cranberries and continue to cook at slow boil for 10 minutes; watch it carefully, stirring to prevent scorching. Add sugar and bring back to boil, cooking 10–15 minutes or until mixture thickens. Spoon into clean jars and refrigerate.

Life in "Our Kitchen"

I'm 28, the youngest of eight children, and I love to reminisce about my childhood. The strongest memories of life in our kitchen are, of course, of my mother and the food she made. They went hand in hand.

We are an Acadian family, so one of the meals we enjoyed the most often was "chicken fricot," a familiar dish to anyone from this region, and many other regions of the Maritimes. Basically, it is chicken soup, but you can't call it that because … it's not. We also enjoyed râpure, poutines and crêpes. Unfortunately, it was such hard work to make these dishes that we didn't get to have them very often. Something we got to sink our teeth into more frequently was Mom's homemade bread, biscuits, cookies and sweets.

I can still see myself, on a cool spring afternoon, jumping off the bus, running down our long lane, through the door … and it would hit me. The best scents this side of heaven. I'm sure of it! A big batch of fresh biscuits, another bowl overflowing with soft chocolate cookies just out of the oven!

Six loaves of bread, the crusts crackling under the melted butter Mom spread on them. Where do I start? Hurry, hurry! Decide!

Too late. In comes my brother, throws his books on the kitchen table, and pushes me aside. His hand plunges into the soup pot Mom uses to put the biscuits in while they cool. One, two, three. Only three? He must be having a bad day. He splits them in two and lines them up in a straight row. Armed with a knife, he thickly spreads peanut butter on each half. He goes down the line until the last biscuit is gone and washes it down with a glass of Tang. Then he is out the door again, on his bike, and down the road to play "common ball."

I loved watching Mom bake or cook, especially before I was old enough for school and I'd be home with her all day. When she made chocolate cookies I would anticipate that moment when she would sift the flour all over the chocolate gooey mixture. It looked like snow-covered mountains! Chocolate mountains, that is. Being the only one at home, I got to eat what was left over in the bowl!

Life was sweet.

— Lisa Arsenault, Tignish, Prince Edward Island

MOM'S DUMPLINGS IN CARAMEL

"We kids would never worry when the meat seemed a little scarce. If the larder was down Mom would always make sure that a filling sweet rounded off a meal. She could scratch something wonderful out of nothing. When we had it, she would serve it with the cream jug. My kids like it with ice cream."

— CBM, Nova Scotia

1 ½ cups	brown sugar	375 mL
2 tbsp	butter	30 mL
1 cup	hot water	250 mL
1 tsp	vanilla	5 mL
½ cup	white sugar	125 mL
2 tbsp	butter	30 mL
½ cup	milk	125 mL
1 tsp	baking powder	5 mL
1 cup	flour	250 mL
	pinch of salt	

Combine first 4 ingredients. Boil. Mix rest of ingredients, then drop by teaspoonful into the boiling syrup. Bake at 350°F for 30 minutes, or until light brown.

Living History

Children love to be doing and involved, whether they are starting seedlings for transplanting to summer gardens or doing things to protect the environment.

For a great April project, have them bring home the plastic cups from fruit, pudding and gelatin snack portions that they carry in their lunch. Punch holes in the bottom of each cup and place in old rectangular cake pans or reusable trays also salvaged from grocery store purchases. Great for starting seeds.

When it comes time to transplant, consider giving each child a container or two to work with. You can get a head start on the season by muscling the containers into the kitchen or a porch — out of danger of frost. Do it right and you just might find them creating wonderful pots full of eye appeal to grace your patio or deck. Just think how thrilled they will be!

A remarkable colonial document, the diary of Simeon Perkins is preserved in Liverpool, N.S., along with his home, which is open to the public. The widower, 27, came to the raw new settlement in 1762 to open a store and engage in the fishery. A true entrepreneur, he added lumber and shipbuilding and soon owned and operated a fleet of ships. He held many offices and responsibilities in the community.

In 1775 he took a second bride, Elizabeth Headley, and soon had a family of two sons and six daughters. Perkins' diary covers a period of 46 years, giving great insight into home life as well as early days in Liverpool. Privateers, the American Revolution and the Napoleonic Wars were part of their lives but for me the household, and particularly the kitchen is the lure.

It is amazing to be able to stand in the very room where the Perkinses entertained 16 for dinner in 1801, knocking out a wall to accommodate the large number and rebuilding it after the festivity.

The original kitchen featured a bake oven next to an open-hearth fireplace. The room was the centre of a great deal of activity. There was always a large number of people who took meals here in addition to the couple's eight children. Perkins wrote that when he was building a ship he provided board for most of his workers; thus carpenters, caulkers, sailmakers and others took their meals at Perkins House in addition to guests there for meals and overnight stays.

Mrs. Perkins had at least one hired woman, and usually a hired man. Even so, it must have been quite a chore to prepare meals on an open hearth. The cook was at the whim of the fire, with little control over heat that could only be regulated by moving the cooking utensil.

Pots were designed to sit or hang over the fire, and pans were placed at the edge or held over the flames with long handles. Cast iron pots and pans were excellent for long, slow cooking: durable, with an even heat spread. They were also heavy and tended to rust.

In 1792 an addition built on the back of the house expanded the kitchen. It had a large fireplace in the middle. When we visited, this room had a display of dyeing, bringing to light yet another aspect of kitchen life. Wool was spun, fabric dyed, garments stitched, socks knitted, all often by the warmth of the kitchen fire.

The good folks at Perkins House gave me a book filled with recipes that represent the heritage they work to preserve. They suggested I select one that reflects the close relationship between Perkins and New England, which he left in 1762; it was hard, because *Perkins' Hearth Cookbook* is chock full of great recipes from the region.

This is my choice:

Clam Fritters

"And if we've a mind for a delicate dish
We go to the clam banks."
— "The Forefather's Song," 1630

Recipes such as this one, of the sea, would have travelled with those leaving the American colonies for what was to become Canada. It was contributed to *Perkins' Hearth Cookbook* by Mabel Murray Kirkpatrick (née Ford), a descendant of *Mayflower* passengers who landed in Plymouth Colony in 1620 and ancestors who appeared in the original Liverpool, Nova Scotia, "warrant" of 1759.

2 or 3	small eggs	2 or 3
2 cups	shucked raw clams	500 mL
1 cup	flour	250 mL
1 cup	milk	250 mL
1/2 tsp	salt	2.5 mL
1/4 tsp	pepper	1 mL

Chop clams very finely. Make a batter by beating eggs, add flour gradually. Add milk slowly, salt and pepper, then chopped clams. Stir all together. Drop by spoonfuls into deep, hot fat that will colour a 1-inch cube of bread golden brown in 60 seconds, or cook in frying pan holding 1 1/2 inches of hot fat. When brown, turn and brown on reverse side. Drain and serve piping hot.

A charming way to bring "country" to your garden is to put a mailbox on a post for the birds to build a nest. Now tie that to the longing for spring that we all experience this month and you have a perfect kitchen table project. A visit to local flea markets or second-hand stores is sure to turn up an old junker mailbox. Get out some paints, turn creative and pretty one up, ready to "plant" as soon as the snow goes.

Seafood Smarts

Fish commonly called "scrod" got its name from the Middle Dutch word "schrode," meaning a strip or shred. On the Atlantic coast, scrod may be immature cod or haddock weighing 1 1/2 to 2 1/2 pounds. Sometimes the term is applied to cusk of about the same weight, or to pollock weighing 1 1/2 to 4 pounds.

A Lobster is a Lobster

Fish, naturally, is a staple food for the dwellers on New Brunswick's coast. They eat it both fresh and salted, summer, winter, spring, and fall. It comes sometimes in surprising guises. For instance, should you see Richibucto goose noted on your hotel menu, do not let the appetizing thought mislead your palate into expecting the breast of one of the numerous honkers that frequent the bay. If you do you will be disappointed, for Richibucto goose is salt shad! Just as Digby chicken is salt herring, and Shippagan turkey is salt cod.

There are no euphemisms for lobster. There need be none. Such lobsters! The whole New Brunswick shore literally crawls with them. One day three of us stopped at a restaurant in a north shore village. The French proprietor mentioned that the lobsters were very good, "Just right size. Fresh out of the water." So we ordered lobster. They were sweet, and firm, and tender, and, oh, so flavorful. We complimented the *maitre.* He raised his eye and invoked *le bon dieu.* Then we ordered a second round. Coffee and apple pie completed the ample luncheon. Our friend stepped up to the desk and asked for the check. The maitre handed him a chit marked "$.75."

"No," said our friend. "I'll pay for all three."

The Frenchman adjusted his spectacles and squinted at the check.

"That's right," he said. "Three lunches. Twenty-five cents each."

— Lowell Thomas and Rex Barton in "Along the Chaleur Shore," *In New Brunswick We'll Find It* (1939)

TREACLE TART

A staple in Maritime homes, simple-to-make sugar pies had several variations in ingredients and name, dependent on region, culture and era.

One of my fondest memories is of treacle tart. Sweet and sticky, it was made with golden syrup and just melted in my mouth. You only need a small piece — it's decadent. This recipe comes from a Cape Bretoner, Mrs. J. A. Russell. The only change made by my family was the occasional addition of raisins.

	pastry for 1 pie (open)	
⅓ cup	treacle, golden, corn or maple syrup	80 mL
1 cup	bread crumbs	250 mL
3 tbsp	lemon juice	45 mL

Line pie plate with pastry, spread bread crumbs inside, drip treacle over crumbs. Squeeze lemon juice over. Trim pie with pastry cuttings (shapes cut from leftover pastry). Cook 30 minutes in oven at 350°F.

LASSY TART

This Newfoundland version also pops up in the Maritimes.

	pastry for double pie crust	
1	egg	1
1 cup	soft bread crumbs	250 mL
1 cup	molasses	250 mL

Line 8-inch pie plate with pastry, cut pastry strips for top from remainder. Beat egg. Add molasses and beat well. Stir in bread crumbs. Pour into unbaked crust, top with strips of pastry and bake at 400°F for 20 minutes.

RITA'S BROCCOLI-CAULIFLOWER SALAD

This recipe was passed along, to me after I enjoyed this salad at a writers gathering in Nova Scotia. I was told it came from "Rita in Dieppe," so I named it for her. I find it especially enjoyable at this time of year when one longs for fresh vegetables. Make the dressing first; refrigerate for at least three hours to blend the flavours. When ready to serve, toss with salad.

DRESSING:

1 cup	mayonnaise	250 mL
4 tbsp	sugar	60 mL
2 tbsp	red wine vinegar	30 mL

Combine and chill 3 hours.

SALAD:

1	head of broccoli, separated into florets	1
1	head cauliflower, separated into florets	1
6–7	slices bacon, cooked crisp and crumbled	6–7
½	large red onion, sliced thin or chopped	½
1 cup	grated cheddar cheese	250 mL

Mix all ingredients together and add dressing just before serving.

Those Who Provide Nourishment

It wasn't just the family income that kept rural folks "down on the farm." It was also the weather. There were many days when going out for groceries was simply impossible. Deep snow was not removed from roads as quickly or as efficiently as it is today. It could be weeks, or even months, between trips for supplies.

Even today, the worst travelling time can be spring — especially for those who live on dirt roads in Prince Edward Island, where clay becomes a slippery quagmire that defeats even the biggest vehicles. Those charged with providing nourishment had to know how to plan, and more importantly how to make do. If you ran out of one thing you had to substitute another.

One woman in my past was a shining example of how talented these past-generation cooks were. Hazel Falconer lived on a farm on Caribou Island, Nova Scotia. She was a wizard with ingredients. She knew how to fix things that didn't work, how to substitute, what did what. In another life she would probably have been a food chemist or scientist. Although Hazel is no longer with us, her knowledge of the kitchen lives on through her daughters.

That was the old way: mother passed her kitchen skills on to her daughter. This is a practice more of us need to follow. It not only prepares children for life beyond our care, but quality kitchen time also creates a bond with our kids that is only gained by "doing" together. Learning kitchen skills has another, as important, benefit to our children: it teaches them confidence and self-sufficiency. It is my experience that a person at ease cooking is almost always ready to tackle new and different things.

PORRIDGE BREAD

In days when pots and pans were very expensive and hard to come by, any baking container possible would be used. This old-fashioned bread is enough to fill three large juice cans (smooth-sided).

1 ½ cups	hot water	375 mL
⅓ cup	shortening	80 mL
½ cup	molasses	125 mL
1 tbsp	salt	15 mL
1 cup	rolled oats	250 mL
2	packages yeast, dissolved in ½ cup lukewarm water	
2	eggs, beaten	2
5 ½ cups	flour	1.5 L

Grease 3 large juice cans. Mix first 5 ingredients together. Let cool. Mix in yeast mixture, then eggs, then flour mixture, 1 cup at a time. Divide dough into 3 balls and knead each one for 5 minutes, then place into a can. Let it rise 1 hour in a warm (not hot) place. Bake in 350°F oven for 45 minutes to an hour.

— Helen Grant Collection

Poutine

Now this is something food writers do: order one dish over and over again, to use as a measuring stick. I have one friend who always orders a "side" of mashed potatoes when reviewing a restaurant. It not only tells her about their food preparation techniques (instant, fresh-mashed, creative with perhaps some garlic or parsnips mashed in, dry, creamed, or old and tired), but also, in fine dining establishments where such things are not on the menu, their flexibility and dedication to pleasing the customer.

One summer I used this as an excuse to order and enjoy poutine, a concoction of French fries, homemade gravy and cheese curds. The variations around the region are legion.

"Down Nakawick they make hamburger

poutine. It's really good. We make an Italian poutine with spaghetti sauce and hamburger. With the cheese it's really good," said Amanda Bowmaster, a waitress at the Springwater Restaurant at Four Falls, between Aroostook and Grand Falls, N.B. They also serve Gralvaude Poutine, with chicken and peas, and Poutine avec Viande Fumée, with smoked meat.

Big Al's Acadian Restaurant and Lounge in Tatamagouche, N.S., serves Poutine with Fingers and Dipping Sauce. Now think about this … a platter of fries smothered in cheese and topped with hot gravy (to melt the cheese), with deep-fried chicken fingers on the side, along with a nice, rich sour cream dipping sauce. Truly wicked. And too good.

I have to say I am totally confused about the word "poutine." According to one of my favourite cookbooks, *A Taste of Acadie* by Marielle Cormier-Boudreau and Melvin Gallant, poutines made from puréed or grated potatoes, flour or bread were used as dumplings or as the pastry for pies, and could range in flavour from salty to sweet. They go on to say that Poutines Râpées, a potato dumpling with a mixture of seasoned pork in the middle, is considered a national dish by Acadians in southeastern New Brunswick. This is, they say. one of the few French dishes to survive the transition to the New World. How the heck the word gets used for fries smothered in cheese and gravy is beyond me!

You can make the fries version easily at home, piling up fries, cheese and gravy. You should use cheese curds to do it right, but lower-end restaurants use grated mozzarella.

Beans, Beans, Beans

Asked about kitchen traditions, one New Brunswick old-timer quickly responded, "Beans and wieners on Saturday night." He said it was a staple, served with homemade brown bread with molasses drizzled on instead of butter. Saturday was a going-to-town day and it was an easy meal for Mom to make after a hectic day shopping and "stuff."

"We kids were some proud to be allowed to slice the wieners and stir them into the beans," he recalled. "Mom poured a big glass of milk for each of us, Dad would slice the bread and voila, supper was ready. If the weather was fittin', neighbours would come in the evening for card play around our huge kitchen table. Each lady would bring squares or biscuits and jam and the kettle would sing on the wood stove to make continuous pots of tea."

…

Rooting around in the Yarmouth archives, we came across an old scrapbook dating back to the 1950s. This clipping was stuck, with dozens more, on the pages of an old telephone logbook:

"Friday — even if it should fall on the 13th — will be a lucky day for the family if they get Libby's Baked Beans for luncheon. And you'll be lucky if you have enough to go 'round, if you serve them in hot baking powder biscuits from which the centres have been removed. Replace the top, put a little butter on top of each, and serve surrounded with more beans. You don't need to waste the biscuit centres, just steam them up and serve them instead of dumplings with your next meat stew."

There can be no doubt that beans are an important part of Maritime kitchen lore. They could be grown, dried and easily stored. Hearty and nourishing, baked beans were set to cook while other chores were tended to. We even named a war after them! According to Colleen Whitney Thompson's book, *Roads to Remember*, the Pork and Beans War began in 1837. Folks in what we now know as Maine and New Brunswick disagreed over the border. Lumbermen on both sides got in on the action. What historians call the Aroostook War amounted to some fist-fighting and general harassment between opposing lumber camps. In 1842 the Ashburton-Webster Treaty ended the argument by firmly declaring the border.

The lumber camps were home to Bean-hole Beans — so named because a hole was dug, a fire lit and, once a bed of good red coals formed, the tightly lidded pot of beans was set in, covered with dirt and left to cook for 24 hours. They were much favoured for their distinctive flavour. Some say a slug of hot rum, presumably added to the beans, improved things even more.

There are so many versions of baked beans that I hesitate to select a recipe to include in this book. Soldier, navy, pea or white beans could be used. Salt pork, an onion and a touch of dry mustard are standard, but when it comes to the sauce there are many combinations of brown sugar, molasses, maple syrup, tomato sauce and even ginger.

Lumber Camp Beans

Soak a pound of soldier beans overnight. In the morning, simmer until the skins start to peel, then drain and rinse several times in cold water. Place the beans in a large oven-proof crock. Mix in $1/4$ pound of salt pork that has been cubed, a cooking onion, chopped, 3 tablespoons brown sugar or maple syrup, a good teaspoon dry mustard, $1/2$ teaspoon black pepper and the same amount of powder ginger, and a quarter cup, plus a little less than a half cup of molasses. Cover all with boiling water. Cover tightly and place crock in a 350°F oven for 7 hours. Serve with johnnycake, cornbread or ploye, with molasses on the table.

OLD-STYLE ACADIAN-STYLE BAKED BEANS

Keep in mind that the salt pork listed here is the old kind with a rind, which is removed.

1 $1/2$ cups	dry, small white beans	525 mL
$1/2$ lb	lean, salt pork	250 g
$1/2$	medium onion, chopped fine	$1/2$
$1/4$ cup	molasses	50 mL
$1/2$ tsp	dry mustard	2.5 mL
$1/2$ tsp	black pepper	2.5 mL
	salt to taste (optional)	

After supper, cover beans with cold water and leave to soak overnight in covered pot. Next day, drain. Remove rind from pork, slice pork as thin as possible; flatten with mallet or knife as necessary. Starting with pork, create alternating *layers of pork, beans and onions so that you end up with $^1/_3$ of pork set aside. Combine molasses, mustard and pepper, drizzle over top. Add enough boiling water to bring up to top layer, then top off with remaining pork. Cover and place in preheated 350°F oven for 5 hours. Check periodically, add water when needed. Uncover pot for final 30 minutes' cooking time.*

Boston Sandwiches

A Blue Ribbon Mayonnaise brochure, yellowed with age, was found near Edmunston, N.B. Someone had marked an "X" beside this recipe, with the note "Good for G." Have visions of some woodsman named Gabrielle or Gordon or … Gerhard opening his lunch pail to these unusual sandwiches, made on a hearty molasses brown bread. All you need: baked beans (leftovers), horseradish, mayonnaise, brown bread and lettuce.

Mix together the beans, horseradish and mayonnaise. Spread thickly between slices of bread, putting a leaf of lettuce in each sandwich. Cut in triangles and serve.

SAUTÉED COD TONGUES

Serves 4

Cod cheeks, cod tongues, cod roe … words sure to send many a Maritimer into some degree of nostalgic rhapsody. For those who lived by the sea, these were sought-after delicacies.

It was cod that attracted the first Europeans to our shores. So plentiful were the fish that men sailed across the Atlantic in search of them some 400 years ago. Those early fishermen would come on shore to air- and sun-dry cod on racks to preserve it for the long journey home. Salt cod was a staple both at home and for export until the past decade or so, when the mismanaged fishery failed.

A lady in Cape Breton told me that although cod tongues became a delicacy, the reason that people started eating this unlikely bit of the cod was less prosaic. The fish were gutted, heads removed and the rest was sold, dried or salted. Not folks to waste anything, fisher families took the cod cheeks and tongues home for their own dinner. Today they are hard to find, usually available only from September to May.

1 lb	cod tongues (if frozen, defrost completely)	450 g
1 cup	milk	250 mL
2 tsp	salt	10 mL
	flour	
1	egg	1
2 tsp	water	10 mL
	fine bread crumbs	
	cooking oil	

Rinse cod tongues in cold water, drain and soak for about an hour in milk to which the salt has been added. Drain, dry well on absorbent paper. Dredge in flour. Beat egg and water together. Dip tongues in egg mixture and roll in bread crumbs. Heat oil in heavy skillet, add tongues a few at a time, fry until golden brown on both sides. Serve hot, with lemony butter, made by heating butter and stirring in lemon juice to taste.

Cornbread

Two cups Indian, one cup wheat;
One cup sour milk, one cup sweet;
One good egg that you will beat.
Half cup molasses, too,
Half a cup sugar add thereto;
With one spoon butter new,
Salt and soda each a spoon;
Mix up quickly and bake it soon;
Then you'll have corn bread complete,
Best of all corn bread you meet.

— Exmouth Street Methodist Church Ladies, New
Brunswick, 1909

— Ellah Liscombe

Cod Roe

Roe came to be highly valued by fisher families, who fried it up for breakfast, lunch, dinner — or supper. One fisher's wife told me about her method of cooking roe: She would gently wash the roe, then tie it loosely in a cheesecloth bag and drop it into boiling water for half to three-quarters of an hour, depending on the size. When ready to make a meal she would press the roe quite flat, using one plate upon another. These row patties, cut if need be, were dipped in egg and then in fine bread crumbs and fried in drippings (fat from bacon or salt pork). The golden brown morsels were served with fried potatoes, with crumbled bacon or pork scrapple (bits of salt pork) sprinkled over the dish.

CHANCES SHIPWRECK CASSEROLE

Serves 6

The adage that too many cooks spoil the broth does not apply to learner cooks participating in a program designed to get them cookin' and send meals home for a nominal fee while teaching about nutrition and "shopping smart ." CHANCES — Caring, Helping and Nurturing Children Every Step — is held in community kitchens in Charlottetown to help parents meet the basic food needs of their families. They go away feeling that they have contributed to the cost and in the preparation of meals for their own families, as well as those of classmates. It's a wonderful program that brings people together to cook and to share the results of their labours.

"On the cooking side it is an opportunity to realize that the most cost-effective way to feed their family was making (a meal) from scratch rather than buying it from the frozen-food section," says Barb Macnutt of the P.E.I. department of education.

This is one of CHANCES' favourite recipes:

1 lb	ground beef	450 g
1 tbsp	vegetable oil (optional)	15 mL

1	onion, chopped	1
1 cup	frozen peas and carrots, combined	250 mL
6–8	potatoes, peeled and sliced	6–8
1	can tomato soup	1
	a pinch of pepper	

Preheat oven to 350°F. In a large fry-pan over medium heat cook ground beef and onion, using oil if necessary. Drain off excess fat. Mix in frozen peas and carrots. In a deep casserole dish, place half of the sliced potatoes. Spoon beef mixture over potato. Place remaining potatoes over beef mixture. Pour tomato soup over top of potatoes. Sprinkle with pepper.

Bake for 1 1/2 hours.

Around the Kitchen Table

In the years just after our family emigrated to Canada, many hours were spent visiting relatives. We were, after all, a close-knit unit exploring life in a new country and we didn't have money for going out. For a time my grandparents shared a house with my aunt, uncle and cousins, just a block from our home. One fond memory of this time is of Nanny, our grandmother, serving us three kids special treats in their tiny kitchen. Egg and Soldiers was one of our favourites. The egg was soft-boiled, perfectly cooked for her charges, with the yolk runny and the white firm. The soldiers, well-buttered bread cut into sticks perfect for dunking into our egg, were, for some reason, a real treat. The bread was firmer and tastier than the store-bought version we get today.

An evening treat, usually enjoyed after wrestling or hockey (which Nanny religiously watched every Friday night, with the family gathered around) was a mashed-banana-and-shaved-chocolate sandwich. I seem to remember the cousins sprinkling sugar on theirs!

...

Back of the loaf is the snowy flour,
And back of the flour the mill,
And back of the mill is the wheat
and the shower
And the sun, and the Father's will.

— Wesley United Church
U.C.W. Cookbook

Fish Fry

For cooking any fish. Clean, dip in beaten egg to coat, then into fine bread crumbs, flour, cornmeal or oatmeal. Dust with salt and pepper, and pan-fry in drippings, butter or oil. I love mixing a little butter into my oil, for added flavour with a few less calories.

April

Recalling childhood treats is a grand way to loosen tongues at family gatherings. Try it some time — be sure to have ingredients on hand so folks can recreate favourites. The results can be hilarious … and you know some of those old concoctions still prove decadently delicious.

Most of us have family stories relating to meals of which the basis was bread. Bread and molasses for many Maritimers, bread and drippings in mine. Old pioneer diaries often recorded having little to eat besides bread, especially during the long, cold winters. Even with these memories of bad times, we Canadians have a long-standing love affair with bread. Why, it was even a good trading item!

Jack and I have a saying: "Everything tastes better between two slices." We confess to loving sandwiches and accept that they become very personal — so personalized that we seldom prepare sandwiches for each other, at least not when anticipating a decadent munch-down (versus a filling-the-hole/stuff-it-in-type fast meal).

I have a number of favourites:
- sockeye salmon mashed with malt vinegar (not mayonnaise), tomatoes and alfalfa sprouts on toasted 12-grain bread
- Marmite and very old cheddar cheese on a toasted scrumpet (a cross between a biscuit and a crumpet)
- extra old cheddar cheese and sliced beetroot (in vinegar, not pickled with sugar) on toasted dark rye
- Bovril on toasted anything
- once a year, on Boxing Day, I absolutely must have leftover turkey with lettuce, and Marmite in a sandwich made with toasted homemade bread spread with the drippings and jelly from the turkey

My husband, now, his bread of choice is Grainhouse Bran because of its low sugar content, a good sourdough, or rye. He piles onto it:
- sliced vidallia, Spanish or red onion or dill pickle with peanut butter
- sliced cheese and lettuce — 'cause it keeps his blood sugars in check
- sliced cheese and a fried egg — 'cause he just plain likes the taste
- dill pickle, cold meat, tomato and lettuce
- vegetarian specials
- summer sausage (the real kind, not modern imitations) with a good strong English-style mustard, lettuce and, maybe, cheese

NEW BRUNSWICK "HAM" BURGERS

4	slices cooked ham	4
1	cup celery	250 mL
1/2–2/3 cup	sweet pickle	125–160 mL
1/4–1/2 cup	chopped onion	60–125 mL
	salt and pepper to taste	
1/4 tsp	dry mustard	1 mL
1/2 cup	mayonnaise	125 mL
2	hard-boiled eggs	2

Chop all ingredients medium-fine, mix well with mayonnaise. Fill hamburger buns, place on cookie sheet. Cover with aluminum foil (it is important to cover tightly). Bake in 400°F oven till hot (15–20 minutes).

May

— Things wild and wonderful,
from fiddleheads to lobster,
grace our tables.

Pioneer spirit must have been very strong to endure the rigorous conditions of their lifestyle. The day was a busy one filled with domestic tasks from laundry to bread making. Doing the laundry itself was an all day job. Housewives carried the water, heated it in the boiler and pots on the stove and scrubbed and rinsed each garment before hanging the clothes out to dry. When the weather was bad the kitchen was used to dry the clothes. Clothes racks, some of which were hung from the ceiling, were laden with clothes. Women took pride in the laundry. The earlier you had the clothesline full the better.

— New Perth: Link with the Past, various authors

If any one food symbolizes New Brunswick it is the fiddlehead. Prior to the arrival of Europeans, Maliseet and Mi'kmaq First Nations were using symbols of new-growth ostrich ferns on their artifacts, clothing and canoes. They recognized its benefit as one of the first vegetables of spring, saying it cleaned the body and prepared it for the upcoming season. In the spirit of sharing that often occurred between Native and settler, Europeans acquired a taste for this gastronomic delicacy, said to taste between asparagus and spinach. It was the Europeans who gave these ferns the moniker "fiddlehead," naming them for the carved end of the violin neck that they so closely resemble.

Like early peoples we, too, acquired the taste. We get fresh fiddleheads a few times a year, often picking them up at Moncton's Farmers Market. I try to save a few for Sunday breakfast, lightly cooking them along with those being prepared for Saturday dinner, to save time in the morning. Sauté and fold into scrambled eggs or incorporate into an omelette. Either way they're wonderful.

FIDDLEHEADERS BREAKFAST

Now that we are on a healthy eating regime, we try to add vegetables to breakfast by sautéeing a few mushrooms, fiddleheads and yellow peppers in a second fry-pan to serve alongside and reduce the number of eggs from the four we used to use to three. Small steps!

	button mushrooms	
	diced yellow pepper to taste	
	olive oil	
1/3 cup	fiddleheads, precooked until just tender	75mL
1 tsp	lemon zest	5 mL
1 tbsp	butter	15 mL
3	large eggs	3
2 tbsp	water (substitute milk if desired)	30 mL
2 tbsp	grated cheddar cheese	30 mL
	salt and pepper to taste	
	grated cheese, lemon zest curls	
	or chopped chives, to garnish	

Sauté mushrooms, fiddleheads and yellow pepper in olive oil while heating second frying pan over medium-high. Lightly beat eggs with water. Melt butter in second pan until it foams, then add 1/3 cup fiddleheads. Stir in lemon zest, pour egg mixture over all. As eggs cook, lift edges so that mixture runs underneath until no liquid remains; cover and cook for a minute or two until eggs set. Add cheese to half the omelette, pepper and salt to taste. Fold the other half over, turn off heat. Leave in pan 2–3 minutes to allow cheese to melt. Divide vegetables onto two hot plates, divide omelette, sprinkle garnish over all and serve with toast.

…

If the fiddlehead is picked when very young, the stalk will be as tender as the head. If late, and the green is old, only the heads are tender and can be eaten. Shake out each stalk and head carefully, so as not to break off head. To remove brownish scale, wash well in several waters — warmish water is good — and lift greens up and out of the water. Let stand in salted cold water a half-hour or so before cooking. Cook in a small amount of boiling water only a few minutes until the stalks are tender. Drain. Season with salt and pepper, butter, a few drops of vinegar or lemon juice. Ideal for a Spring supper — serve poached eggs on cooked fiddleheads. Sprinkle lightly with paprika or seasoning salt.

— *The Atlantic Advocate's Holiday Book*

May

Salmon and Fiddleheads

Fredericton, or more accurately the Saint John River Valley, is one of the best spots anywhere to enjoy fiddleheads. The folks at Kings Landing, who share the following recipe, say that the combination of salmon and fiddleheads was introduced to early settlers by the First Nations living along the river. The Maliseet living near Kingsclear annually invite folks to share a salmon and fiddlehead dinner with them as they celebrate St. Anne Day.

The Kings Landing recipe:
Cut the salmon into steaks, dip them in flour and fry crisp and brown in a little butter at medium heat 5 minutes, then turn and fry another few minutes, depending on thickness, until the fish flakes. Salmon can be steamed in its own juices by covering the cooking vessel tightly and baking in a hot oven (450°F) or over an open grill, about 10 minutes per inch of thickness. A white sauce is delicious over salmon. Fiddleheads are best boiled or steamed (5 minutes or more, until just tender), but Mr. Valentine (an 1820s carpenter characterized at Kings Landing's Fisher House) probably would have fried the greens at the same time he cooked salmon. Fiddleheads are wonderful simply steamed or cooked in a little boiling water. Once steamed, toss them in with minced garlic that has been sautéed in butter. Squeeze a little lemon juice over and season with pepper. Also great in quiche, on pizza or stir-fried and sprinkled with sesame seeds.

Living History

Kings Landing Historical Settlement in Prince William, N.B., takes visitors through accurate presentations of early kitchens of the 19th century. More importantly, a visit to this living museum that recreates New Brunswick life from the early 1800s to the 20th century is just plain good fun for everyone in the family.

Nineteenth-century residents of the Saint John River Valley were faced with constant change and development. After the American Revolution more than 6,000 Loyalist families came as refugees, followed by thousands more immigrants from the British Isles. As recounted in the book, *From the Kitchens of Kings Landing,* the first years in this new land were difficult and nourishing food was important. By 1800 farms and settlements had been established. The port of Saint John provided word of new innovations, many of which brought about radical changes to the kitchen; better-quality pots, heating and cooking stoves made life a little easier in the home. "Cookstoves with adjustable heat revolutionized cooking. Sautés, sauces and souffles could now be prepared by anyone fortunate enough to have one of the new ranges. Cooking was no longer searing purgatory. These stoves replaced hearths in most Victorian homes by the 1860s. Other gadgets that helped the farm wife included sausage makers, apple peelers, hash choppers and meat grinders."

As you wander through Kings Landing you will see the evolution of the 1800s kitchen. In the 1820 Fisher House, home of a carpenter, cooking was carried out on the large hearth that dominated one side of the kitchen. Strength and endurance were required to handle the heavy, cumbersome cast iron pots and other iron utensils — trivets, spits, pokers, hooks and shovels — forged by the local blacksmith. Morehouse House, of the same era, features a summer kitchen, equipped with a bake oven and a reflector oven for roasting meat, as well as a winter kitchen.

The 1830s Lint House was home to Catherine and Lawrence, a shoemaker who on cold days worked at his trade in the kitchen, and their three children. The home of Thomas and Jane Jones was built around a spring so there would be a constant water supply for the kitchen. Typical of many houses in the Saint John River Valley, it was built into the side of a hill; thus, the pantry and milk room stayed quite cool. Another home built in a hill, the Long House, has its kitchen, dominated by a large cooking hearth, in the basement. During the winter the kitchen would have been a warm, cheery work area for the family. This kitchen, more than any others, makes me feel I want to stay, to work there.

The 1850 Heustis House was home to older, more affluent owners, with two bedrooms off the kitchen for a hired girl and domestic worker. The pantry beside the bedrooms housed foodstuffs and utensils including a dough box, a flat wooden box with a cover in which bread dough was placed in a warm area to raise for baking.

The 1860s Joslin Farm House kitchen was well equipped with the latest stove of the time, a New Brunswicker manufactured in Saint John. A firebox in the front at the bottom heated a warming oven and bake oven as heat rose.

These are typical of the treasures from the past to be found throughout Kings Landing. It is a place that plays to the senses. Walk into any of these homes and enjoy the visual feast of hanging herbs, costumed women going about their kitchen duties, even cakes, pickles, flavoured vinegars or jams. Savour the scent of stews simmering or desserts baking; feel the warmth of the kitchen on a cool day or the coolness of water from a spring on a hot one. For that is what Kings Landing gives — experience. Each home has a component of costumed players well versed in the era they represent. Since many live on-site, these kitchens are operational. You're likely to enter in the middle of preparation, or as the resident "family" and workers sit down for a meal. Unfortunately you can't join them. That is not allowed. However, you can partake of the cuisine represented throughout the settlement at Kings Head Inn.

The area has a long history of taverns, inns and hotels that stretches back to the early settlements of the Loyalists. Travel was slower then, and although the temperance movement gave innkeepers much grief they still offered plenty of food and drink and warm hospitality. William Baird, in *Seventy Years of New Brunswick Life*, described his meal in such a place: "Everything to satisfy a hungry man is here: ham and eggs, fowl, venison of moose or deer (found within a hundred yards), pies, doughnuts, and the inevitable apple-sauce …"

The cooks at Kings Landing, whether working to interpret the social history within the houses or to prepare meals for the public in the inn, are the heart of the settlement. For a look at Saint John River Valley's culinary past, a taste of flavours of yesteryear, take a step back at Kings Landing. Many of the recipes prepared in the settlement are to be found in their cookbook and they have kindly allowed us to reproduce a few below.

COLCANNON

This traditional Irish dish used vegetables that could have survived through winter in cold storage. It was, I'm sure, being prepared during one of our visits.

1 lb	cabbage, coarsely chopped	450 g
2 lb	potatoes, peeled	900 g
1	small onion	1
¼ cup	butter	60 mL
2 tbsp	cream	30 mL
	salt and pepper	

Boil cabbage and potatoes in large pot until tender. Sauté onion in butter in large frying pan. Add cooked potatoes, cabbage and cream. Mash mixture together, add salt and pepper to taste, serve. Or: boil potatoes and greens, or spinach, separately; mash the potatoes; squeeze the greens dry; chop them quite finely and mix them with the potatoes with a little butter, pepper and salt; put it into a well-buttered mould; let stand in a hot oven for 10 minutes.

HUNTER'S PIE

Also known as Irish Stew.

4	mutton chops	4
24	potatoes, cooked and mashed	24
¾ cup	mutton or beef gravy	175 mL
	salt and pepper	

Braise or lightly brown chops with a bit of fat, seasoned well. With a little water added, stew over low heat for half an hour, or until cooked. Boil, mash and season potatoes. Butter your mould (casserole dish), line it with half the potatoes; put in the mutton, cover it with potatoes. Bake for half an hour in a moderate oven (375°F) oven, then cut hole in top and add some good gravy to it.

Sporting Life

Sport fishing, and fishing lodges, hold an important place in New Brunswick history. By the mid-19th century the inland fishery was not just a food source but also a leisure pursuit for residents and tourists alike. In fact, it brought a touch of elegance and luxury to the woodlands. Food and nourishment took on great importance right from the first as adventurous individuals pursued the thrills of finding the very best fishing spots.

Consider the words of Lieutenant Campbell Hardy of the Royal Artillery, who in 1855 penned a book, *Sporting Adventures in the New World*, recording his quest for the mighty salmon:

"Our tea having been all exhausted the Indians made a decoction of burnt biscuit boiled in water, which they called 'coffee.'

"A few potatoes, which had hither to escaped notice in the bottom of one of the sacks, were discovered with delight, and immediately roasted."

…

By the 1860s a rising middle class took to the rivers, lakes and forests for fishing excursions, travelling by horse and wagon, ferry, steamboat and railway. The hardiest used birchbark canoe and portage to reach remote locations.

Angling trips became the base of an industry and spinoffs such as superb recipes for salmon became legendary. Fishing camps such as Stanford White's two New Brunswick camps on the Restigouche River, Camp Harmony and Kedgwick Lodge, provided luxury in the wilderness. particularly in the 1890–1930 era, a golden age for river camps. Clientele that included Joseph Pulitzer II, the Carnegies and Vanderbilts and many more members of the American and Canadian elite led to luxurious silverware, porcelain and, more important, service. Behind the scenes, a parallel society worked to create an atmosphere of luxury in the wilderness.

For local residents the lodges meant employment. Northern New Brunswick was an economically depressed region at the time, so summer work in the kitchens was highly valued.

An exhibit at the Museum of Civilization in Hull, Quebec, compared life in the fishing camps to the British television series *Upstairs/Downstairs*. An exhibit pointed out that the days were hard — long hours over a wood stove in the July heat, or washing and ironing clothing and bedsheets. Nonetheless, veteran employees looked forward to the return of the "sports" in the spring, often developing lasting friendships with employers.

Grilled Salmon

Today we are truly blessed by the ready availability of Bay of Fundy farm-raised Atlantic salmon, one of the most delicious and healthiest seafoods. To my mind the best way to cook it is on the barbecue or pan-fried so that it develops a crisp, flavourful outside while remaining moist and tender inside. In days past, fish cooked in a heavy (cast iron) pan or griddle were referred to as "grilled."

Place fish fillets or steak on the hot pan or grill, which has been oiled. It takes only 3–4 minutes a side (depending on thickness), so cook when everything else is ready to serve. If desired, season with pepper, chives, dill or — our favourite — lemon and ginger. We serve it with a squeeze of lemon juice, but you may prefer herb butter made by blending softened butter with any fresh herbs. Keep it simple. It's delicious!

Planked Fish

If there is one way we can almost guarantee those sport fishermen enjoyed salmon it would be planked. This method of cooking, which began with First Nations who split wood and fastened salmon sides to it to cook over an open fire, has been rediscovered. We recently enjoyed cedar-planked salmon at Rodd's Miramichi River Lodge in Miramichi. This first recipe, from "SMA in Moncton," is a 1920s New Brunswick version I can just picture being served at those luxurious fishing camps.

"A fish plank should be made of hardwood, 16 inches long and 12 inches wide. Heat it very hot, place the fish skin-down, dust with salt and pepper, baste with melted butter, and put it in the under oven of the gas stove, or before a wood fire, or on the shelf in a coal oven. Cook quickly for 15 minutes; baste again, decorate with duchesse potatoes pressed through a star tube; put it back in the oven and cook until the potatoes are brown. Garnish with parsley and lemon and send to the table."

And another from SMA:

Broiled salmon outdoors — A 3- to 7-pound salmon is ideal for broiling on an open fire. Split the fish through the back from head to tail. Remove head and backbone. Place the fish skin-down on a hardwood plank, or split a log a few inches longer and wider than the fish. (An open-fire toaster may be used.) Secure with skewers and place strips of bacon or salt pork about 2 inches apart over the fish. Then stand before an open fire. Allow about 10 minutes for each inch of thickness of fish."

The Farmers Market

Every Saturday morning that we are on the Island, Jack and I head for the Charlottetown Farmers Market. Usually among the first customers, we find this one of the highlights of our week as we meet old friends and new. We spend about 70 percent of our food dollar here, buying directly from the producer. Organic beef with a flavour that stores can't offer, vegetables and fruits grown right in Prince Edward Island, baked goods to die for, fragrant herbs, freshly harvested trout and char, even fresh lettuce in the middle of winter and wild boar, elk or buffalo on occasion. Not to be overlooked are foods prepared by our ethnic community to enjoy on the spot or take home. For us, breakfast is a predetermined menu: coffee made with freshly roasted beans and thinly sliced smoked salmon on a toasted homemade bagel spread with cream cheese, with just a touch of lemon juice, thin slices of red onion and capers. If we don't afford any other treat in a week, we afford this one!

We Canadians are blessed with some of the best smoked salmon in the world and the East Coast is home to some of the best smokers. The variety of species of salmon, different water conditions where it grows and numerous methods of smoking and curing are factors that influence the taste, texture and quality of what you buy. Sometimes it takes a bit of experimenting to determine which is your favourite. Not an unpleasant task, I say!

Smoked Salmon Cukes

If you can't visit the market for salmon on a bagel, then try serving these treats to those you love — they're that good. Serve them on a cucumber slice for something cool and refreshing, or on a favourite cracker or bagel crisp in cooler weather. Garnish with dill weed and/or capers. All you need: thinly sliced smoked salmon; cream cheese, softened; fresh dill, chopped; capers (optional).

Arrange the salmon slices on a sheet of plastic wrap to make a "sheet" of salmon. Mix dill and cream cheese, then spread over salmon. Carefully roll salmon like a jelly roll. Fasten the plastic wrap around the roll. Refrigerate for several hours so that it firms up. When ready to serve, remove wrap and slice thinly, creating spirals to place on crackers or cucumber slices. Can be frozen if salmon has not been previously frozen.

Seafood Smarts 🍴

Processed salmon textures and flavours vary according to the salt curing (brining process), time and temperature of the smoking or drying, type of packaging or storing and shelf life.

KIPPERED or HOT-SMOKED: curing is done in a brine solution and smoked at high temperatures, creating a moist, tender and flaky salmon with a strong smoked flavour. A coating of coarsely ground black peppercorns transforms Kippered Salmon into "Pastrami Salmon."

LOX or NOVA LOX: cured in brine and soaked to remove salt, it may be lightly smoked at very low temperatures. Lox is less expensive to buy but often salty. It may contain food colouring.

NOVA or NOVA SCOTIA: mild curing and cold-smoking. Not necessarily from Nova Scotia; the name has become symbolic of the type of processing. Sometimes called "Novi."

SCOTTISH, IRISH, NORWEGIAN and ICE-LANDIC: sides are cured and cold-smoked, using nothing but natural ingredients — a skill perfected through centuries of experience. The smoking gives the distinctive, soft aroma of wood smoke and the unique silky, sashimi-like texture and flavour.

DRIED or JERKY: a combination of lox and kippered processes is used to create various types ranging from very smoky and moist to firm, chewy or even a rubbery product.

RETORT POUCH or CANNED: brined, lightly smoked and packed in vacuum packages or cans to ensure a stable shelf life without refrigeration.

When buying smoked salmon, read your label and get to know your smoker. There is a huge difference in quality out there in the marketplace.

First Feed

In May the first feed of the fishing season often includes lobster. In fact, on Mother's Day it's a must! The first feed of the season is traditionally to treat Mom. Many head for the famous lobster suppers that are held specially for that day. Others do as we do: they head on out to the pounds or wharves to pick up lobster and perhaps a few mussels or clams as an appetizer. The menfolk usually cook up the crustaceans — a simple procedure that can be done on the stove, or outside over a camp stove. These days you can rent terrific stands with a big pot over a propane burner.

There is no substitute for live lobster — freshly cooked if you plan a traditional down-east lobster feed. That type of meal is accessible to anyone within a reasonable distance of an airport. Live lobster can be shipped from the East Coast in the quantity you want, with just a phone call or fax and a credit card number.

Not a whole lot is needed to create a lobster supper. Fresh bread or rolls and butter, your favourite salads and some melted butter round out a meal where crackin', pickin' and munchin' the world's best finger food is just plain good times.

How to Cook Fresh Lobster

Traditionally, lobster is served freshly cooked in the shell. A meal in itself, and lots of fun, it is the perfect food for a festive occasion. When buying, look for active lobsters. The tail should curl back if pulled straight.

To cook, bring to a boil enough salted water to cover lobster (2 tablespoons salt per quart of water—noniodized sea salt is best). Holding by its back, plunge the lobster, claws first, into the water. Cover and return to boil. Lower the heat to bubbling simmer and cook 12–20 minutes, depending on size. Done when an antenna easily comes free when tugged.

Eating lobster seems tricky for the uninitiated. Approach it right and it's a piece of cake. Hold by the body, using the other hand to twist off the claw and knuckle. Watch for the pointy bits on the knuckles. Break each segment apart. If you find it hard, insert the handle of a spoon into the joint and twist. Crack claws with a nutcracker or heavy knife, on a cutting board. Remove meat with a fork or small pick. Twist the tail to remove it from the body. Break off the flippers and push out meat from the tail end. The top of the tail meat will peel back to reveal a dark vein in the centre; remove it before eating. The shell covering the body can be removed by grasping the legs and lifting it away. Inside, break apart the ribs for more white meat. The green tomalley and red roe are delicacies. For a final morsel, break off the small legs and nibble or squeeze out the meat. Do the same with the flippers. Enjoy!

…

Melted butter is traditionally served with lobster, but if you are watching fat try following the tradition from the Pictou area of enjoying plain white vinegar or mayo (low-fat) mixed with a little mustard for dipping. Or try combining tomato sauce or ketchup with mayo. A little experimenting and you have a great dip for lobster or crab. Or you can go a little more fancy.

Lemon Pepper Butter

A nice addition to a lobster dinner, or to use as a dip for shrimp or artichokes, this seasoned butter can also be used to flavour vegetables, brush over broiled fish or meats, or even spread on toast. It stores well, so can be made ahead and refrigerated in a tightly covered container until needed.

1 lb	butter	450 g
¼ cup	snipped chives	60 mL
1 ½ tsp	grated lemon peel	7.5 mL
2 tbsp	lemon juice	30 mL
1 tsp	fresh ground black pepper	5 mL

Cream butter in a small bowl until light and creamy. Add other ingredients, blending thoroughly. Store as above.

Surf and Turf in lean years — canned tuna and beef gravy on a bun.

Table Talk

A young mother of four, heartbroken when her youngest died from drinking contaminated milk, vowed to do everything she could to help others avoid similar tragedies. In 1897 Adelaide Hoodless called a meeting in Stoney Creek, Ontario, to share ideas about educating women in modern homemaking skills and working together to improve the living conditions for their families, their communities and the world. At this founding meeting of the Women's Institute the first steps were taken toward accomplishments few people realize must be credited to united women of Canada.

Maritime women were quick to join the WI movement, which was rooted in the belief that by working together women with vision could bring about change and improvement. Considering Hoodless' background, it is not surprising that the institute became key to the campaign to pasteurize milk. Other achievements affect all of us and how we carry out our daily lives. In Prince Edward Island, for instance, the institute organizes Cleanup Day in May. Folks all over the Island literally clean roadside ditches. No sluggards here: it's why the Island always looks so lush and clean. Each spring we get a spit-and-polish job!

The institute also lobbied hard for wrapping of bread, painting white lines to divide highways, and for signs at railway crossings. Other causes included music as part of the school curriculum; mandatory stopping by other drivers while school buses load and unload; requiring drivers to have insurance before obtaining their licence; breathalyser and blood tests for suspected drunk drivers; dental and medical inspections in schools; tuberculosis tests for people handling food; and establishment of higher-level learning institutions.

Good works are not the only thing that happens when WI members gather. Lunch follows the meetings, allowing hostesses to impress upon those present just how talented they are in their kitchen. When I asked my good friend Debbie Gamble-Arsenault of the Alexandra WI, in Prince Edward Island what her favourite lunch was, she didn't hesitate in naming dessert:

We were sitting on a kitchen porch, relaxing on a 90-degree, bug-free, glorious Prince Edward Island spring day, when "Mom" got rather agitated. In her 70s she is a bit of a stickler for how things should be done so I figured one of us had incurred a little wrath.

Not us.

"Just look at that," she sputtered. "Why doesn't someone do something to stop them?" pointing to the sky. "Those damn (she's a dignified lady of the truest order but she was mad!) planes. Look at them making all those clouds. The sky was pure blue, now they are making it all cloudy!"

"It's been so nice, too," she moaned. "Now this lovely weather is over."

Her daughter and I looked at each other and snickered. We shouldn't have; the sky never did clear. It turned cool and wet. Go figure. Jet planes!

JOAN JUDSON'S LEMON PINEAPPLE SAUCE

Served over angel food cake it is just too delicious!

1 package	lemon pie filling (the cooked kind)	1 package
4 cups	Cool Whip (use the light version)	1 litre
19-oz	can crushed pineapple	540 mL

Prepare lemon pie filling mix according to package directions. Cool. Add crushed pineapple (you can drain the can or add the full contents, depending on how thick you want the sauce to be). Fold in Cool Whip. Chill for a couple of hours or overnight, serve over slices of angel food cake. Scrumptious!

...

In the fair land of Nova Scotia, there is a ridge called North Mountain overlooking the Bay of Fundy on one side and the fertile Annapolis Valley on the other. Here Joshua Slocum grew up. On both sides of his family were sailors. His father was a good judge of a boat, but the farm that "some calamity made his" was an anchor to him.

Not so his son: the "wonderful sea" claimed him from the first.

Slocum was the first man to sail alone around the world, completing his voyage in 1898 in the 33-foot *Spray*. A writer as well as a sailor, he left a legacy of his voyages including the most noteworthy work, *Sailing Alone Around The World*.

Leaving Boston on April 24, 1895, he sailed east, first to Nova Scotia. After overhauling the *Spray* at Briar Island and visiting friends at various ports of call, Slocum put into Yarmouth for several days on account of fog and headwinds. While there he took in butter and a barrel of potatoes, filled six barrels with water and for $1.50 purchased the old tin clock that was to gain fame as his navigational instrument.

"My chrono is a one dollar tin clock! And of course in no time at all — I have to boil her often to keep her at it, from noon to noon," he wrote. On shipboard the day begins at noon. The noon sight, an ancient element of navigation, is a simple and convenient way of determining location.

The log of his first day in the Atlantic in the *Spray* reads in part: "9:30 am sailed from Yarmouth. 4:30 pm passed Cape Sable. Before the sun went down I was taking my supper of strawberries and tea in smooth seas."

He also wrote of fruitcake. One given to him by Lady Sterndale of St. Helena near the end of his trip lasted to be enjoyed with his first cup of coffee in Antigua, West Indies — quite a record. "The one my own sister made me at the little Island in the Bay of Fundy, at the first of the voyage, kept about the same length of time, namely, forty-two days."

Putting Up

When Doug Deacon decided to convert a one-time general store in Mount Stewart, P.E.I., into a restaurant he was amazed at the evidence of locally produced products he found. Signs were preserved and hung on the restaurant's walls. Some of the bottled and canned goods still line shelves, making for an interesting as well as scrumptious visit.

Mount Stewart Strawberry Growers Exchange offered Strawberry Preserves and the Mount Stewart fruit growers also "put up" Pure Cranberry Jam. As well, onions manufactured by "Bow's, Mount Stewart, P.E. Island" were actually preserved "boiled onions" — you can repeat the recipe below by selecting small onions, preboiling them whole until tender.

Green Thumb

Plant your herb and vegetable gardens as close to your kitchen as possible. Not only will your gardens be more convenient, but when you see them more often you will be more likely to do the weeding, pruning and harvesting needed to keep them looking good, and to notice any insect problems early.

Medicinal Receipts

" Mayapple, also known as wild lemon, raccoon berry, mandrake or Podophyllum peltatum, *was highly valued in days past. The root of the plant had considerable medicinal qualities, being helpful as a cathartic and emetic (causing vomiting) medicine and useful as an intestinal purge."*

— Shelburne Historical Society

Burn the Bologna

Bologna is a staple in many Maritime kitchens, ranked right up there with bacon or sausages. Sliced thick from a whole piece, it is pan-fried to a crisp brown. As one trucker put it in a New Brunswick truck stop, "Eggs over easy, but burn the bologna." Also known as tube steak, Newfie steak and in one P.E.I. home "meat with the rag." Bologna can be habit-forming when fried up in a hot pan till it is slightly crispy on the outside.

Flights of Fancy

As we continue to develop an outdoor kitchen for our wildlife friends, our efforts have turned to vines. This year we added honeysuckles to grow over the arbour just outside our kitchen window. We are told the trumpet-like flowers will attract orioles and hummingbirds, and many birds will enjoy its berries and nest in the vines.

Next week Virginia creeper will go in to provide a haven for chipmunks and even more berries. Downy woodpeckers, quail, chickadees and grosbeaks are just a few of the feathered friends who enjoy the creepers' blue berries.

The following is from a Bow's sign:

BOW'S BOILED ONIONS
Patent Process
THE LIQUID SHOULD BE SAVED FOR FLAVOURING SOUPS, MEATS, ETC.

AMBER ONIONS
COMBINE 2 TABLESPOONS MELTED BUTTER WITH 1 ½ TABLE-SPOONS LEMON JUICE AND 3 TABLESPOONS HONEY. ADD BOILED ONIONS AND KEEP OVER LOW HEAT ABOUT 8 MINUTES UNTIL ONIONS ARE GLAZED.

Guess-Work Cooking

She guessed the pepper, the soup was too hot;
She guessed the water, it dried in the pot;
She guessed the salt, and what do you think?
For the rest of the day we did nothing but drink.
She guessed the sugar, the sauce was too sweet,
And by her guessing, she spoiled the meat.
What is the moral? 'Tis easy to guess:
A good cook measures and weighs for her mess.

— Recipe scrapbook bought from
an auction dealer

Around the Kitchen Table

Bessie, of Murray River, Prince Edward Island, recalled her own special memories in a story, "Old Times Town and Country," which was part of a collection, "People and Stuff," gathered up by one R. C. Montgomery.

"We didn't have Best Yeast in those days. When our mother wanted to set her bread, she would give us a cent and a pickle bottle and send us for a cent's worth of yeast. There were women who made the yeast and sold it to make a few cents for themselves. We would put the cent in the bottle. Of course, usually the woman would take it out, but one time she didn't. We took a lunch to school. School would go in at 9:00 o'clock and come out at 2:00, so we would be hungry. Well, one day my sister took her lunch, a nice slice of bread — a good thick one. She took one bite, then another and there was the cent the woman forgot to take out of the bottle.

"My mother often spoke of the fun they had on moonlight nights when it was lobster-time. They would go to the shore with a basket and a stick to get lobsters. They would put the stick in the water and the lobster would grab it and they would haul him out! Then they would build a big bonfire and boil them. All the neighbours would be there. They would sit around and sing Gaelic songs and eat the lovely lobsters."

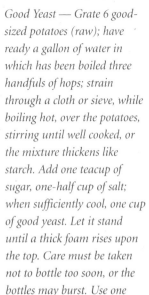

Medicinal Receipt

Good Yeast — Grate 6 good-sized potatoes (raw); have ready a gallon of water in which has been boiled three handfuls of hops; strain through a cloth or sieve, while boiling hot, over the potatoes, stirring until well cooked, or the mixture thickens like starch. Add one teacup of sugar, one-half cup of salt; when sufficiently cool, one cup of good yeast. Let it stand until a thick foam rises upon the top. Care must be taken not to bottle too soon, or the bottles may burst. Use one coffee cup of yeast to six loaves of bread. If kept in a cool place, this yeast will last a long time, and housekeepers need not fear having sour bread.

May

June

— Strawberries, socials and
succulent seafood celebrate the
long days of summer solstice.

MARRIED WOMAN'S CAKE — *One pound of true love, one pound of perfect trust and confidence, one pound of cheerfulness, a pinch of unselfishness, a sprinkle of interest in all your husband does. Method: Mix all these well with one gill of oil of sympathy, put into a tin of contentment, spice with a bright fireside and bake well all your life.*

— Mrs. Duston, *The Modern Cookbook for New Brunswick*

My fascination with old scrapbooks revealed a tattered magazine clipping titled "Tops for Breakfast." Nearest I can figure the clipping, part of a find in an "old stuff" store in southern Nova Scotia, dates to the 1950s. The food spatters on this one indicate its advice has been well used. I've excerpted a few of the neatest ideas. "Well-dressed foods, like well-dressed women, always attract attention. It's the tops and toppings that show off your foods and make them interesting and gay." Here are some different toppings you'll enjoy with your breakfast foods.

- Want a tangy bite to awaken your early-morning appetite? Make waffle sauce of orange-cranberry relish thinned with maple syrup.
- For a spicy, heart-warming breakfast, serve a topping of molasses, ginger, nutmeg and cinnamon on French toast.
- Topped scrambled eggs lately? You might want to experiment with a tomato sauce, a pineapple sauce or a cheese sauce.
- Add a gourmet touch to the morning slice of ham by spreading it with a tart jelly or jam before broiling. Apricot, peach or apple are all good with ham. Spicy applesauce over fried ham will perk up your rating as a breakfast cook, too.

This is the season when we can start moving outside for breakfast. Summer mornings are, in fact, my favourite time to enjoy the backyard. Don't hesitate to experiment with a breakfast barbecue. Ham, sausages, bacon, even frozen waffles, and of course anything toasted cooks up great. Add strawberries or other fruit and voila, breakfast with the birds.

Entertaining Royally

All of New Brunswick was agog with excitement in the late 1930s when King George and Queen Elizabeth came to visit. Probably one of the most excited was Mrs. Gilks who entertained the royal couple to tea. The Gilks' home in Doaktown, chosen as a stop for refreshments, between Newcastle and Fredericton, was a wise choice indeed as their lodge was known for their hospitality and, as one reporter put it, "so thoroughly Canadian." "Mr. and Mrs. Gilks are both New Brunswick born and their whole-hearted hospitality is marked with a simplicity of living that makes one feel instantly at home. It is typical of real Canadian rural home-life," reported Evangeline, a "home-baking" columnist.

"Sitting in the chair Her Majesty had occupied, looking out at the New Brunswick forest, it was not difficult to understand why Her Majesty, after sitting a while in the living room, came quietly into the cosy dining-room, and, placing her gloved hand upon the table said, 'I think I should like to have my tea here.' Although it had been planned to serve tea in buffet style, a few deft changes were made and Their Majesties sat down just as you or I would at the dining room table which was decorated simply with purple and white lilacs.

" 'I would have liked to serve a lot of real Canadian cooking,' Mrs. Gilks was reported as saying, 'but of course it was afternoon tea and the menu was restricted.' The honor came to us because we are half-way between the two cities, and we have a small place, although it is well known. Sportsmen come here from all over the continent during the hunting and fishing seasons. They like my home baking and the table I set.' "

The day Evangeline had luncheon at Gilks House there were Parker House rolls, plain rolls, banana bread and oatmeal cookies on the table in generous quantities. "They were so good it was hard not to reach for them between each course. Some of the sportsmen say they like hunting but declare they really come to get Mrs. Gilks' baking. Even the excitement of deer hunting or fishing for the famous Miramichi salmon would be greatly added to by the thrill of coming in at night to enjoy those fresh crisp rolls and other delicious baked products."

Mrs. Gilks, who did all of her own baking, said you need experience to turn out good baking. "You need to know not only how to bake, but what to buy to get the best results."

MRS. GILKS' BANANA BREAD

1/4 cup	butter	60 mL
3/4 cup	white sugar	175 mL
2	eggs	2
1 1/4 cups	flour, well sifted	300 mL
1 tsp	cream of tartar	5 mL
1/2 tsp	soda	2.5 mL
1/4 cup	hot water	60 mL
	salt	
2	bananas (ripe), mashed	2

Cream butter, sugar and salt. Add part of the flour that has been well sifted with cream of tartar. Add the well-beaten eggs. Add soda that has been dissolved in the hot water. Add bananas and remainder of flour. Bake in loaf tin 3/4 hour at 350°F.

Honey, I'm Home

Honey is an important part of life in the Maritimes and has a special link to June, the honeymoon month. It was the accepted practice in Babylon 4,000 years ago that for a month after the wedding the bride's father would supply his son-in-law with all the mead he could drink. Mead is a honey beer, and because their calendar was lunar-based this period was called the "honey month," or what we know today as the "honeymoon."

Just in case you feel adventurous, here is a recipe for mead that, when published in 1936, was said to be "old-fashioned."

Old-Fashioned Mead

Ingredients — Honey, hops, ginger, allspice.

Method — To every gallon of water allow four pounds of honey, and for a hogshead allow half a pound of hops, three-quarters of a pound of bruised ginger, and a quarter of a pound of allspice. The honey and water should first be boiled for 1 hour and skimmed, then the spices added and boiled for about 10 minutes. As it will probably be inconvenient to boil enough to fill a hogshead, put part into the cask and fill up every day until the cask is full. Having boiled the liquor, strain it, add the yeast on toast, and let it remain 2 days, then skim it off and put the liquor in the barrel; when the cask is full and the mead has done fermenting bung it down closely. Bottle in one year.

— Home Management

...

I've been fascinated by the number of older homes, especially in the country, which have hops growing as a vine on their porch or a fence, giving evidence to past tendencies to brew up a batch of beer.

"JUNE 19, 1879 — At candle liting up drove James Johnsons with a Bee Hive of Bees for me."

— Diary of Robert Jackson
1871–1882

"At candle lighting? What a nice expression! Robert lived in a 'do it yourself society', if you want sugar, tap the trees and boil the sap, if you want honey, hive the bees, if you want bread, grow the wheat and take it to the mill to get ground, then bake it."

— commentary by Morris Ellis, found in Moncton library

Maid of Honour Tarts

I acquired this recipe in a manner typical of the Maritimes: a friend received it from a friend who had these tarts at a bridal shower.

¼ cup	butter	60 mL
½ cup	sugar	125 mL
1	egg, separated	1
½ tsp	almond extract	2.5 mL
¼ cup	rice flour	60 mL
½ cup	flaked coconut	125 mL
	strawberry or raspberry jam	
12	3-inch tart shells, unbaked	12

Cream together butter and sugar, beat in egg yoke. Add almond extract and rice flour. Beat egg white until stiff, fold into creamed mixture, stir in coconut. Spoon about 1 teaspoon jam into each tart shell, top with 1 tablespoonful coconut mixture. Bake at 375°F for 20–25 minutes until topping is set and golden brown. When cool, dust with sifted icing sugar.

Living History

Kitchen gardens of Loyalist families were vital for medicinal as well as culinary reasons. Samples of several such gardens can be found in the Maritimes. One, the Loyalist Garden at Ross-Thompson House in Shelburne, N.S., is a mini-celebration of a family history.

The white strawberries growing there were brought to the museum from the property of Bertha Hamilton Snow in Villagedale and are known botanically as *Fragaria* and *Fragasubala*. Bertha was a descendant of Alexander and Anna McGeorge Hamilton, who came to America from Scotland between 1772 and 1774. After serving as a guide and assisting recruiting corps of volunteers for the Guides of Pioneers to serve with the British army during the American Revolution, Alexander brought his family to Shelburne in 1783.

The strawberries have many medicinal qualities. The leaves may be boiled and applied as a poultice to take away burning. The infusion will "strengthen the gums, fasten the teeth and stop the flow of blood." The berries will "quench thirst and stop the inflamation of the stomach." Distilled water (of the white strawberry) "is good against the passion of the heart, revives the spirits and makes the heart merry."

These strawberries, along with mayapples, yellow loosestrife and *Rosa mundi* are featured in the fabric Loyalist Garden, developed by the Shelburne Historical Society. *Rosa mundi* is thought to have been developed by crossing the red rose of the House of Lancaster and the white rose of the House of York, the two English royal houses that were the protagonists in the War of the Roses that effectively ended in 1485. The rose was perfected in 1551 and is the first of the striped roses. For early settlers this 16th-century "Apothecary's Rose" was highly valued for its hips, which are rich in vitamin C.

Strawberries and the socials that celebrate their arrival are one of the joys of June, with its long evenings and early mornings perfect for heading out to the picking fields.

Strawberry shortcake, the most popular of June desserts, is made with a tea biscuit, split and filled with juicy crushed strawberries, topped with more, along with ice cream or whipped cream.

Sunshine Strawberries

Fine-flavoured, large strawberries are most delicious when preserved in the sunshine. Hull, measure and allow an equal quantity of sugar. Dissolve sugar in just enough water to melt it, then cook it almost to the thread stage (220°F). Add berries and simmer gently about 10 minutes or until fruit is tender. Do not stir; try to keep the fruit whole. Pour strawberries onto large platters or shallow pans, cover with mosquito netting or glass and stand in the hot sunshine for 2 or 3 days, when mixture should thicken and jelly. Bring in each night. Put into sterilized jars and seal with paraffin.

Sweet pitted cherries, raspberries and blackberries may be preserved in the same way. Fruit may also be dried in a very low oven (110°F) instead of by sunshine.

Strawberry Sauce

Hull and cut in halves a quart of strawberries. Add a cup and a half of sugar and set in a warm place for a few hours to extract the juice. Pour over ice cream and decorate with whole berries.

— found in an old scrapbook purchased near Tatamagouche, N.S.

From My Kitchen Window

One of the most delightful occurrences at this time of year is the arrival of the hummingbirds. Feeders hung near a kitchen window will lure them close enough for a close look at these beautiful creatures. My friend Helen, who lives near Pictou, has been entertained by two families of hummingbirds who do daily battle for possession of her feeder. They whiz around the pool like little feathered kamikaze missiles. A few tips from devotees: change the nectar every few days because in the hot sun it can ferment — tipsy hummingbirds whizzing about could be dangerous.

To make hummingbird nectar, mix one part granulated sugar to four parts water. First boil the water; then add the sugar, stirring to dissolve thoroughly. Let the solution cool. Store unused solution in the refrigerator.

Rhubarb

Rhubarb, I'm told, originated in the Orient and made it to North America in the days when men wore frock coats and carried muskets. The importance it played in the Maritimes is evidenced by the rhubarb patches found near most rural kitchens.

The tart juice was often made into a refreshing summer drink by cooking it with plenty of water, then pressing through a sieve to extract the juice. The resulting nectar was mixed with a little sugar and water. Then, of course, the folks used to preserve fruits by making wine. My dad used to make rhubarb wine, which was lovely. This older method is fun to read, if not practical to make today when ingredients such as isinglass are hard to find. It brings home the fact that scales were a common measuring tool.

Rhubarb Wine

To every gallon of water add 10 pounds of rhubarb, cut in thin slices; let it stand 9 days, stirring 3 times a day. Squeeze through a cloth, and to every gallon allow 4 pounds of lump sugar, the juice of 2 lemons and rind of 1, and an ounce of whole ginger. To every 9 gallons allow an ounce of isinglass, which is to be dissolved over the fire in a pint of the wine liquor, and when cold stirred into the wine. Put into a cask, and when done fermenting bung it down, and leave till the following March before bottling. If kept until the following Christmas it is somewhat like champagne. The ginger can be omitted."

— Home Management

Oven-Stewed Rhubarb

"Mother used to make stewed rhubarb in the spring. We children liked it because she made it nice and sweet, even though she served it over custard, cake or ice cream. This holds its shape, and doesn't go into a water mush like rhubarb boiled on top of the stove. If any was left we would have it on toast for breakfast."

— CBM

Wash stalks and cut into one-inch pieces. Butter a casserole. Add a layer of rhubarb and cover with sugar. Repeat to fill, ending with sugar as the top layer. Use about half as much sugar as rhubarb. Let stand overnight (or several hours) to allow the juice to be drawn from the rhubarb by the sugar. Bake at 300°F about 20 minutes, or just until tender. Test with a knife. When cool, add a few drops of almond extract and more sugar, if desired.

Rhubarb Pie

"Cut the large stalks off where the leaves commence, strip off the outside skin, then cut the stalks in pieces half an inch long; line a pie dish with paste, put a layer of the rhubarb nearly an inch deep; to a quart bowl of cut rhubarb put a large teacupful of sugar; strew it over with a $^1/_4$ teaspoon salt and a little nutmeg grated, shake over a little flour; cover with a rich pie crust, cut a slit in the centre, trim off the edge with a sharp knife, and bake in a quick oven."

— Mrs. Flynn's Cookbook

Some old recipes for rhubarb pie called for the addition of raisins.

RHUBARB RELISH

Excellent with ham or burgers.

2 $^1/_2$ cups	diced rhubarb	625 mL
	(fresh or frozen)	
2 $^1/_2$ cups	chopped onion	625 mL
1 cup	cider vinegar	250 mL
2 cups	brown sugar,	500 mL
	lightly packed	
1 $^1/_2$ tsp	salt	7.5 mL
$^1/_2$ tsp	ground cloves	2.5 mL
$^1/_2$ tsp	cinnamon	2.5 mL
$^1/_2$ tsp	allspice	2.5 mL

Combine all ingredients in saucepan. Cook, uncovered, over low heat for 1 $^1/_4$ to 1 $^1/_2$ hours or until of desired consistency. Stir occasionally. Cool and store in covered container in refrigerator. Makes 2 $^1/_2$ cups.

Fries with the Works

Folks "up west" in P.E.I. claim to be the originators of this dish, which shows up on many menus these days. I'm not sure where the idea came from, but I can tell you they are some good. After a chilly run with our motorcycle touring club it sure is nice to haul in the Starlite Diner in Summerside for this tummy warmer. They say there is no secret — just good fries, nicely browned onions and great-tasting gravy. All you need: fries; peas; fried onions; hamburger, cooked and broken into bite-size pieces; gravy. Pile on a plate in the order given.

BACON LAMB ROLL

Serves 6–8

2 lb	ground lamb	900 g
1 $^1/_2$ cup	cracker crumbs	375 mL
1	large onion	1
3	eggs, well beaten	3
1 tsp	salt	5 mL
$^1/_2$ tsp	nutmeg	2.5 mL
$^1/_2$ tsp	pepper	2.5 mL
$^1/_4$ tsp	thyme	1 mL
$^1/_4$ tsp	allspice	1 mL
6	bacon strips	6

In a large bowl, combine all ingredients except bacon. Shape the mixture into a loaf with your hands. Lay the bacon in a baking dish, place the lamb mixture on top and wrap the bacon around the loaf. Place the seam side on the bottom of the dish. Bake at 350°F for 45–50 minutes, or until done to desired browness. This roll is delicious when sliced cold for sandwiches.

— Fresh from the Market

June

Mrs. Flynn

Katherine Lewis Flynn opened our eyes to the cooking activities of the early 20th-century housewife in Prince Edward Island with her book *Mrs. Flynn's Cookbook: Selected and Tested Recipes*, published by the Ladies of St. Elizabeth's and Society in aid of St. Vincent's Orphanage in 1930. Born in Cardigan in 1874, "Katie" grew up proud of her Scottish heritage. Her marriage to a Canadian National Railway station agent took her to live in many communities. Wherever she went, her cooking skills quickly became known. Mrs. Flynn's fruitcakes were said to be the pride of many a church tea, hand-dipped chocolates her fame.

Her cookbook emphasized being practical. She said, "Neither time nor labor has been spared in selecting the choicest bits of the best experience of those who have long travelled the daily round of household duties."

Stewed Whole Spring Chicken

Dress a full-grown spring chicken the same as for roasting, season it with salt and pepper inside and out; then fill the body with oysters; place it in a tin pail with a close-fitting cover. Set the pail in a pot of fast-boiling water and cook until the chicken is tender. Dish up the chicken on a warm dish, then pour the gravy into a saucepan, put into it a tablespoonful of butter, half a cupful of cream or rich milk, three hard-boiled eggs chopped fine; some minced herbs and a tablespoon of flour. Let it boil up and then pour it over the chicken. Serve hot.

— Mrs. Flynn's Cookbook

Boston Boulettes

Should any chicken be left, it would be made up for a meal the next day.

½ cup	cold cooked chicken	125 mL
½ cup	diced cooked celery	125 mL
¼ cup	chopped pecans	60 mL
¼ tsp	salt	1 mL
	crumbs	
	buttered Boston Brown Bread	
	pepper	
	white sauce	
	beaten egg	
	watercress	

Mix together the chicken, celery and pecans. Season with salt and pepper. Add enough white sauce so that the mixture may be easily handled and holds its shape. Spread on a plate to cool. When cool, form into tiny balls, roll in crumbs and egg and fry until golden brown. Serve on a bed of watercress, accompanied by thin strip of buttered Boston Brown Bread.

— Mrs. Flynn's Cookbook

Dulse

If there is one ingredient sure to be found in the kitchens of Grand Mananers, it's dulse. This sea vegetable grown at low tide is harvested by hand and sun-dried on a drying ground made especially for drying dulse. Sold worldwide, dulse is grown in several areas, but that grown on Grand Manan Island in New Brunswick is said to be the most delicious and sought-after.

Since my experience with dulse is limited to the occasional chew or enjoyment of a recipe prepared by an expert, I contacted a couple of Grand Mananers to see how they use dulse.

Heidi Ingalls, general manager of Atlantic Mariculture Ltd., said visitors to Grand Manan will easily see harvesters at work gathering dulse at low tide and spreading it to dry.

"Islanders are very accommodating and most enjoy chatting with visitors about their livelihoods."

DULSE SOUP (OLD SCOTTISH RECIPE)

Serves 6

Atlantic Mariculture Ltd. was started by a group of biologists and harvesters who believe that natural food products can be harvested, husbanded and nurtured in the sea with minimum upset to the near-shore ecology. They cultivate organically grown vegetables that convert sunlight and natural nutrients from the fertile garden of the sea into nutritious and tasty food products. Dulse is hand-picked by experienced harvesters and taken to nature's own solar drier — the sun-heated rocks of the drying field.

This is their recipe, as is the following Super Seafood and Chicken Stew.

1 cup	cooked dulse	250 mL
1 tbsp	melted butter	15 mL
6 cups	milk	1.5 L
2 cups	mashed potatoes	500 mL
	juice of 1 lemon	
	pepper to taste	

Simmer the milk, cooked dulse and mashed potatoes together for about 20 minutes, then either beat well or liquidize in blender. Season to taste, add melted butter and lemon juice and beat again. Heat up and serve immediately.

Hot Dogs

Back in 1936 the Canadian Bakers' Association, extolling the virtues of all manner of things that used its baked products, gave instructions on "Hot Dogs":

"For the informal party, there's often no substitute for 'Hot Dogs' or 'Red Hots.' Have ready fresh bakers' rolls (long shape), wieners and prepared mustard or chili sauce. Prick wieners and boil until plump. Heat rolls.

"Assemble by splitting roll almost through, inserting wiener, and dressing with prepared mustard, chili sauce or a finely-chopped mustard relish. A long strip of dill pickle may be inserted with each wiener."

Toasted Dulse

Place a handful of whole-leaf dulse on a paper plate. Place in microwave for about 40 seconds. Great treat!

SUPER SEAFOOD AND CHICKEN STEW

1 cup	olive oil	250 mL
4 cups	hot water	1 L
2 lb	boiler-fryer chicken cut up small	900 g
1 cup	fresh or frozen green peas	250 mL
⅓ cup	dulse, coarsely chopped	80 mL
or ¼ cup	dulse flakes	60 mL
¼ cup	parsley, coarsely chopped	60 mL
1 tbsp	finely chopped onion few shreds (only a few) saffron	15 mL
2	cloves garlic, crushed	2
2	ripe tomatoes, peeled and coarsely chopped	2
1	lobster tail, cooked and pieced, or equivalent crab meat	2
1	large can of shrimp (fresh are better)	1
7-oz	can pimentos, whole	213 g
12–16	clams in shells	12–16
1½ tsp	salt	7.5 mL
1 lb	white meat fish (cod, haddock, sole)	450 g
2 cups	uncooked rice	500 mL
½ cup	sliced boiled ham or smokey sausage (optional)	125 mL

Heat olive oil in large skillet. Add chicken and ham or sausage and cook about 10 minutes, turning chicken to brown on all sides. Add onion and garlic. Cook 2 minutes. Add next 4 ingredients, cover, cook 5 to 10 minutes or until clams open. Remove clams and keep warm. Stir rice into mixture. Add peas, dulse, parsley, water and saffron. Cover and cook 25 minutes. Mix in lobster or crabmeat, half the pimentos and clams in shells. Heat until very hot. Serve garnished with remaining pimentos. If the light fish is used, add it with shrimp.

ROLAND'S "FIT FOR ANY KING" DULSE CHOWDER

Serves 8

The folks at Roland's Sea Vegetables, also on Grand Manan, say, "dulse is eaten as it is, like you would a potato chip. It is delicious toasted on an electric burner for about four or five seconds or in a microwave for 45 seconds. It can also be chopped up and put into salads or soups as a seasoning."

Simple Pleasures

2 cups	milk	500 mL
2	cans condensed cream	2
2	cans chicken soup	2
2	6-oz/170 mL cans of clams, undrained	2
1 oz	dulse	28 g
10-oz	can of peas, undrained	284 mL
1 cup	white wine (dry)	250 mL
	pepper to taste	

In saucepan or Dutch oven, stir milk into condensed soup. Add dulse, cook and stir over medium heat. Simmer uncovered for 10 minutes, stirring occasionally. Add undrained clams, peas, wine and peppers. Simmer 5 more minutes and serve.

BAKED SCALLOPS

1 lb	scallops	450 g
½ cup	flour	125 mL
2 tsp	dulse flakes	10 mL
¼ tsp	pepper	1 mL
4 tbsp	cream or canned milk	60 mL
4 tbsp	fine bread crumbs	60 mL
4 tbsp	butter	60 mL

Roll scallops in mixture of flour, dulse flakes and pepper. Place scallops in pan, add cream, bread crumbs and butter. Sprinkle with dulse flakes. Bake at 400°F for 20 minutes.

DULSE SALAD

Serves 8

Dulse is a highly digestible and protein-rich sea vegetable whose nut-like taste will enrich almost any dish.

3 oz	dried dulse, chopped finely	75 g
2	apples, sliced	2
3	large carrots, grated	3

Green Thumb

This summer night Tipsy did her "gotta go out now or I'm gonna die" routine at about 11 p.m. Being a dutiful mom, I slipped on my sneakers and off we went. It was a beautiful evening, relatively cool after a sweltering hot day, although very humid. Living on the outskirts of town as we do means a superb view of the stars. I sauntered along enjoying the air, the sounds, the breeze and the warm fuzzies that come from knowing the neighbours are settling into bed after a day in the sun. As I neared home the humidity turned to mist — almost drizzly rain. With it came the most delightful scent. The closer I got, the more delightful. It seemed to be drifting down my driveway. It was! Basil, thyme, tarragon and rosemary all planted in clay pots on the deck beside our kitchen door were scenting the air. Since then I've come to savour that scent on many summer evenings, brushing my hand over the plants if no breeze releases their scent. Frankly, if I never use the herbs in the kitchen it's worth the effort of planting them just for their aromatic contribution to my enjoyment of summer.

1 cup	alfalfa sprouts	250 mL
½	ripe avocado, cut up	½
¼ cup	currants	50 mL

DRESSING:

⅔ cup	safflower oil	160 mL
4 tbsp	soy sauce	60 mL
juice of one lemon		

Shake dressing ingredients together. Mix salad ingredients. Toss together.

Pictou Clamfest

Our first visit to Caribou Island, in Northumberland Strait near Pictou, N.S., stays strong in my mind. Our friends Helen and Roy Grant had invited us to visit Helen's family farm during their annual visit back home.

Meals in the Falconer kitchen were a marvel to me. So was clam-digging. We had such fun learning the intricacies of figuring out where the clams were — you stomp on the sand to see where squirts appear, then dig furiously to catch the clams before they get too deep. We filled a bucket, which our hosts insisted we take back to our campsite. The hunt had been great, but we were not sure what to do with them. Soon my gregarious husband was out soliciting advice.

"Feed 'em cornmeal overnight," we were told. "Cleans 'em out. Gets rid of the grit."

Getting rid of grit sounded good to me, so we happily went off to buy those critters their last meal.

Clean as they were, we still had the problem of what to do with them. My Britishness would not allow them to be wasted! The problem was solved when a couple from Quebec strolled past our campsite. As campers are wont to do, we struck up a conversation and invited them to sit down in our camp kitchen for a coffee. When they spied the clams they went wild. When we explained our dilemma and offered the clams to them they happily accepted, insisting that we join them that evening for a clamfest. We did.

Clam chowder, steamed clams, fried clams and even a dippy thing with clams chopped into it were all served up with riotous good humour. A couple next door brought along guitars for a singsong and it turned into one of those special times forever remembered.

Eat fish live longer
Eat oysters love longer
Eat clams last longer.

— seen in Lunenburg

Steamed Clams

Done in seaweed on outdoor fireplace. Build fireplace with stones on beach. Prepare fire. Place a large piece of tin or an "oven grate" about 1 foot from base of fire. Put layer of seaweed on top of grate and then clams, alternating with more clams and seaweed. Leave clams on fire for 10 minutes. They will steam open.

CLAM CHOWDER

Serves 8

The original recipe for this chowder called for a quart of clams cleaned and picked over, boiled and chopped, liquor reserved. We usually use canned clams for chowder. If we have fresh, they seem to get steamed and scoffed with no leftovers!

2	cans clams, reserve juice	2
4 cups	potatoes, cut into cubes	1 L
1	cube (1 ½-inch) salt pork, diced	1
1	onion, diced	1
8	common crackers, split in half	8
4 cups	milk, heated	1 L
2 tbsp	minced celery	30 mL
1 tbsp	minced green pepper	15 mL
1 tsp	salt	5 mL
⅛ tsp	pepper	0.5 mL
1 tbsp	flour	15 mL
2 tbsp	melted fat (butter is best)	30 mL

In a soup pot, fry out salt pork. Add onion, celery and green pepper, cook until lightly browned; meanwhile, parboil potatoes, then brown in fat. Add clams and 2 cups boiling water. Cook 10 minutes. Add milk and crackers (these are large, hard crackers, which were often used in the past as a thickener). Cook 3 minutes. Add milk. Combine butter and flour; use to thicken juice or liquor reserved from clams, add just before serving. Do not boil: the clam broth tends to curdle the milk. Season to taste.

Around the Kitchen Table

As a devotee of sitting around the kitchen table for a good natter, it amuses me that my good friends Paul and Jean Offer have banned such behaviour at their B & B, The Doctor's Inn, in Tyne Valley, P.E.I.

As Paul tells it, "Confusion can sometimes be unavoidable in a B & B kitchen. Since we provide evening dining for our guests, we sometimes get in over our heads. One evening when Jean was working at her 'other job' I agreed to do dinner for two — no problem for me. But by the time that everyone had checked in I was doing dinner for seven! Mass hysteria! But I had the time. Until — the father of the family of five asked if he could use the kitchen sink to open some P.E.I. oysters. Now we've got a problem — an unknown entity in a known kitchen. A long story, shortened down to the fact that dinner was served — almost on time and almost done right, and everyone was happy.

"Later that year we received a letter from the family with 'Thank you' and a copy of a menu from 'father's well-known San Francisco restaurant.' He had added their evening menu from The Doctor's Inn to his own, which we took as a great compliment, until we read at the bottom 'And Paul even allows guests in the kitchen while he is working!'

"When we first started our B & B we had to create our own system — the rules we tried to work by.

"We quickly discovered that it didn't work that way. Our guests always seemed to enjoy our kitchen while we were working there. We thought we had that problem licked when we moved the paperwork table and chairs out of the kitchen. It didn't take long to realize we were defeated: when one couple came in, the gentleman went to our back porch where we keep the firewood for the kitchen stove and came back with a log to sit on and the wife sat on the flour barrel (the whole time, we thought she was going to fall in).

"We grow what we have trialed to be the vegetables with the best flavour. But every once in a while we run out of our own and have to resort to 'commercial purchases.' When our own carrots are gone we use the 'tasteless' boughtens; we spruce up the flavour by adding a little butter and some chopped parsley, either dried or fresh.

"Onions can be sweetened by marinating them in a mix (don't worry about measuring) of vegetable oil, vinegar and a little sugar."

Medicinal Receipts

Dandelion Wine — *The arrival of flowers provides opportunity for preparing a tonic for the blood such as this one found in* The New Cookbook:

Four quarts of dandelion flowers; cover with one gallon of water and boil; strain, and when luke-warm add six lemons, four pounds of white sugar and half royal yeast-cake; let it stand about ten days, or until done working, then strain bottle and seal.

Living History

This recipe comes from Green Park Shipbuilding Museum and Historic Yeo House in Green Park, P.E.I. The immaculately restored house reveals a wonderful vision of the lifestyle of the "ship barons" of the 1800s. During the summer you can tour the Victorian house, or attend one of the "kitchen chatter" blueberry socials or other events. You will usually get to sample something yummy from the kitchen. One night I was there to give a reading from my ghost-story book and we had cookies and scones baked in the open-hearth fireplace. Delicious!

I especially liked this recipe because it works as well over a campfire as it does cooked in the hearth at Yeo House. You can also make the scones on top of the stove, cooking them in a skillet.

SKILLET SCONES

½ cup	butter	125 mL
2 tbsp	white sugar	30 mL
1 cup	milk	250 mL
1	egg	1
3 tsp	baking powder	15 mL
2 cups	flour	500 mL
⅓ cup	currents	80 mL
½ tsp	salt	2.5 mL

Mix as for biscuits. Roll out, cut into squares. Bake on greased skillet until brown on one side, then flip and cook the other side.

Beat eggs with milk, add onion and potato chips. Mix gently and drop by tablespoon onto a well-buttered griddle. Brown lightly. Turn gently. Brown the other side. Serve with commercial sour cream or on buttered rye toast. Or: omit the onion, fry quickly like small pancakes, dust with cinnamon and sugar or serve with blueberry jam in the manner of small Swedish pancakes.
   Makes about a dozen 3-inch pancakes.

Clive Doucet's Cape Breton

It wasn't like anything I had seen at home. It was a very large room with light spilling in through two windows. Wooden tongue-and-groove strips acted like a kind of skirt around the walls and above this skirt the walls were painted white. The kitchen table was small and set on casters so that it could be moved around easily. The stove, or what I guessed to be the stove, had truly grand proportions, taking up almost all of one wall. There were six round burners on the top, a large plate warmer above, a hot water tank at one side of the oven and the fire box at the other. I found a closet tucked beside the stove that discreetly stored the wood. The rocking chair beside the stove must have been Grandfather's. Along one side of the room there was a row of hard-backed chairs. A simple, wooden crucifix hung on the wall. A counter ran from the edge of the kitchen sink along the entire length of that wall with a neat row of cupboards below and above it. The refrigerator looked as it did at home, modern, white and stuck in a corner. Above it, on a shelf, was a large collection of coal oil lamps. All in all, without people, it was a bright but utilitarian room. Only the doors leading off to other parts of the house betrayed the kitchen for what it was — the heart of the house.

— Clive Doucet,
My Grandfather's Cape Breton

...

It was the summer of 1958. Twelve-year-old Clive Doucet had just arrived at his grand-father's home on Cape Breton Island — sent from Ottawa to spend the first of many summers on the farm in Grand Etang. In his book he gives us a sensitive and lively glimpse of Acadian life. His description could be of many a rural Maritime kitchen.

   As he continues he speaks more of the kitchen. Of the merry crackle of that wood stove, of a room "baking-bread warm with the aroma of dinner all around," of that table piled high with all manner of good things — golden brown bread, oven biscuits, fresh butter, freshly sliced bananas and thick whipped cream. And he speaks of fricot, which his aunt described as a potato-and-chicken soup.

FRICOT AU POULET

Chicken Fricot from the wife of Percy Mallet in Shippagan, New Brunswick. Percy says it is always better to prepare the meal a few hours before serving. "In doing this, your fricot will be much more tasty. Bon appétit!"

✳ About Fricot

Acadian chicken stew in the Bouctouche area of New Brunswick is traditionally made in a slightly different way than the recipe to the right.

A whole chicken is simmered with salt and pepper until cooked. Then bone the meat, strain the broth if desired. Return the meat to the broth, along with 2 large onions, minced, 6 cups chopped potatoes and a table-spoon of savory. Carrots, turnips and salted herbs, or dumplings, can be added.

8	pieces skinless chicken	8
2	large carrots, cut in small pieces	2
2	large onions, cut in small pieces	2
6	potatoes, cut in pieces, and water	6
2 tbsp	summer savory	30 mL
¼ lb	butter	100 g
1 tbsp	oil	15 mL
	salt and pepper	

In large saucepan, brown onions and carrots in butter and oil. Add chicken and brown. Add enough water to cover chicken, savory, salt and pepper; simmer until chicken is cooked. Add potatoes and water to cover, boil until potatoes are tender. If there isn't enough salt and pepper, add some.

PÂTÉS À FRICOT (DUMPLINGS FOR STEW)

1 cup	flour	250 mL
½ tsp	salt	2.5 mL
3 tsp	baking powder	15 mL
½ cup	water	125 mL

Mix dry ingredients. Add wet, mix. Drop by teaspoonfuls into the stew and simmer for 7 minutes. Alternatively, you can roll the dough quite thin, cut into 1/2-inch squares and add to the stew.

JULIE'S SALAD SUPREME

If I have a signature dish, one I can always count on to be a hit, hold well and be easy to prepare, this is it. Jack and I prepared it for the International Association of Culinary Professionals in New Orleans and the great Julia Child complimented us on it. One of life's precious moments! Weeks later, culinary students prepared it for a tasting, cutting everything so small it was like coleslaw! Don't do that!

Frozen lobster meat, thawed and drained, is perfect for making salads and sandwiches, as is leftover cooked lobster.

7 oz (1 cup)	cooked lobster meat, cut into bite-size pieces	200 g
4 oz	smoked turkey or smoked salmon, diced into 3/4-inch chunks	125 g
1	Belgian endive	1
2	green onions, sliced	2
1/2	medium red, yellow or orange pepper, diced	1/2
1/3 cup	cashew pieces	80 mL
1	small head Chinese cabbage (sometimes called napa cabbage)	1

DRESSING:

3/4 cup	mayonnaise	175 mL
1 tbsp	soy sauce	15 mL
1 tsp	honey	5 mL
	dash of sesame seed oil	
1/4 tsp	ground ginger	1 mL

Mix dressing ingredients. Heat frying pan over medium heat, add cashews and stir until brown (optional); set aside half for garnish. Reserve 2–3 lobster claws and outer leaves of endive for garnish. Line bowl with cabbage leaves. Slice remaining endive and cabbage across the leaves. Toss vegetables, seafood and meat with dressing in a separate bowl until well covered. Place in bowl with cabbage, garnish and chill until ready to use. Serves 2–4 as a meal, 4–8 as an appetizer or side salad.

Great-Gram's Tasty Fish Cakes

Take the remains of any cold fish leftover, a bunch of sweet herbs, bread crumbs, cold potatoes, a sprig of parsley, one or two eggs, salt and pepper, with a pint of water. Carefully pick the flesh from the fish and mince it very finely; mix it well with equal quantities of bread crumbs and cold mashed potatoes, season highly with salt and pepper. Put the bones, head and trimmings of the fish into a stew pan with the sweet herbs, parsley and a little pepper and salt; pour over it about a pint of water and let it simmer quietly for an hour and a half, or longer if not done enough. Make the minced fish, bread and potatoes into a cake, binding it with well-beaten white of an egg; brush it over with the beaten yolk, strew well with bread crumbs, fry it lightly. Pour over it the strained gravy; set it over gentle fire to stew slowly for nearly 20 minutes, stirring occasionally; garnish with slice of lemon and parsley.

Living History

I was on a mission. After hearing whisperings about a regional dish said to be done "when the little eyes are looking at you," great sleuthing and a hot tip from New Brunswick Tourism guru Valerie Kidney led me to the New Brunswick Botanical Garden in St-Jacques.

An unlikely place to find a kitchen and the answers to a culinary mystery, thought I. Didn't take long to realize my mistake. For here I found the heart of Madawaska, the northwestern part of New Brunswick that boasts a culture and unique French heritage all its own. Madawaskans, or Brayonne, speak their own dialect.

At the gardens I was met by Irene LeChant, who had promised to introduce me to "ploye" or "plogue," a thin buckwheat pancake unique to Madawaska. Irene explained that buckwheat flour is milled to a consistency favoured for ploye.

When the batter is poured on the grill it is a greenish yellow colour. The pancake is not turned: it's "done" when the top becomes riddled with holes — "little eyes looking at you." Ploye is to the Madawaskan what the biscuit is to others.

"Our ancestors used ploye instead of bread to accompany a meal; good with meat pâté, or maple syrup and even maple sugar when you have it," explained Irene. As I was presented with a sampling to try, she urged, "Be creative with it."

In my case I was served lavender and rose syrups (we were in a botanical garden!) as well as traditional pâté, molasses, maple sugar and butter. I must say I tried every one and it was all delicious! Every single bite!

Ploye are also traditionally served with baked beans, pea soup and "cretons."

Why are these delicacies, best described as a buckwheat crêpe-like pancake, called "ploye" or "plogue"? It is thought the word came from the English word "plug," defining the plug, or bung, that is put in the hole in a barrel to seal it.

"It's weird, we speak a mix," said Irene. "The definition of the English word is 'to cap or close,' so when we eat a ploye it 'fills up a hole' (in our belly). 'Ployé' or 'pleye' is an Acadian word for 'bending'; perhaps why we roll them like we do.

"Ploye is considered the bread of the poor, doesn't cost much to make and fills us up. It is a symbol of the Madawaska region."

Ploye is not a regular menu item in the botanical gardens restaurant. However, they sometimes prepare it for bus tours and if you phone ahead may do it for you. It's a culinary adventure I recommend.

While there, do check out the wonderful displays of herbs, vegetables and fruits in the gardens. I was fascinated with plots of tea (angelica, borage, camomile, lemon balm, bee balm, lemon catnip, coffee chicory, vervain) and condiment plants (garden sage, thyme, lemon carpet, broadleaf, French tarragon, fennel, rosemary, parsleys, marjoram, lemon grass, basil).

We have two recipes for ploye — slightly different.

LE JARDIN BOTANIQUE PLOYE

2 cups	buckwheat	500 mL
1 cup	flour	250 mL
1 tsp	salt	5 mL
2 1/4	cups cold water	560 mL
2 1/4	cups boiling water	560 mL
2 tsp	baking powder	10 mL

Mix. Let it rest 15 minutes. Put on griddle, 2–3 minutes to cook. Done when it's a little brown on bottom and all same colour on top, with little holes.

SPRINGWATER PLOYES BRAYONNE (PANCAKES)

This recipe was given to me by a waitress at the Springwater Restaurant in Four Falls, N.B. In her family, ploye was eaten as a "bed lunch" with molasses.

1 cup	buckwheat flour	250 mL
1/2 cup	flour	125 mL
3 tsp	baking powder	15 mL
1 tsp	salt	5 mL
3/4 cup	cold water	175 mL
1 3/4 cup	boiling water	425 mL

Mix dry ingredients well, add cold water and mix well to make a thick dough. Gradually add boiling water, just a bit at a time, so that you get a thin dough. It must be mixed well. Drop a thin layer of dough onto hot pan, cook without turning. You should get a dozen or more ployes from this amount of batter.

Incidentally, at the Springwater toast is buttered bread browned on the grill. Cretons with headcheese was also on the menu. It's one of those neat little "finds" that foodies enjoy so much.

Berrylicious

When raspberries, blackberries and blueberries come in I go slightly mad, I love them so much. One little trick keeps my addiction fed for months to come. Using small pickling jars, start layering berries as you get them. Remove leaves, stems or obvious dirt, but don't wash, then keep them in the freezer. I used to do this in plastic freezer bags, but found the berries got squashed, or too much moisture got in when opening and resealing.

Company claim to love my mixed berry desserts and they are simple to prepare. Cake, custard, ice cream, even low-fat puddings are made special with the addition of a sprinkling of berries and a few flakes or curls of white chocolate. Chill a chocolate block. When it's time to prepare your meal, use a vegetable peeler on the chocolate: short pulls result in flakes; slow and sweeping pulls give you curls. Curls are fragile, so use a toothpick to move. Chill until ready to serve. Use berries frozen. By the time the first spoon goes in, they are thawed. You can also combine with fresh fruit. A peach, for example, will serve six to eight for dessert if divided.

Fruit tip — measure berries or rhubarb into specific quantities, put in small freezer bags, removing as much air as possible before sealing. Place small bags into big, strong, clear freezer bags. Write on the bag "$1/2$ cup blueberries" or "1 cup cranberries" or "1 pound of" whatever. Just remove what you want for baking or a dessert. No fuss, no muss. I love making lemon cranberry muffins, so I premeasure the right quantity of cranberries, freeze, then pop them into the muffin mix — still frozen. Muffins turn out great.

Raspberry Velvet Cream

For this you need 2 cupfuls of ripe red raspberries. Pick them over carefully, hull and wash very quickly so they will not get watersoaked. Stir in $1/2$ cupful of sugar. Cover, let stand for at least 2 hours (an hour or two longer is all the better). Rub them through a rather fine strainer. Now put $1/2$ cup of sugar and $1/4$ cup of water in a saucepan, let boil until it will thread when dropped from the point of a spoon. Beat the white of 2 eggs very stiff, pour in the syrup gradually, beating all the time. Beat 1 cup cream until stiff, fold into egg mixture; last of all, stir in the raspberry pulp very lightly. Freeze, then let stand for 3 hours for flavour to ripen.

BLACKBERRY CRUMBLE

Blackberries evoke childhood memories for me, especially as they are as readily available along walking trails and lanes as they were long ago.

1 lb	blackberries, (picked over and rinsed) clean of dust (substitute other fruits if desired)	450 g
6–8 tbsp	sugar	90-120 ml
$1/2$ cup	butter	125 ml
1 $2/3$ cups	whole wheat flour	400 ml
$2/3$ cup	rolled oats	150 ml
$1/2$ cup	soft brown sugar	125 ml

Preheat oven to 350°F. Line bottom of pie pan with blackberries and sprinkle sugar all over. In a crock mixing bowl, cut butter into flour and blend until crumbly. Stir in oats and brown sugar until well mixed. Sprinkle over berries. Bake 40–45 minutes until top is golden. Delicious served with cream.

BLACKBERRY AND APPLE PIE

1	pastry for deep dish pie	1
1 $1/2$ lb	tart apples (Gravenstein or Granny Smith), cored and sliced	700 g
1 lb	blackberries, picked clean	450 g
5 tbsp	sugar	75 ml

Dry fruit well. Arrange in pie crust and sprinkle sugar over. Cover with pastry, sealing edges and making slit in top. Bake until fruit is tender and crust lightly golden. Remove pie from oven, sprinkle with sugar. Excellent hot or cold, served with cream (from a pitcher, not whipped).

BLACKBERRY SAUCE

Given to me by an Irish lady who was visiting her now-Canadian daughter in Cape Breton. Hearing I'm a sucker for blackberries, and knowing they were growing just a nice walk away, she suggested we gather some, then made the sauce to serve over ice cream. It was simply delicious and remains in my personal cookbook as a reminder of our first Cape Breton holiday.

1 ½ lb	blackberries, ripe and well picked over	700 g
3 cups	confectioner's sugar, sifted	750 mL
2 tbsp	blackcurrant liqueur	30 mL
	juice of ½ lemon	

Purée fruit with the sugar (use a food processor if you wish). Strain to remove seeds, mix with other ingredients. Taste; you might want to add a little sugar. Serve with ice cream, hot custard, over or under a slice of complementary cake and so on. A favourite dessert of mine is to put a piece of stale cake in a dish, pour over with hot custard, then blackberry sauce. Pop 2–3 fresh berries on top and you have a wonderful mix of flavours in a satisfying dessert.

It was a desperate search for food that started a migration that brought thousands of immigrants to North American shores. Potatoes were a staple food of most Irish until crop failure created a great famine. Prior to the potato, the staple was a mix of meals (oat, wheat and barley) made into a porridge known as "stirabout."

One of my pet peeves is finding good stuff overlooked in the bottom of the salad bowl at cleanup time. Thus, I tend to make individual salads, ensuring everyone a taste of the shrimp, scallop, chicken, cheese, croutons — as well as each veggie — depending on the creation of the day.

POTATO FARLS

Irish immigrants brought with them many wonderful things to do with potatoes.

2 tbsp	butter, melted	30 mL
2 cups	mashed potatoes	500 mL
	pinch salt	
1 cup	plain flour	250 mL

Mix potatoes, butter and salt together, working in flour quickly. Knead lightly, divide into two. Flour a board, roll out each half into a circle. Cut each into quarters. Carefully cook each side for about 3 minutes in hot bacon fat, using a heavy frying pan.

The Crock-Pot

W

e love pasta, and dishes like this one just seem to fit well with summer. What we don't like is creating the steam and heat in the kitchen on hot, muggy days, so I purchased a good Crock-Pot that we plug in outside. It works great for potatoes, corn or vegetables, teaming well with a barbeque. Chili, many meat dishes and any number of things that I would normally cook in the oven all work well. The Crock-Pot keeps food warm right there beside, or on, the picnic table. Another thing it cooks well is pasta. I have a Crock-Pot that can be used as a deep fryer. I just leave the basket in when cooking pasta — when done, lift and voila, it's drained.

TOMATO ROTINI

Serves 4

Perfect to use up those juicy tomatoes that all seem to ripen at the same time. In our house we have one olive lover and one olive hater, so I serve olives on the side. They should really be stirred in when heating the sauce.

¼ cup	extra virgin olive oil	50 mL
2 cups	fresh tomatoes, chopped fine with all juice, or	500 mL
2	8-oz cans crushed tomatoes	2
1 cup	feta cheese, crumbled	250 mL
1 cup	black olives, drained and sliced	250 mL
16-oz	package rotini pasta, cooked	500 g

Heat olive oil in a sauté pan, stir in tomatoes, olives and cheese and heat through. Toss into pasta until mixed well. Serve immediately.

OLD WORLD SAUTÉED SCALLOPS

Use your favourite mustard in this French recipe, which combines the big scallops the region is known for with fresh spinach. Short cooking time makes it perfect for summer.

12	large scallops	12
2 tbsp	olive oil	30 mL
6 oz	spinach (select smaller leaves)	150 g
6 tbsp	whipping cream	90 mL
1 tbsp	Dijon mustard	15 mL
½ tsp	curry powder	2.5 mL
	salt and black pepper to taste	

Heat oil and sautée scallops 2 minutes on each side. Remove, keep warm. In same pan, sauté spinach 1 minute, season to taste. Add cream, mustard and curry powder, cook an additional 2 minutes, add scallops. To serve, place 3 scallops on a bed of spinach and rim with sauce.

ICED RUM TEA

Serves 8

Maritimers have a close relationship with rum. Back in the days of Prohibition a whole segment of communities became rum-runners. Low-cut boats ran in front of the law to import the illegal bringer-of-good-cheer. Often casks of illegal rum were hidden in the kitchen to protect the family from the "law."

It's a sure thing some crept into the larder, especially at times of celebration — especially if that celebration was for another successful smuggling operation.

15 oz	light rum	450 mL
1 qt	tea	950 mL
3 tbsp	lemon juice	45 mL
4 tbsp	sugar	60 mL
	lemon slices	
	ice cubes	

Combine sugar and lemon juice with tea and refrigerate until cool. Pour into large pitcher, add rum and ice cubes. Stir. Add lemon slices.

Herbs 🌿

Cut a piece of tulle, 18 x 14 inches, spread on top of fabric one kind of herb, scattering leaves. Make sure herbs are clean, dry and good quality. Roll tulle loosely. Tie ends shut with twine. Keep it in refrigerator for a couple of weeks until dry. Crumble and store in labelled jars, use all winter long.

Miracle Cookies

This 1936 recipe from rural Nova Scotia "is nice to make in the morning of a hot day for it doesn't much heat the kitchen." All you need: 1/4 pound sweet milk chocolate; 1 cup toasted coarse bread crumbs; chopped nutmeat (optional).

Cut up chocolate, melt over hot water. Mix in crumbs (and nutmeat, if used). Drop by spoonfuls onto greased pan. Let stand several hours or overnight, to set. The nutmeat, whilst not necessary, adds interest; walnuts, pecans, almonds, filberts, peanuts — broken or chopped — are suitable.

Green Thumb 🌱

When cutting fresh flowers, instead of those fancy, expensive flower preservers I use a homemade one that contains 3 items found in every home. I fill my vase with water (8 oz), add approximately 1/2 teaspoon of regular household bleach, a teaspoon of sugar (sugar cubes work great). Flowers tend to last 2–3 weeks this way, sometimes even longer. Use double bleach if you keep your vase of flowers in direct sunlight.

The Soup

*One morning in the garden bed
The onions and the carrots said
Unto the parsley group;
"Oh, when shall we thee meet again,
In thunder, lightning, hail or rain?"
"Alas;" replied in tones of pain
The parsley: "In the soup."*

— Mrs. Flynn's Cookbook

July

Potatoes

By midmonth we start to watch the market shelves for freshly dug new potatoes. Tiny nuggets of goodness. We love them pan-roasted or boiled with a sprig or two of fresh mint from the herb pot or, better yet, on the barbecue, drizzled with a little olive oil and sprinkled with lemon pepper, then double-wrapped in foil. Other herbs, coming in now, marry well with new potatoes — especially tiny reds. Chives work well, or try fresh dill. Parring a band around the middle of each potato prevents splitting.

CHIVE-AND-LEMON NEW POTATOES

Serves 6

2 lb	new potatoes, scrubbed clean	900 g
1/3 cup	butter	80 mL
1 tsp	grated lemon rind	5 mL
1 tbsp	lemon juice	15 mL
1 tbsp	chopped chives	15 mL
	pinch of salt and pepper	

Place potatoes in large pot, cover with water, bring to boil. Simmer, closely covered, until tender. Drain, place in serving dish, keep hot. Melt butter, stir in lemon rind and juice. Pour over hot potatoes. Sprinkle with chives, salt and pepper.

GRANDFATHER'S POTATO SALAD

"This recipe was one that my grandfather made. I made it at the Charlottetown Sobeys' cooking class because it would've been his birthday. I enjoy this potato salad because it is not made with mayonnaise."

— Arne Fulton, Executive Chef, Rent A Chef, "The Culinary Adventure Company," Gagetown, New Brunswick

10–12	baby red potatoes, cut in half	10–12
1 lb	fresh asparagus, cut into 1/2-inch pieces	450 g
1/2 cup	oil	125 mL
1/4 cup	Spanish paprika	50 mL
1/4 cup	chopped fresh parsley salt and pepper, to taste	50 mL

Cook potatoes until desired tenderness, immediately place under cold running water until thoroughly chilled. Drain, add remaining ingredients. Mix well and serve.

RADISH SPREAD

We tend to use radishes as a finger food or chopped into a salad, but by grating them we create a great ingredient with tang. My appreciation for such things came in the kitchens of the Prince Edward Hotel (now the Delta) in Charlottetown, where I spent hours with the head chef as he developed dishes to tempt the Japanese visitors who come to P.E.I. on an Anne of Green Gables pilgrimage. Spread on bread (pumpernickel or rye) triangles, crackers or even cucumber slices.

16	radishes, cleaned	16
2 tbsp	butter	30 mL
6 oz	cream cheese	150 g
1 tbsp	chopped parsley	15 mL
1 tsp	chopped chives	5 mL
1 tbsp	lemon juice	15 mL
1 tsp	lemon zest	5 mL
	salt and pepper to taste	

Grate radishes in a food processor or by hand. Place mixture on paper or cloth towels and squeeze to remove as much moisture as you can. Cream butter and cheese until fluffy. Add parsley, chives, lemon juice, salt, pepper and half the radishes. Use as a spread, topping with remaining radish.

Ginger Beer

A glass of homemade ginger beer with a lump of ice is always a pleasant drink on a hot day. Take an earthenware kettle, slice 4 lemons, place them in the kettle, add 1 1/2 pounds loaf sugar, 1 1/2 ounces root ginger, slightly bruised. Pour over these ingredients 2 gallons boiling water; when nearly cold, pour in a dessertspoonful of fresh brewer's yeast. Cover with thin cloth, let stand 24 hours. Strain, bottle, store in a cool place.

Ginger Cordial

One gallon of whisky, 8 lemons, 4 pounds of sugar, 1/4- pound of whole ginger biscuit, 1 quart of water added to the sugar, and 4 pounds of red currants made in summer. Put the whisky, lemons and ginger in a crock and let it stand for 3 days, stirring every day ; then strain and add the sugar, which has been dissolved in the quart of water. Stir until all is well mixed; then bottle. Ready for use at once.

Planning a party? Take a hint from fisherfolk, who have been known to fill old dories with ice to chill the pop and beer at a summer "do": fill something around home that is "fun" as well as practical. For a kids' party it could be an old red wagon or even a wading pool. For grown-ups use a half barrel, buckets (nothing too deep, 'cause you can't reach the pop without soaking your boobs), or a wheelbarrow works wonderfully. If it leaks, line it with strong garbage bags.

Any time you want a new, unusual drink — at least to you — check out the old cookbooks. You'll find a great change from over-sweetened bottled concoctions we are bombarded with!

Living History

On a sunny day in the year of the new millennium costumed ladies, gentlemen and children strolled into the gardens of Ardgowan National Historic Site in Charlottetown to celebrate the launch of a new book, *Ardgowan: A Journal of House and Garden in Victorian Prince Edward Island.* I had asked my good friend Chef Stefan Czapalay to cater for the Victorian Garden Party using recipes from the era of Confederation, 1860–1875. Those recipes presented a challenge for Stefan's cooks and apprentice chefs. Not because they didn't have the skills — as trained preparers of food they certainly know what they are doing — but, as Stefan said, cooks of days past relied on now-forgotten methods and ingredients to create flavour. Consider this excerpt on picnics (these 1860s folks also knew how to organize!):

Plain, substantial food, simple and well-cooked should be chosen, with sweet and simple dainties to top off with. This can be divided up among the party by the one who is most executive, with the ladies to furnish the substantials and the gentlemen the beverages. The men assume the expenses of the boats or other conveyances.

One girl may promise to furnish a certain proportion of the rolls or sandwiches, and another, part of the cake. Others may promise cold or potted meats, sardines, stuffed eggs, Saratoga potatoes, olives, pickles, fruit, lemonade and cold coffee. Salad may easily be carried if the lettuce and chicken or lobster are arranged in a dish set in a basket, and the dressing contained in a wide-mouth bottle or pickle jar.

To begin with the substantials, a cold roast, a boiled tongue, deviled eggs, are simple and tasty. The roast may be sliced off before going, and carefully wrapped up, but the tongue should be carried whole and cut up when required, or it is apt to become dry. The eggs are easily prepared, being hard boiled, cut lengthwise, the yolks taken out, mixed in a bowl with pepper, salt and mustard, and a few drops of Worcester and put back in the whites.

Different kinds of sandwiches may be served. For one time there may be finger-rolls, split, the inside hollowed out and filled with chopped chicken or tongue, and the two sides tied together with the narrowest of ribbon. Again bread and butter, cut wafer thin and rolled, may appear. Sweetbread sandwiches, sardine sandwiches, egg sandwiches, are delicious and easily prepared variations upon the everlasting ham and tongue. Very dainty sandwiches are made of two thicknesses of thin bread and butter, with a layer between them of cream cheese and chopped water cress. The fruit should be heaped in a basket or arranged as a center-piece with flowers.

For the sweets some plain cake and bon-bons, and a box of crystallized ginger are all-sufficient. Cold tea, with lemon and ice, is certainly the most refreshing and satisfactory.

If more side dishes are preferred, there are olives, salted peanuts or pecans, gherkins, radishes or club-house cheese and wafers to choose from, and if berries in season are desired, they are best carried in a glass preserve jar.
— *Ardgowan*: "Social Etiquette or Manners and Customs of Polite Society"

The grounds at Ardgowan welcome visitors to step back in time. Perhaps you could use the Victorian formula for preparing an appropriate picnic:

The Victorian Sandwich

The crust is always cut from the loaf before making fancy sandwiches. In choosing what sandwiches to make for certain occasions, the suitability should be considered. Cheese isn't nice for afternoon tea, nor jam sandwiches for supper. A meat sandwich should not be served with sweets, nor a highly spiced one at the end of a meal.

TONGUE SANDWICHES

Tongue can be sliced thinly and spread with mustard. For a more elaborate preparation, mix a cupful of finely chopped tongue with half as much boiled ham, stir in 3 tablespoonfuls of melted butter, beaten lightly, with as much salad oil, $1/2$ teaspoon of made mustard, and $1/4$ teaspoon of paprika. When the mixture is smooth and light, set in a saucepan of boiling water over the fire and cook until it is thoroughly heated. Beat in the yolk of a whipped egg; take from the fire and set by until perfectly cold. Spread between thin slices of bread.

CHICKEN SANDWICHES

Mince up fine any cold boiled or roasted chicken; put it into a saucepan with gravy, water or cream enough to soften it; add a good piece of butter, a pinch of pepper; work it very smooth while it is heating until it looks almost like a paste. Then spread it on a plate to cool. Spread it between slices of buttered bread.

ROLLED CRESS SANDWICHES

Cut fresh bread in as thin slices as possible; remove crusts. Spread with butter; place a small bunch of cress at each end of the bread, extending a little beyond the edge. Roll closely on a damp towel. Additions, your choice of … chopped olives, chopped nuts, asparagus, pimento strips, cheese.

DATE SANDWICHES

Chop dates finely; mix with cream (or a mild salad dressing). Add nuts, raisins, figs or preserved ginger if desired. Spread on bread.

CUCUMBER SANDWICHES

Cut cucumber in thin slices; remove large seeds, cover with diluted vinegar to which a little salt has been added; let stand $1/2$ hour; drain. Place on buttered bread; spread with salad dressing; cover with buttered bread.

LETTUCE SANDWICHES

Use crisp leaves of lettuce, well-dried. Spread bread with butter and, if to your taste, a little salad dressing; place lettuce between slices and keep cool until ready to eat.

CHEESE SANDWICHES

These are extremely nice, and very easily made. Take one hard-boiled egg, a quarter of a pound of common cheese grated, half a teaspoonful of salt, half a teaspoonful of pepper, half a teaspoonful of mustard, one tablespoon of melted butter, and one tablespoon of vinegar or cold water. Take the yolk of the egg and put it into a small bowl and crumble it down, put into it the butter and mix it smooth with a spoon, then add the salt, pepper, mustard and the cheese, mixing each well. Then put in the tablespoonful of vinegar, which will make it the proper thickness. If the vinegar is not relished, then use cold water instead. Spread this between two biscuits or pieces of oatcake, and you could not require a better sandwich. Some people will prefer the sandwiches less highly seasoned. In that case, season to taste.

WALNUT SANDWICHES

Walnut meats with mayonnaise make very tasty sandwiches: so do chopped peanuts or pistachio. The bread should be rather close-grained homemade.

On my travels I pick up greeting cards and postcards with a food theme, such as fiddleheads sketched by a New Brunswick artist. I frame them in good frames with nice mats, to make art prints for my kitchen. Original, unique decorations and a reminder of wonderful memories.

PLUM CHUTNEY

The chef who gave me this recipe says it is perfect with venison, chicken or pork. I agree, but I also think this spicy condiment is especially good with cream cheese and a bagel. When you see those purple plums in the market, get out the canning gear!

4 lb	prune plums, pitted	1.8 kg
2 lb	firm apples, peeled, cored and chopped	900 g
1 1/2 cups	white vinegar	375 g
4 cups	brown sugar, packed firm	1 L
1 tbsp	salt (pickling is best)	15 mL
1 1/2 tsp	ground allspice	7.5 mL
1 1/2 tsp	ginger	7.5 mL
1 1/2 tsp	ground cloves	7.5 mL
1 1/2 tsp	cinnamon	7.5 mL

Place fruit and vinegar in large jam-making kettle. Bring to boil; take down to simmer for one hour. Leave uncovered, stir as needed. After 1 hour stir in remaining ingredients, bring back to boil, simmer again for another hour or until thickened. Bottle in sterilized jars, filling almost to top. Seal immediately, store in cool cupboard.

August

— A golden month of ripening crops, outdoor feasts and working to keep the kitchen cool.

The well-being and success in life of every individual bears a closer relation to food than to any other single factor known. Sleep, fresh air and exercise are absolute essentials to health, but these are not capable, singly or combined, of outweighing for any time the ill-effects which eventually follow a wrong use of food.

— *The Canadian Cook Book*

SMOTHERED TOMATO RAREBIT

One of the best breakfasts of my life was served up at a tiny country eatery we came across when cruising years ago. I haven't been able to find it since and fear it's long gone. The breakfast lives on, though, for those folks opened my eyes to a new way to use an old family favourite, Welsh rarebit. We love this cheese concoction poured over crusty toast and browned in the oven for an evening treat. It's also delicious as a breakfast celebration of tomatoes ripening on the vine. We like it with a dark rye bread placed in the centre of the plate and smothered with rarebit, popped under the broiler to brown (optional), then surrounded by chilled beefsteak tomato slices. The hot/cold sensations and the flavour mix are wonderful.

All you need: ripe tomatoes, sliced bread or English muffins, toasted; Welsh rarebit, as follows. Assemble as described above.

WELSH RAREBIT

Unlike cheese sauce, made with milk, this hearty concoction marries cheddar with beer. To be authentic (and rich), use an "old" or "extra-old" cheddar and a hearty beer.

2 lbs	cheddar cheese, diced or grated	900 g
1 tbsp	butter	15 mL
½ tsp	salt	2.5 mL
½ tsp	paprika	2.5 mL
1 tsp	dry mustard	5 mL

Simple Pleasures

¼ tsp	Tabasco or Worcestershire sauce (depending on taste)	1 mL
1 cup	beer	250 mL

Melt cheese and butter in double boiler over gently boiling water. Add seasonings and beer, stirring constantly until smooth.

…

In the 1930s a Prince Edward Island recipe suggested that Welsh rarebit be served "on top of fried rounds of bread."

From My Kitchen Window

AUGUST 11, 1999 — "Julie, come quick!" my husband called. It was just after 6 a.m. and I was getting into my clothes. Half-dressed, I ran to the kitchen, expecting to see a minor catastrophe that needed cleaning or something. I didn't need this; I was on my way out the door.

"Cover your eyes," he ordered, and handed me a small rectangle of almost-black glass. Positioning me at the window over the sink, he pulled my hand up so the glass was covering my eyes. "Now look!" he said. I did and saw it: A solar eclipse, happening right outside my kitchen window.

We hadn't thought it would be visible from the house because of the lie of the land and the trees, thus my frantic dressing routine — I was heading down the road for a good

viewpoint — but there it was. Even through our number 14 welding goggle glass, another memory to store away in my "cool" collection of neat things viewed from my kitchen window. Now we have the viewing glass ready for when the next eclipse comes along. All I have to do is figure out where to put it, so that we can find it should such an event occur when we're home!

Snacking with Samhire and Goosetongue

Having reached the stage in life where we really treasure relaxing over the paper on weekends, I have one must-buy on my shopping list. *The Moncton Times & Transcript* is, in my lowly opinion, one of the best newspapers produced. One reason for this sweeping statement is a chap by the name of Nelson Poirier, who writes a column entitled "New Brunswick Nature Scope." He has the ability to present fascinating glimpses of nature that I so appreciate that I treat his columns as keepers, living in hope that one day he will publish them in a book.

It was from Nelson Poirier that I learned about samphire and goosetongue. He wrote that a mere 30 to 50 years ago the two words were well-known in many Maritime kitchens. Even though they are not heard of as much today, he says the greens are still out there, as abundant and flavourful as ever.

"As a child," he wrote, "I well recall the pot of samphire greens my mother would prepare in a very large pot. We'd use them as a constant finger nibble for the next few days as the cooled drained pot was simply left on the stove to forage into. It often surprises me these freely available sea salt flavoured tid-bits seem to have been forgotten about in more recent times."

Like the fiddlehead (ostrich fern), these tasty morsels from Mother Nature's food hamper have not been successfully cultivated, so we have to harvest them from her "organic" garden. In fact, Poirier says, if you're really looking for truly organically grown natural foods it just may be time to revisit the samphires and the goosetongues, aka seaside plaintain. Both plants grow along the seacoast in the tidal flats, salt marshes or salty mud flats, making them fairly accessible to harvest. You may also find them in a market.

Poirier stresses that, as with any wild edible, you must make certain of correct identification before eating them. To learn more, use good edible-plant field guides.

"Samphire greens can be eaten raw after a thorough washing, however, the popular preparation method is steaming for 5 to 10 minutes. Another method is bottling stems in pickling solution in jars for winter use," says Poirier, although in his home they never got that far! "Each stem contains a slender woody stock. Pick the stem by the base and bite lightly pulling on it, pulling the fleshy part from the woody centre. Samphire greens are an absolute delicacy and should be tried at the earliest opportunity. Remember not to add any salt to overpower the delicate already sea-salted morsels."

Edible Flowers

Watched an organic farmer make a salad today. She placed a metal bowl — you know, the stacking kind — inside another that had ice in the bottom. A mix of fresh lettuce was broken into the top bowl. Fresh dill was torn into tiny sprigs and sprinkled over it. As I watched, she reached over to a bouquet of flowers and began plucking: a petal here, a sprig there, tiny flowers. Rich yellows, reds, blues and whites were sprinkled over the top of the salad and an elegant masterpiece was born. A few minutes' preparation, accompanied by a friendly chat, and she had a delicious treat that she served with a simple vinaigrette.

Do it yourself by buying those handy bags of mixed salad greens, a sprig of fresh herbs and some organic, edible flowers that have not been sprayed. Edible flowers include all culinary herbs and scented geraniums, bachelor's button, snapdragon, begonia, tulip, calendula (petals), viola, cornflower, violet, fuchsia, dandelion (petals), gladiolus and many more. For a tasting of edible flowers and a gourmands' introduction to herbs, consider joining a tour with Clarice Hambly of Howe Bay, P.E.I., head gardener at the Inn at Bay Fortune. This knowledgeable lady works with chefs at the home of the TV show Inn Chef. She is so talented a gardener that she harvests fresh strawberries and raspberries into November — what a treat!

Good Food, Good Friends

Traditions are wonderful things, especially when they are special times shared with good friends. We count our friendship with Beth and David Smith of Indian River, P.E.I., as one of our life blessings. Many a tradition we have shared with them.

The fruiting of trees down the heritage road that splits their farm signifies a special event for all of us. Jack and I pick up fresh mussels from French River on the way over, so we have all the makings for a true feast. The fellows harvest the garden for the makings of hodgepodge. A glorious walk, accompanied by dogs and occasionally a lovely orange feline, takes us out to gather berries for pie.

In our circle, these berries are called huckleberries. However, I suspect they are really serviceberries, aka saskatoons, Indian pear or shadbush. Whatever, in the annals of our memories they shall ever be huckleberries. They make excellent pies, wine and preserves. The birds love them, too! Since the species takes on forms ranging from 2-foot shrubs to 25-foot trees, there are lots for all of us.

Once all the ingredients are gathered, we head for their delightful farm kitchen. Beth makes the pie (a simple two-crust pie filled with fruit and sprinkled with sugar) — she's the master. David usually washes all of the new veggies while Jack and I supervise. Hey, it's a big kitchen but has small counter space. We do the dishes afterward.

Good food, good friends and the satisfaction of the gathering make for a perfect day.

Medicinal Receipts

Where does everyone run when they get a hurt? To Mom in the kitchen, of course. Treatments have changed, but the lovin' is still the most important part of the "cure." Old cures called for a mix of cider vinegar and water, or cold tea. My grandmother used to dab sunburned backs with a cold tea bag; I don't know if it sped up the healing process, but it sure felt good.

Hodgepodge

As soon as vegetables begin to ripen, Mrs. Maritimer picks a little here and a little there, until she has enough for this old-time treat.

Take any combination of new vegetables from the garden (small potatoes, peas, green or yellow string beans, tiny carrots, onions, little squash, etc.) and wash. Cook in a small amount of water, starting with the vegetables that take longest to cook and adding the others so that they are all cooked at the same time. Once done, drain, reduce heat. Add butter and cream, season with salt and pepper and serve hot. Quantities depend on what you have in the pot, but generally speaking, use two tablespoons of butter to one cup of cream.

August

Huckleberry Beef

Huckleberries (or saskatoons) make a very impressive addition to beef or game. Pan-cook medallions of meat to your preferred doneness, add a nice red wine sauce (stirring to deglaze the pan) and add huckleberries. Simmer for a few minutes and serve. Excellent with wild rice. An earthy meal reminiscent of days past.

Around the Kitchen Table

The signs are all there ... Delicious aromas waft from rural kitchens, the very best flowers are cosseted in the garden. Over dinner, discussions focus on a horse's performance, coat quality of cattle or the chances of Mom bringing home a first-place ribbon. It's obvious: Old Home Week is just around the corner.

Anyone living close to town kept a pretty open-door policy. Years ago, rural folk would come in bringing cattle, horses, sheep, chickens, crops and more to be judged. Women, particularly members of the WI, have been busy making their best pickles, cakes and breads.

This has long been the time when folks "away" come home. In days past there would be strangers to put up, as well. Fellow exhibitors and workers from the shows and midway needed a place to stay. Special excursion trains brought people to town for this most important social event of the year.

The house packed, Mom would spend hours in the kitchen feeding the multitude that descended. Meals were exciting. Formality was dropped and everyone gathered around the kitchen table to share the love of being together at this stimulating time.

In 1997 Syd Clay wrote a wonderful account of a visit to town for "Ye Olde Home Week" in the *Charlottetown Guardian*, recalling that weeks later in the fall those friends and relatives who had enjoyed the hospitality of their city kin during Old Home Week dropped in for another visit. They just happened to have a few sacks of potatoes, carrots and turnips and maybe a chuck of pork in the back of the truck.

"The kids went out to play and fight. The grown-ups sat around the kitchen table recounting the memories of Old Home Week, the exhibits and who won the prizes in the Women's Institute building, the vaudeville and the races. As the women got up to prepare the supper, someone said, 'How long do you think it will be before we get television on the Island?'"

Blueberries

Blueberries, nature's gift, grow abundantly and can easily be picked. Of course, today you have to be sure that you are not poaching someone's crop — it's not like it was years ago.

When Europeans arrived in the New World, they found Native people had a particular fondness for these little blue berries that were an important part of their diet, both in

Blueberries

I'm sorry, blueberries, that I must leave you.
Vacation comrades of a summer hour,
Gay little children of the upland pastures,
Lovely as any flower!

I met you on a ramble that first morning,
Inside the pasture bars.
Your blue frocks and blue jackets trim and dainty,
Your eyes like stars.

Such pleasures as that pasture held abundant —
Sweet fern, shy paths, roses and veery's nest!
But blueberries that lay beyond the balsams —
Of all the treasures you were the first and best.

You did not fear me when I took you from it,
But tumbled from your places in a trice;
And when I ate you — like some green ogre —
Still other ripened for the sacrifice.

Good-by blue sky, blue hills, blue spattered pasture
Good-by to you, blue everlasting sea!
The city calls. Should I be late next summer,
Blueberry bushes, watch and wait for me!

— Frances Crosby Hamlet

In 1803 Luke Harrison, of Maccan in Cumberland County, N.S., wrote a letter describing, among other things, the wild fruits that "grow in the woods, such as cherries and blueberries." Today blueberries are commercially harvested on the same Harrison land. By the 1880s they were an important source of food and income. In Lunenburg and Yarmouth areas, early records show pickers were paid two to five cents a quart. Berries were taken by tugboat to Liverpool, where shopkeepers sold them from wooden barrels by the scoopful. Others would peddle blueberries from door to door from picking baskets, and even maple sap buckets. Housewives could buy a quart for two to three cents in 1914–15.

Blueberry picking was an excursion, especially for women and children, who would start early for the field carrying a lunch. Others, particularly in the Yarmouth area, would go out to the barrens, a trip of about 10 miles, for days at a time. Ox teams, picking their way around rocks, followed the trail almost all day to get to the picking areas, where tents were set up and the camp kitchen readied.

Usually three or four families made up a picking party, although there could be as many as 40, ranging from babies to grandparents. Families took utensils and provisions: home-baked bread, home-canned meats, salt herring, potatoes and so on. They usually had one hot meal a day, cooked over open fires. Salt fish and potatoes were supplemented with fresh meat only when their "hunter" brought in moose or trout. He would be paid in blueberries.

The work was hard, living conditions

fresh and preserved forms: dried, for use in soups, stews, perhaps teas, and pounded into meat that was then smoke-dried.

Blueberries were undoubtedly among the first familiar foodstuffs found by colonists, since they were almost identical to hurtleberries, plentiful in England and Scotland.

primitive, yet families looked forward to "berry picking time," their family outing for the year.

Buyers came each day. If the harvest was good, pickers remained out in the barrens for four to five weeks, relying on supply wagons to bring provisions.

During the First World War, a Yarmouth resident suggested drying should be done more extensively. Done by spreading berries in the sun for several days on a cheesecloth-covered frame, then packing them away in a cool, dry place, this made it possible to send berries overseas. To use, the berries were set into water for a few hours to rehydrate. You can try one of those fancy electric dehydrators. Added to cereal or as snacks, dried blueberries make great treats and gifts.

…

Blueberry desserts have been given unlikely names such as "grunt" and "buckle." Both are sinfully delicious.

BLUEBERRY GRUNT

Back when my husband was a farrier and I the lifestyles editor at our local newspaper, I often accompanied him on his rounds. While he and Carol Townshend took care of shoeing her horses, I went to visit her mom in the farm kitchen. The wood stove was a-hummin', the kettle singing and the scent of cooking blueberries mouth-watering. One of the covers was removed from the top of the stove and a cast iron pot dropped into the hole, so that only three or four inches remained above the stove top. Luckily we had timed our visit to coincide with the serving of Mrs. Townshend's Blueberry Grunt. She shared her recipe — which I cook in my boring electric oven — while recounting that when her family moved to the farm they found an old cookbook in the wall of the back kitchen. Since they didn't own a cookbook, it was much treasured.

Funnily enough, it was things friends found in the walls of Island homes that triggered my interest in domestic history. Old newspapers, magazines and catalogues, used as insulation years ago, preserved history for aficionados like me.

1 1/2 cups	blueberries, washed and picked	375 mL
1 2/3 cups	water	400 mL
2/3 cup	white sugar	160 mL
1/4 tsp	salt	1 mL
1 1/4 tsp	baking powder	6 mL
1 1/3 cups	flour	325 mL
1 tbsp	shortening	15 mL
1/3 cup	milk	80 mL

Mix up the berries, water and sugar in oven pot or casserole dish. Bake at 400°F 5 to 10 minutes, so the berries soften and a nice juicy mixture forms. Mix remaining ingredients into a dough and drop by spoonfuls onto berries. Return to oven and bake for 25 minutes or until browned lightly.

A Lunenburg recipe for Blueberry Grunt called for layers of berries and biscuit dough, with sugar sprinkled on each layer and moistened with water. It was said to be important not to remove the lid during the 20-minute cooking time or the dough would get soggy and heavy.

BLUEBERRY BUCKLE

There are dozens of recipes out there for "Buckle" aux Bleuets. This simple one from an Acadian kitchen represents them all.

1/4 cup	shortening	50 mL
1/2 cup	sugar	125 mL
1	egg	1
	dash of salt	
1 1/2 tsp	baking powder	7.5 mL
1/3 cup	milk	75 mL
1 pint (2 cups)	blueberries, picked over	500 mL
1/3 cup	butter	75 mL
1/3 to 1/2 cup	sugar	75–125 mL
1/2 tsp	cinnamon	2.5 mL
1/3 cup	flour	75 mL

Mix together the first 6 ingredients, spread in an 8 x 8-inch baking pan. Spread blueberries over all. Cut together the last 4 ingredients, sprinkle over berries. Bake in 350°F oven for 45 minutes.

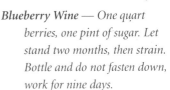

MEDICINAL RECEIPTS

Blueberry Wine — One quart berries, one pint of sugar. Let stand two months, then strain. Bottle and do not fasten down, work for nine days.

— R.C.M., Sussex, in a New Brunswick cookbook dated 1920.

This wine was listed as a dish for invalids. Personally I prefer to take a couple of aspirin and eat my blueberries fresh. Then I buy my blueberry wine from Rossignol Winery in Prince Edward Island.

Zucchini

Love 'em or hate 'em … before you nix one of the garden's most prolific producers, do give zucchini in all its forms a try. Harvest babies, which are wonderful in salads, with dip or as a low-cal munchie. Slightly bigger ones are great grilled on the barbecue. Just cut lengthwise, brush with olive oil, sprinkle with seasoning (such as lemon pepper) and pop them on the grill. When dealing with smaller zucchini, try teaming with small yellow squash — textures and colours complement each other.

The humongous zucchini that gardeners are always trying to give away later in the year can be sliced and grilled, or pan-fried in a little olive oil. Or try a traditional favourite, pickles that can be pulled out in the winter when you really appreciate a bit of the garden.

Heard on a CBC Radio call-in show out of Halifax: "In our neighbourhood you don't dare leave your car unlocked for fear someone will fill it with zucchini."

AUGUST 1980 — Spent a week at Three Brooks, Nova Scotia, my annual gift to myself. My friend Helen and I went into our pickle-making frenzy. Since we spend most of our time gabbing in the kitchen anyway, it's good to be creating.

SANDY'S ZUCCHINI RELISH

5 cups	ground zucchini (with skins)	1250 mL
2 cups	ground onion	500 mL
1	green pepper, ground up	1
1	red pepper, ground up	1
2 1/2 tbsp	coarse salt (pickling salt)	35 mL

Let stand overnight. Next day drain, rinse with cold water. Drain again. Put this mixture in a large (Dutch oven-size) pot. Add the following:

1 1/4 cup	white pickling vinegar	300 mL
2 1/2 cups	sugar	625 mL
1 tbsp	celery seed	15 mL
2 tsp	cornstarch	10 mL
1 1/2 tsp	dry mustard	7.5 mL
1 1/2 tsp	turmeric	7.5 mL
1 1/2 tsp	nutmeg	7.5 mL
1/4 tsp	pepper	1 mL

Cook 30 minutes over medium heat, at a gentle boil. Bottle it. Makes approx 5 pints. Can be doubled.

FRESH PINEAPPLE CHUTNEY

The original recipe has a chopped green pepper and a half clove of garlic. We left it out and wrote "Really good" on the recipe card.

1	small pineapple	1
2 cups	golden raisins	500 mL
2 cups	light brown sugar	500 mL
3/4 cup	red wine vinegar	175 mL
1/2 cup	dark rum or orange juice	125 mL
1/2 cup	pecans or walnuts, coarsely chopped	125 mL
1/2	clove garlic, crushed	1/2
2 inch	cinnamon stick	5 cm
1 tsp	pickling salt	5 mL
1/4 tsp	ground ginger	1 mL
1/4 tsp	allspice	1 mL
1	green pepper, chopped1	

Cut pineapple into 3/4-inch cubes. Combine about 2 1/2 cups pineapple with all other ingredients, except green pepper, in a large, heavy-bottomed saucepan. Bring to a boil; boil gently, uncovered, about 1 hour, or until as thick as you like. Add green pepper for the last 10 minutes of cooking. Spoon into sterilized jars, leaving 1/2-inch space at top. Seal each jar as it is filled. Process for 10 minutes in boiling water bath. Makes 2 pints.

PELLAR'S WIFE'S CUCUMBER RELISH

7	large cucumbers	7
4	large onions	4
2	red peppers (hot)	2
2	green peppers (sweet)	2
3 cups	vinegar	750 mL
1 1/2 cups	hot water	375 mL
4 cups	white sugar	1000 mL
1 1/2 cups	flour	375 mL
1 tsp	turmeric	5 mL
1 tbsp	mustard (dry)	15 mL

Put vegetables through food chopper. Sprinkle with salt and leave overnight. Drain. Make a dressing by combining the vinegar, hot water, sugar, flour, turmeric and mustard. Mix together and boil 5 minutes. Add vegetables and boil 5 minutes more. Cool a little. Put in bottles, but don't cap until cool. Makes 7 pints, plus a little bit.

PEACH CONSERVE WITH RUM

4 cups	coarsely chopped peaches	1000 mL
1 cup	crushed pineapple, drained	250 mL
1	orange	1
1	lime	1
1/2 cup	chopped maraschino cherries (optional)	125 mL
2 tbsp	finely chopped ginger	30 mL
1/2 tsp	salt	2.5 mL
3 cups	white sugar	750 mL
2 tbsp	light rum (optional)	30 mL

A preserve-maker in Oromocto, New Brunswick, covers young grapes with pantyhose to protect them from the birds. As the grapes grow, the pantyhose stretch, allowing the sun in but making it difficult for the birds to steal the crop. Read about it years ago, but the vision of grapevines decorated with pantyhose always stuck with me.

Combine peaches, pineapple, finely grated peel and juice of orange and lime, cherries, ginger, salt and sugar in heavy-bottomed saucepan. Bring to boil; boil gently, uncovered, until thick, about 30 minutes. Remove from heat , skim off foam. Add rum, return to a boil. Pour into hot sterilized jars, leaving a ^{1}/2-inch space at top. Seal each jar as it is filled. Process for 10 minutes in boiling water bath. Spoon over toast, biscuits or ice cream. Makes 3 pints.

SPICED PEARS AND GINGER

Very nice with chicken.

4	pears, peeled, quartered and cored	4
1 cup	sugar	250 mL
^{1}/2 inch	cinnamon stick	1.25 cm
4 cups	water	1000 mL
1 tbsp	lemon juice	15 mL
2 tbsp	finely chopped ginger root	30 mL
^{1}/2	lemon, sliced	^{1}/2

Place pears in bowl containing 2 cups water and the lemon juice. Combine remaining 2 cups water, sugar, ginger and cinnamon stick in large, heavy-bottomed saucepan. Bring to boil, stirring until sugar is dissolved. Add drained pears and unpeeled lemon slices. Simmer 15 minutes or until pears are tender. Remove cinnamon stick. Pack pears in sterilized jars. Boil syrup over high heat for 5 minutes to thicken. Pour over fruit, leaving a ^{1}/2-inch space at top. Seal each jar as it is filled. Process for 20 minutes in a boiling water bath. Makes about 7 ^{1}/2 pints.

Living History

Between Caraquet and Grande-Anse lies one of the best places to experience and learn about the Acadian culture — the past that led them to where they are today, the food that nourished them. The Acadian Historical Village/Village Historique Acadien revives the old trades, the costumes and traditions that characterized Acadians in New Brunswick between 1770 and 1939. To appreciate the uniqueness of the Acadian community one needs to understand its history, for it was what went before that moulded home life.

The birth of the Acadian people can be determined very precisely to the first half of the 17th century, as pioneers, coming from the western provinces of France — Basque country, Flanders and elsewhere — established themselves on the shore of what they called Baie Française, now the Bay of Fundy, and formed the first white community in North America. They gave their new country the name "Acadie."

After only a few generations they considered themselves a distinct people, refusing to bear arms in the wars between the French and English. Regardless, a century and a half after their installation in the territory the Acadians were victims of a deportation order. Eventually they returned, but original lands were taken by others; circumstances had changed.

It is the second settlement period that is recreated at the Acadian Historical Village, illustrating the bare essentials of life during difficult times. This very deprivation became a cause for pride and built a far-reaching social community.

Today, the Acadians who at the time of deportation numbered hardly 15,000 souls are close to two million. Many offshoots from the original tree have taken root under faraway skies. In Louisiana, they number over one million. They are found in all Canadian provinces, the Falkland Islands, in France and New England.

But it is chiefly in the Maritimes that they have affirmed their identity. While many sites in the region commemorate, celebrate and capture their past, the village outside Caraquet brings it to life in a remarkably authentic way.

Our visit began with a stay at Château Albert. Leaving the modern world in a vintage automobile, we began a magical interlude. The dining room menu is based on the customs of the 1900–1910 period, with certain adjustments intended to suit the needs of today's clients: for example, pork fat is used with more restraint. Fish cakes or beans are typical lunch fare, while a musical supper is likely to feature roast venison, codfish in cream sauce, roast chicken with brown gravy, simmered eel or other traditional Acadian dishes.

Our dinner conversation naturally turned to food and kitchen lore. I heard about Pet de Soeur, similar to cinnamon rolls. The story is that nuns gave these treats to their favourite students and thus it was named Pet de Soeur, which translates to "Nun's Farts."

Between each course we were entertained by local musicians. Soon couples were waltzing between the tables. One of the two waitresses took to the floor. The other reminisced. "It brings back memories of an earlier time when my father and mother would take to the floor," she said. "Soon he would hold his hand out to me. A turn around the floor and I felt like … well, like a grand lady, even if only for a minute. A sinkful of dish was waiting. Those turns around the kitchen made me feel good about myself, at one with my world. It was a great gift my parents fed to me in our kitchen."

Soon we were off for a wonderful night-time experience. The peace and quiet of this circa1910 hotel was something seldom experienced in this day of constant electrical hum and noise.

Since our visit to the village coincided with La Fête Nationale — the Acadian national holiday, held August 15 — we followed woodland trails to a special breakfast held in the heart of the Acadian Village: scrambled eggs, sausages, a biscuit and baked beans served free to the first 700 who arrive for the celebration.

Peeking through a window I observed an old friend, Richard Chiasson, dressed in his chef's whites and overseeing breakfast preparation. He and a surprisingly small team met the formidable task of appeasing the appetites of those early risers.

Richard is the executive chef in charge of food service at the village. He and a staff of 55 feed more than 100,000 visitors each summer. There are various food outlets, but it is obvious that his pride and joy is La Table des Ancêtres Inn.

In this ancient Acadian house, cooking is traditional 18th- and 19th-century Acadian, simple and hearty: Sunday soup, clam fricot,

dried codfish and lard, rolls, molasses cake. With few ingredients and straightforward cooking methods, old-time cooks turn out interesting dishes that you can enjoy — as long as you can get in.

It was here I first experienced Poutine à Trou, a poutine or pastry filled with apples, cranberries and raisins. A hole in the top serves two purposes: it lets steam out during baking, and then allows the cook to pour in a sweet syrup. Absolutely wonderful. I also had my first, and probably my last, Poutines Râpées, a potato dumpling with seasoned fatty salt pork in the centre.

"The old Acadians went by inventiveness. What was not there we can not use," said Richard, talking about the dishes offered at the hotel and La Table des Ancêtres Inn. "They are all authentic presentations. We use a natural style of cooking. Summer savory, salt and pepper were the only flavourings they had." A huge amount of research has gone into presenting accurate meals. Ranking up there with the actual eating is the magical experience of visiting recreated kitchens and gaining knowledge from costumed players in homes throughout the village.

"Before the deportation they have found trays of carrots, but afterwards they were not seen until around 1901. No one knows why carrots disappeared for so many years," said Richard.

"The fishermen bring in cod which is split, soaked in heavily salted water and spread on racks covered with pine needles to dry. Why pine? You would not want the fish to take the taste of the wood — rather the pine needles."

Incidentally, the folks at the Acadian Historical Village told me the best reference book for Acadian cooking is *A Taste of Acadie*, by Marielle Cormier-Boudreau and Melvin Gallant. It is a good read, with good information on the many natural ingredients favoured by the Acadians, and it's now available in many city markets.

Following our Acadian Village adventure we headed for Caraquet to participate in the Tintamarre, a colourful, lively traditional party. Thousands of citizens adorned in the Acadian colours of red, white and blue, making as much noise as possible. At the chiming of the church bell household utensils and whatever else does the job — pots and pans, drums, foghorns, tin horns, whistles, not to mention human voices functioning at the highest decibels possible — all make noise until the bells peel again. Concerts, parties and celebrations follow, making for a magical event that cannot be described but should be experienced.

Our Acadian adventure took us to many fine eateries in northeastern New Brunswick, offering up traditional dishes, seafood to die for and experiences to treasure. At Kouchibouguac National Park we visited Le Bon Accueil Restaurant. Operated each summer by four women of the community, it seemed an unlikely spot to find the wonderful Acadian dishes we did. I would drive back there for their chowder and Poutine à Trou any time. In Bouctouche, the characters at Le Pays de la Sagouine brought housewives to life in this fictional village on the Île aux Puces (Isle of Fleas). As well as fun history lessons, a recipe for molasses cake (which follows) and fine music, we enjoyed some great laughs before moving on to Le Vieux Presbytère de Bouctouche, a restored 1880 manse, for a fine dinner and overnight stay.

POUTINE À TROU

Our Acadian tour began and ended at the Delta Beauséjour Hotel in Moncton. This recipe comes courtesty of Louise Arsenault, a staff member who says, "These are indeed a treat for Acadians. My grandmother would make them for special occasions and would also make a few with apples only, for the kids who did not like raisins. The ingredients can vary slightly, as you can opt not to include the cranberries."

DOUGH:

2 ½ cups	flour	625 mL
4 tsp	baking powder	20 mL
½ tsp	salt	2.5 mL
¼ cup	milk	50 mL

FILLING:

4–6	apples, peeled and cut into small pieces	4–6
½ cup	raisins	125 mL
½ cup	cranberries	125 mL

SYRUP:

1 cup	packed brown sugar	250 mL
¾ cups	water	175 mL

For the dough, sift and mix dry ingredients, blend in shortening and gradually add milk.

The dough should be similar consistency to tea biscuit or baking powder biscuit dough. Roll out to form a dozen 5- to 6-inch circles of dough.

Place apples, cranberries and raisins on the dough. Moisten edges with milk or water to seal and form a ball with each circle. Place folded side down on a baking sheet. Make a small (1/2-inch) hole on the top of each. Bake these poutines at 350°F for 1/2 hour.

While baking make a syrup by gently boiling water and sugar for 5 minutes. Remove cooked poutines from the oven when done, pour syrup into each, using hole on top. Serve warm or cold.

MOLASSES CAKE

"Amicalement Dolinda Pays de la Sagouine"

2 cups	molasses	500 mL
1 cup	white sugar	250 mL
1 cup	melted margarine	250 mL
1 cup	black tea (lukewarm)	250 mL
5 cups	flour	1250 mL
1 tsp	baking soda	5 mL
1 tsp	cinnamon	5 mL
1 tsp	ginger	5 mL
1 tsp	salt	5 mL
4	eggs	4
1 cup	raisins	250 mL

Bake at 275°F for 1 hour, then up the temperature to 300° for additional 15 minutes.

Crab

Sometimes I'm called upon to act as a guide to chefs or food writers visiting my home province. Invariably the experience involves lobster fishing. We head for the wharf at 4 a.m. or so, and spend the waking hours on the sea. A magical experience on a calm day. We won't talk about days when winds and waves play havoc with tummies!

One of the things that invariably comes up with lobster traps is rock crab. These crustaceans, abundant in the waters of Prince Edward Island, are commercially harvested, and a bycatch of the lobster fishery. They are also delicious.

In the true style of fisherfolk we head to the galley to boil up a feed for breakfast at sea. What a treat — lobster and crab cooked in seawater. Yum! Fortunately, consumers can now buy frozen rock crab, whole (in shell) or as processed meat in cans or vacuum packages. It is a tasty ingredient that is often overlooked because of the popularity of its cousin the lobster, but shouldn't be.

Crab-Stuffed Baked Potatoes

Serves 6

6-oz	package rock crab meat	170 g
6	potatoes, baked	6
1 tbsp	butter	15 mL
3/4 cup	sour cream	175 mL
1/4 cup	grated onion	50 mL
1/4 tsp	pepper	1 mL
1/4 cup	diced mushrooms	50 mL
1/2 cup	grated cheddar cheese	125 mL

Preheat oven to 375°F. Cut baked potatoes in half lengthwise, carefully scoop out insides, reserving skins. In a bowl combine potato, butter, sour cream, onion and pepper. Beat until smooth. Fold in crab meat and diced mushrooms, put mixture back into potato skins, dividing equally. Sprinkle with grated cheese, place on baking sheet. Bake for 10–15 minutes until hot. Serve at once.

ROCK CRAB SALAD

Serves 6

1 cup	rock crab meat	250 mL
1 cup	chopped celery	250 mL
1/2 cup	chopped green pepper	125 mL
3/4 cup	sliced mushrooms	175 mL
1/4 cup	chopped onion	50 mL
3	tomatoes	3
	salt and pepper to taste	
2 tsp	vinegar	10 mL
1/4 tsp	sugar	1 mL
1/4 cup	mayonnaise	50 mL

Combine all ingredients in bowl and toss to mix well. Chill thoroughly. Serve on lettuce.

— Recipes courtesy Prince Edward Island
Department of Fisheries and Aquaculture

September

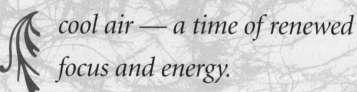

— Bountiful harvest, crisp, cool air — a time of renewed focus and energy.

*y inspiration for cooking comes from what is on hand.
And in the Maritimes, ingredients appear in the natural order of things.
When the smelts are running we eat smelts; when the apples are red we
pick them; and when a generous, but anonymous, neighbour leaves a bushel
(make that 35.23808 litres) of rhubarb on your back porch we have pie for
the next few days and preserves for the rest of the year. For the rest, we have
to be patient like our forebears, and eat what is in season and on hand.
The real Maritime foods are gifts from the sea, forest, shoreline, and field.*

— Judith Comfort, of Medway Harbour, Nova Scotia, speaking at Cuisine Canada's "Northern Bounty"
conference. Her topic, "Some Good! The Maritime Harvest," is a natural for the author of numerous
cooking and travel books, including *Some Good!*

BEGGAR'S BREAKFAST

Serves 4

Once upon a time lobster and crab were so plentiful that they were used as
fertilizer on farm fields. Any child who took lobster sandwiches in his or her
lunch can was immediately labelled as poor — perhaps how this dish got its
name. Lobster could be used at breakfast without anyone outside the household knowing. How things have changed! Today a lobster or crab breakfast is
a treat indeed.

	4 oz	cooked crab or lobster meat	100 g
or	1	live lobster	1
	1 ½ cups	whipping cream, divided (reserve 1 tbsp/15 mL)	375 mL
	1 tsp	cornstarch	5 mL
	½ cup	grated Canadian Emmenthal cheese	125 mL
	1 tsp	chopped, fresh tarragon	5 mL
		salt and pepper	

September

12	eggs	12
¼ cup	milk	50 mL
1 tbsp	butter	15 mL

In saucepan, heat cream (less 1 tbsp [15 mL]). Blend cornstarch with remaining cream; add to sauce and bring to boil. Stir until thickened and cooked. Reduce heat; add cheese and stir until melted. Stir tarragon, salt, pepper and lobster meat into sauce. Simmer 15 minutes.

For each serving, beat 3 eggs with 1 tbsp (15 mL) milk. Melt butter in an 8-inch omelette pan. Prepare omelette, folding over twice to form cigar shape; roll onto warm plate. To serve, split top of omelette and fill with 1/3 cup (80 mL) sauce. Serve with toast.

Oysters

Every so often I find myself pulled into unexpected food experiences. Such was the case at a Prince Edward Island shellfish festival. My good friend Chef Stefan Czapalay and his charming wife, Sharlene, had a demonstration kitchen set up and were giving sessions on how to prepare Prince Edward Island's marvellous mussels and oysters. I was there to take pictures. Next thing I knew, I was topping bruschetta, filling little tarts, passing samples and just generally having a grand time.

I have a passion for cooking demonstrations. Some of the best chefs and cooks in the region often put themselves out, leaving their establishment and a myriad of chores, to get out there and extol the benefits of the products of the region. The thing these presentations do for you, the observer, is dispel the myths.

Cooking oysters scare you? Trust me: once you catch a demo and have a chance to sample, you realize those fears are groundless. On the slim chance that you don't like something it's no sweat, no money out of your pocket, no hours spent labouring in the kitchen. But the treasures you come away with … Ahhhhhhhhh.

Demo kitchens, part of many of the great festivals of our region, celebrate all manner of foods: clams, oysters, scallops, apples, potatoes, lobster.

The following oyster recipes are courtesy of Stefan, then of Summerside, now of Halifax. Please note they contain some of his own oils and dressings as ingredients, but in brackets he also tells you what to substitute, so go for it.

HERB-CRUSTED OYSTER ON TOMATO BRUSCHETTA

6	Malpeque oysters, shucked	6
6	baguette rounds, toasted	6
1	clove garlic	1
1	yellow tomato	1
1	red tomato	1
6	basil leaves	6
	chopped parsley	
	salt and pepper	
	flour	
	lobster oil (substitute clarified butter or vegetable oil)	
1 tbsp	Essence of Thyme balsamic vinaigrette (make your own by blending balsamic vinegar, olive oil, grape seed oil and various spices)	15 mL

Make concasse: Cut tomatoes in quarters, scooping out seeds. Dice tomato and toss with chopped basil, salt, pepper and balsamic vinaigrette. Roll oysters in flour with chopped parsley. Sauté in nonstick frying pan in the oil until golden brown. Season with salt and pepper and reserve, warm. Place a heaping spoonful of tomato concasse on toast round that has been rubbed with the garlic clove and place one oyster on top of each piece.

PUMPKIN AND OYSTER TARTS

12	unsweetened 2-inch/ 5-cm tart shells, precooked	12
½ cup	small diced pumpkin (blanched)	125 mL
½ cup	small diced potatoes (blanched)	125 mL
¼ cup	red peppers, diced fine	50 mL
¼ cup	green onions, diced fine	50 mL
	salt and pepper	
12	oysters, shucked	12
	Essence of Thyme citrus vinaigrette	
	("Of course we always promote our own product! But a squeeze of fresh lemon, a squeeze of fresh lime, 1 teaspoon orange juice and 1 tablespoon olive oil, blended, may substitute."	
	— Stefan)	

Drizzle raw oysters with citrus vinaigrette and let stand 2 minutes. Season with salt and pepper, toss all ingredients together. Place in tart shells and enjoy.

OYSTER AND MUSSEL CHOWDER WITH PUMPKIN

6	oysters	6
12	mussels	12
6	mini pumpkins the size of baseballs, hollowed out	6
¼ cup	diced pumpkin, blanched	50 mL
¼ cup	diced carrots, blanched	50 mL
¼ cup	diced potatoes, blanched	50 mL
¼ cup	diced onions	50 mL
¼ cup	diced celery	50 mL
	pinch seafood seasoning	pinch
¼ cup	dry white wine	50 mL
1	bay leaf	1
1 cup	cream	250 mL
1 clove	garlic	1 clove
	salt and pepper	
1 tbsp	crab-flavoured oil (substitute olive oil)	15 mL
3 tbsp	butter	45 mL

Mince garlic, gently cook in medium-size sauce pan with oil. Before garlic turns colour, add bay leaf, white wine and mussels. Cover pot and steam until mussels open. Remove mussels from shell and strain liquid. In a new pot, gently cook onions and celery in 1 tbsp butter until translucent. Add mussel juice and bring to boil. Add heavy cream and bring back to boil. Add all vegetables, spice, oysters and mussels. Stir in remaining 2 tbsp butter and immediately serve in the small pumpkins. Prior to serving, place pumpkins in a 350° oven for 5 minutes.

September

135

Succotash

When the new vegetables come in, folks make hodgepodge. Later vegetables cooked in a similar way become succotash. Go figure. Nova Scotian writer Florence M. Hilchey wrote that this was originally a dish prepared by First Nations called "Misickquatash," which was probably high on the menu for the Order of Good Cheer enjoyed by the Champlain settlers in 1606:

Six ears of corn; one pint of string beans, trimmed and cut into short pieces; one tablespoonful of butter rolled in flour; one cupful of milk; pepper and salt. Cut the corn from the cob, bruising as little as possible. Put over the fire with the beans in enough hot water, salted, to cover them, and stew gently half an hour. Turn off nearly all the water and add a cupful of milk. Simmer in this, stirring to prevent burning, twenty minutes; add the floured butter, the pepper and salt, and stew ten minutes. Serve in a deep dish."

— *The New Cook Book* (one of my treasured collectibles from the past)

Living History

I do wonder about the cream and butter — did they have cows available to milk in 1606? To find the answer one would have to go to the actual site of the habitation in Port Royal, N.S. A reconstruction of the original French fur-trading post depicts life amidst the hardships of the New World in 1605–6.

Here French explorer Samuel de Champlain led the colony to celebrate the successful harvest with tables laden with roast meat, fowl and fish, fresh vegetables and fine wine.

The events of 1606 were recorded by Acadian writer Marc Lescarbot, who said that Champlain, to keep his men active and healthy, determined to ward off scurvy by maintaining a good diet throughout the winter. The establishment of the Order of Good Cheer, North America's first social club, enabled him to attain his goal. Champlain was a smart cookie, playing on the competitive nature of men.

Every day a "Grand Master" was chosen and given responsibility for providing food, planning the menu and entertainment. Each was determined to hunt the best game, find the most succulent seafood, provide better ingredients than those before him. In the kitchens cooks prepared fine banquets.

When ready the Grand Master, the chain of the Order of Good Cheer hanging from his neck, lead a procession of cooks, bakers, helpers and members of the order, laden with platters of the daily offering. The Champlain party had much knowledge of farming and harvesting from the land. Undoubtedly the food was seasoned with herbs and washed down with French wine and cider. Each meal was a merry affair lasting several hours.

Yarmouth writer Carol Matthews wondered if they got tired of these daily excesses of clams and mussels, roast caribou with turnips, carrots and cabbage, fresh salmon, moose-meat pie, bear, raccoon and wildcat. I wonder if these famous feasts were for all inhabitants at the fort, or just the elite. We can only surmise.

The first social club in North America is still celebrated, even though it officially lasted only one year in Port Royal. Nova Scotian visitors can become members of the Order of Good Cheer and receive an official certificate, and special Order of Good Cheer dinners are held around the region.

There are those of us who feel that our Thanksgiving should be tied to the Order of Good Cheer — those early inhabitants surely did give thanks that they had the feasting, unlike those of earlier voyagers who starved to death during their first Maritime winter.

Making corn chowder or soup? Take leftover corncobs, put them into a stock pot and simmer for a while. It's amazing how much flavour will be transferred to your stock.

A Wedding Feast

SEPTEMBER 23 — In the year 2000 this day was one of those never to be forgotten for our household. Our only son, John, was home from Vancouver to tie the nuptial knot. A fine wedding it was, filled with pride in our boy, the emotional joy of having many members of our family together for the first time in decades, the heartfelt joining with his bride's family, who welcomed us as an extension of their own large clan.

The closeness and love the Blanchards have for Christine, their youngest, was personified in the kitchen at the reception. Held in a former schoolhouse, now community hall (as is often the setting for such events), the affair was catered by family and friends. Sisters, cousins, friends were not sitting around waiting for the formalities. Instead, the buzz was on in the kitchen as everyone — including the moms — pitched in. Even the newlyweds got involved in the production and serving of the wedding feast.

Salads were made, potatoes cooked outside, hot dogs prepared for the kids, roast beef (prepared by a chef friend), turkey (prepared by the mother of the bride), thick country-style gravy lying beside the jus de jour, pickles, home-baked rolls and a vast array of squares, cookies and cake — all were lovingly laid out for a buffet.

Dishwashing began hours before and continued into the evening. Tired and weary food preparers and cleanup crew ended their day with a glow of satisfaction and the knowledge that they had indeed made this day special for two people they loved. They saved them thousands of dollars and, more importantly, made this wedding a true family affair. We thank them all.

As is the case in kitchens of community halls everywhere, they enjoyed the event in their own special way. This was a time to share family news, to gossip, to reminisce, to simply be with loved ones now scattered, and to get to know the newbies to the family.

So warm was the feeling in the kitchen that many of us kept sneaking in to be part of the camaraderie. Don't feel sorry for those volunteers who toil away in the kitchens of church halls, community centres and such: feel appreciation, give them thanks, but be aware that theirs is a special place.

The Last Days of Summer

With the danger of frost looming ever closer, the rush is on to make the best use of what is in the garden. The pungent scent of pickles is evidence of the rush of industrious cooks to preserve every good vegetable they can. Cucumbers, green tomatoes, everything in the garden finds it way into the pickle pot. The resulting mustard pickles and chow are traditionally served with ham and fish cakes.

CHOW CHOW

Chow is made with what you have in the garden, thus it has many variations. This New Brunswick recipe is not traditional, as most don't use fruit. It is, however, delicious.

15 lb	green tomatoes	7 kg
1 cup	salt	250 mL
6	large onions, cut small	6
2 cups	chopped celery	500 mL
3	pears, cored and chopped	3
3	apples, cored and chopped	3
3	green peppers, seeds removed and chopped	3
3	red peppers, seeds removed and chopped	3
2 oz	mixed pickling spice	50 g

| 6 cups | sugar | 1.5 L |
| 1 ½ pints | pickling vinegar | 700 mL |

Chop tomatoes, sprinkle with salt, soak overnight. Drain tomatoes, pressing to remove water and salt. Add remaining ingredients, cook all together for 2 hours. Fill jars and seal.

Green Tomato Butter

Wash and chop finely 3 quarts of green tomatoes. Cut 3 lemons into the thinnest of slices, removing all seeds. Soak 2 ounces of dry ginger root overnight in cold water, then cut it into half-inch pieces. Put the tomatoes and lemons in saucepan to cook, adding just enough cold water to keep them from sticking; when they have boiled 15 minutes, add 4 pounds of granulated sugar and the ginger root. Simmer gently until thick and rich; if liked, add scant cupful of seeded raisins, chopped, and cupful of English walnut meat cut in small pieces. Continue simmering for 15 minutes, then pour into small pots or glasses, seal when cold. This is a delicious conserve.

Mountain Ash Jelly for Game

This condiment was a must in the past when serving venison. The old recipe reads as follows: "Cover the nut ash berries with water and vinegar. Boil until tender. Mash the fruit, strain twice if you desire it very clear. Boil the juice half an hour or so. Measure and add a pound of sugar to pint of juice, and when it comes to the boiling point pour in glasses. Vinegar according to wish. It may be omitted with good results."

— *A Treasury of Nova Scotia Heirloom Recipes*

Green Thumb

The arrival of fall brings houseplants back into the forefront after being overshadowed during the "garden period." We start bringing things back into the house, take cuttings and generally spruce up the plants. It is a time to share them with friends and at this time of year those cuttings could well be heading off to Upper Canada or even farther. This trick might help get them there safely. Store cuttings in a raw potato to keep them fresh during travel. Slice the potato in half lengthwise and place the cut ends of the cuttings inside the potato. Put a rubber band around the potato to hold it together.

A bayleaf in your flour canister will keep the bugs out all year.

A friend suggested this Scottish jelly, passed down in her family: "If you allow pound for pound of apple juice to rowan juice you will get a delightful jelly. Allow a pound of sugar to each pint of apple juice. You can make the tart jelly to taste — an excellent accompaniment to grouse, venison, and saddle of mutton."

Mountain ash, known as rowanberry to those of Scottish extraction, was often teamed with apples or crabapples when jelly making. In her book *Nova Scotia Down Home Cooking*, Janice Murray Gill suggests using three pounds of rowanberries with one pound of sweet crabapples.

Chopped fruit is covered with water, simmered for 45 minutes or so, then poured into a large jelly bag and hung over a bowl to drip overnight. In one old Nova Scotia kitchen a large hook was screwed into the bottom of a sideboard shelf, providing a handy place to hang the jelly bag.

The secret to good jelly is to resist the temptation to squeeze more from the batch. Don't. Just let it drip. Once you have your juice, measure as you pour it into a clean jelly pot (deep-sided). Allow two pounds of sugar to every four cups of juice. Boil quickly over high heat until a spoonful sets quickly on a plate. Skim off any foam before bottling in sterilized jars, topping as you go.

Venison

Although the days where a hunter had to go out and shoot the family's next meal have long passed, game meats such as venison are still very much a part of Maritime life. Fall hunting season puts meat into many a freezer, and delicious it is. Occasionally friends in Nova Scotia share their venison with us. We have learned to guard it closely — the hard way.

Son John decided early in life that after-dinner snacks should be more substantial and fulfilling than opening a bag of chips or pouring cereal in a bowl. It was nothing for him to cook up a burger or steak from the age of 12 on.

One winter weekend he was with his Boy Scout troop at camp, which happened to be just a half mile or so from home. After a hard day of snowshoeing and orienteering, hunger struck. John to the rescue. Tracking us down at friends', he called to see if he could go home for some food to share with "the guys." Sure, said we, thinking he would grab snack stuff, or at worst a few burgers from the freezer. It wasn't until I went to get venison to thaw for a dinner party that we realized those Boy Scouts had scoffed down every scrap of meat that was supposed to have lasted us a couple of months.

The only excuse we got was, "But Mom, the guys had never tasted venison so I cooked it up for them."

I'm sure those "starving" teens didn't notice the absence of marinades that in days past were used to subdue the wild-game flavour and tenderize the meat. In fact, I would be darn surprised if they noticed anything different about the meat they ate. We sure noticed the great big hole in our winter supply.

The Nova Scotia Department of Agriculture and Marketing suggested the following marinade and cooking instructions for venison.

MARINADE FOR VENISON

2	onions, sliced	2
2	bay leaves	2
	pinch thyme	
3/4 cup	vinegar	175 mL
1 pt	ginger ale	500 mL
1 tsp	salt	5 mL
1	clove garlic	1
2	whole cloves	2
	black pepper to taste	

Cut venison into serving size pieces and place them in the marinade in an earthenware or glass jar. Keep in refrigerator for several days.

CHOPS OR STEAK: *Wipe off pieces with a damp cloth and fry in butter or cooking oil for 15 to 20 minutes on each side.*

SHOULDER OR ROUGHER CUTS: *Braising is the best method. Remove meat from marinade, wipe dry and rub on all sides with seasoned flour (1 cup flour, 2 teaspoon salt and 1/4 teaspoon pepper). Brown meat thoroughly in butter and/or oil. Add onions, carrots and 2 1/2 cups of spiced liquid (marinade), simmer for 3 hours.*

ROAST: *Cook in a slow oven (325°F), allowing 25 minutes to the pound (too hot an oven ruins your roast). Baste frequently with fat from bacon strips, or have the roast well larded. Make gravy and serve meat with a tart jelly.*

Which is where we came in — making the jelly!

Around the Kitchen Table

SEPTEMBER 11, 2001 —
THE DAY WE LOST COMPLACENCY

A few days after the terrorist attacks on the World Trade Center and other American targets, talk turned to the future and uncertainty about what women could do to ensure the well-being of their families in the event of war affecting Canadians.

Although angered and sorrowed at the attacks, I did not feel the same depression and almost terror that others expressed. The reason? I grew up in the aftermath of war.

I was born in England during the Second World War and always felt it impacted my life. My father was off fighting for England. What people forget is that the impact of war continues for years after politicians sign a peace treaty. Life changes. Men returned to a very different home front. Our immigration to Canada was a direct result.

My mother's family lived near Banbury,

on the flight path to Coventry. Mom was the oldest and I the first grandchild. My mother ran the family bakery during the war with very little help — all but a few old men had gone. She not only provided bread for the village and military people, she also worked in a factory making parachutes.

I grew up between the bakehouse and my grandmother's. My early memories are of those places, seldom our own house. Mom was from a large family that suffered casualties in war. Nanny billeted Canadian and American soldiers or airmen. It was a popular spot with so many daughters! Some of those airmen, and their families, are still friends of my family.

I grew up in a waste-not-want-not era. We had no pots and pans to speak of because all metals were collected for the war effort. To get coal for the fireplaces my mom and her sisters walked the railroad tracks and followed the coal wagon when it went by on deliveries, hoping for lumps of coal to fall off.

Food was rationed. One popular family story relates to my early allergy to bananas, which were strictly rationed and only made available for babies and the elderly. From my birth to the end of the war my mom had the special treat of two bananas a week — she and her younger sisters who babysat me still talk about what a treat they were. My grandparents had a huge garden. To get fertilizer the aunts followed the horse-drawn milk wagon. They couldn't go home till the horse pooped. There was great competition on the streets for valuable things like coal lumps and horse poop.

I grew up with the effects of all that. My family always has lots of food. You could go to my mom's today and live for a month on what she has in her cupboards. I don't think you ever forget being without.

For those who feel they have to do something against the possibility of war, the one thing I would say is to lay in supplies of things like canned goods. Establish a rotation system so you use from the front and put new ones at the back.

It's important to gather the family around the kitchen table and look at ways you can become self-sufficient — at least for short times. This is useful in winter power outages, never mind war. It helps economize and teaches children to plan ahead, to cope.

All families should look at having an alternative source of heat, light and cooking. Aside from all of that, get yourself as financially stable as you can.

If you live in a city, then figure out where you can go if you feel the need to get out — and, most important, how you are going to get there. Again, it's not likely to happen, but if you have thought it through and have an action plan in mind it puts your mind at ease. I don't think we have to do these things, but it makes folks like me feel better. An added benefit is that you have a supply of food for weeks when money is short or travelling is bad.

The most important thing is to think it out logically, make a plan — then relax.

· · ·

In recognition of the Maritime women who have coped with war, whether in life before Canada or managing the home front, consider these words: "When the cupboards were getting a little bare there were two meals that I remember, Beans on Toast and Fried Sardines on Toast. Both went down well. Even after the lean times we enjoy them on busy days." Leftover homemade beans were probably warmed and served in this Maritime home. In ours we always used tinned beans (Heinz, in tomato sauce — not the ones with a chunk of pork fat in them). Our sardines were mashed with vinegar, rather than fried.

Substitutes for Butter

Vegetable and animal fats may be substituted, measure for measure, in almost any recipe calling for butter. Chicken fat is a fine shortening for cakes, or baking powder biscuits, but isn't available to most people in sufficient quantity for this purpose. Butter contains more water than other shortenings, and so in substituting for it a slightly smaller quantity of the pure fat shortening is required; but this difference is negligible for practical purposes and can be ignored except when baking very rich cakes.

If a recipe calls for an exceptionally large amount of shortening, or if it is rich in chocolate or nuts, it is well to reduce the amount of butter substitute by one tablespoon for every cupful called for. Remember to add salt — about one teaspoon to every cup of shortening — when substituting some other fat for butter.

In mixing cake, add liquid shortening last except where whites of eggs are beaten separately; they should, of course, be folded in after the liquid shortening.

Cornbread

Two cups Indian, one cup wheat;
One cup sour milk, one cup sweet;
One good egg that you will beat.
Half cup molasses, too,
Half a cup sugar add thereto;
With one spoon butter new,
Salt and soda each a spoon;
Mix up quickly and bake it soon;
Then you'll have corn bread complete,
Best of all corn bread you meet.

—Exmouth Street Methodist Church Ladies, New Brunswick, 1909

Fried Sardines

"Dry sardines on blotting paper, dip in lemon juice, roll in bread crumbs and fry in butter a nice brown. Serve on toast and garnish with parsley."

— Mrs. Flynn's Cookbook

Did you know that Connors Bros. in New Brunswick is the world's biggest sardine canning business?

From My Kitchen Window

A fringe of mist covers the field to the far-off woods, its softness a reflection of the clouds above. Even as the kettle boils the mist dissipates, fading away in the rosy glow of the rising sun. If my vision could pass through the trees, like Superman's X-ray eyes, I would probably see walkers welcoming the new day by striding along Confederation Trail. I often think of them, chiding myself for not being as ambitious.

Ship's Lantern Take On Mushrooms

The village of Hillsborough, New Brunswick, known as Blanchard's Village in the 1700s, was the home of Acadian farmers for about 60 years. Around 1763 some moved up the valley to "The Bend" (what is now Moncton), while others moved across the Petitcodiac River to settle what is now known as Pré-d'en-Haut and Belliveau Village. In 1767 Heinrich and Rachel (Decoeur) Steif, who immigrated from Germany to Pennsylvania and then to Canada, settled their family in Hillsborough. After their arrival, the name "Steif" was changed to "Steeves," thus beginning the legacy of the Steeves family that today has more than 150,000 known descendants worldwide. Imagine cooking for their reunions!

Heinrich and Rachel's son, Matthias, originally built what is now the Ship's Lantern Inn owned by Brenda and Cole Belliveau. We chose the Ship's Lantern as one of our "living food" experiences because of the many interesting opportunities in the area, and the dedication of the owners and staff to helping guests develop an appreciation for those who produce fine ingredients as well as providing culinary activities.

One of those activities will take you to the Hope Mushroom Farm for a chance to see how delicious shiitake and oyster mushrooms are grown.

Brenda Belliveau says, "One key in our kitchen is to buy locally and support local merchants or companies whenever we can. From produce, jams, eggs, turkey, mushrooms and such for the kitchen to stained glass mementoes, soaps and maple syrup, we try as often as possible to promote local producers and artisans.

"Hope Mushroom Farm supplies us with the shiitake mushrooms that we use for several dishes including Wild Mushroom Soup, side sauce for steaks and pork tenderloin.

"Doug Northrup and his staff take great care to ensure that their products are picked at just the right moment and quickly delivered. This operation is not what you would expect: dark, with mushrooms growing in the earth. Rather it is the opposite. The temperature is controlled by computer to maintain a consistent warmth in all seasons.

"The growing methods for shiitake involve a block that is compressed and the culture added, so they look like they are growing from a small piece of dark wood. The shiitake is the closest taste to a wild mushroom that you can get. For special functions we also use oyster mushrooms, which feel like velvet to the touch."

WILD MUSHROOM RAVIOLI

Ship's Inn chef Mike Milton shared this recipe, saying, "If you are making your own pasta, you can dehydrate the stems, grind them into a powder and add them to the flour to give a special flavour to the pasta."

STUFFING:

10 oz	shiitake mushrooms	250 g
1/4 tsp	pickling spice	1 mL
1 oz	dry white wine	25 g
1 tbsp	tomato paste	30 mL
5	fresh spinach leaves	5
1	whole roasted garlic cluster	1
1	small roasted onion	1
1/2	roasted red pepper or pimento	1/2
2 tbsp	pine nuts	30 mL
1 tbsp	olive oil	15 mL
	salt and pepper to taste	
	fresh prepared ravioli pasta or wonton wraps	

In a skillet, place mushrooms, spinach, onion, peppers, olive oil and pine nuts. Heat until cooked, then put mixture into blender or food processor with chopping blade. Add remaining ingredients, except for pasta/wonton, and purée until smooth (if the mixture seems too moist, add some fresh bread crumbs to give more

firmness). Let stand 5 minutes to cool, then stuff ravioli/wonton wraps with mixture. Cook stuffed ravioli/wonton for 8–10 minutes, drain carefully.

SAUCE:

12	large plum tomatoes, skinned and cooked	12
4	chives	4
2 tsp	minced garlic	10 mL
1 tbsp	minced fresh basil (dried can be substituted)	15 mL
4 oz	vegetable stock	100 g
1 tbsp	olive oil	15 mL
1 oz	dry red wine (oak barrel red wine gives the best flavour in your red sauces)	25 mL
1/4 tsp	rosemary	1 mL
	fresh ground black pepper to taste	

Add all ingredients, heat so sauce is hot and bubbling, cook 5–20 minutes, depending on thickness you desire. Spoon sauce over ravioli, top with fresh Parmesan cheese and serve with fresh Caesar salad.

The Salem and Hillsborough Railroad

While in Hillsborough, do check out the Salem and Hillsborough Railroad. Dinner Train excursions are memorable, especially in the fall when the colours are at their peak. There is something rather special about dining as you rock along in original railcars through the lovely countryside.

A sign, KIM AND BESSIE'S MAGIC LITTLE KITCHEN, identifies the on-board galley kitchen where Bessie O'Brien and Kim Elliott reign over food service. Some of the precooking is done in a cookhouse — roasting beef, that sort of thing — but there is still quite a challenge involved in feeding the two sittings of 48 guests aboard a rocking train. Steaks are cooked on-board and as Bessie says, "If we forget some-thing here (at the station), unless we get hold of the flagman here it stays. We do without."

In her 70s Bessie is getting to an age where most folk are retired, but she says even after 12 years on the job she loves it.

"We've had very few complaints," she smiles. "I make my own rolls, which is well publicized. I should be retired and out of here, but they tell me I'm like a fixture and I enjoy it here."

Trains are in Bessie's blood. She worked for VIA Rail, travelling from North Sydney through Moncton to Montreal and back again. Her shift was one night on the train, one in Nova Scotia, one on train, one in Montreal … five days on, five days off for eight years.

"One girl working with us had only been there for a while. Her feet were killing her. We'd finished supper, and I looked in the kitchen where she was supposed to be at the sinks washing pots and pans. There she was up on the counter, the sinks full of hot water and her soaking her feet in them!"

Bessie recalls that her daughter and another woman from Moncton were the first women to go on the trains to work. "I was the third. We didn't get welcomed very good. They didn't want women working on the trains."

There is no doubt that today Bessie is a much-valued part of the crew on the Salem and Hillsborough and over the years she's accumulated quite a repertoire of tales. Like the time she was doing a lobster dinner.

"We had them set up on the plates, all trimmed up with lemon. I put butter in the microwave so we could put it on the plates. When I opened the microwave the butter just came pouring out — the dish had broken. Had quite an interesting few minutes cleaning up all those lobsters and plates.

"Another day I was making cheese sauce for the broccoli. We have a table that comes down over the stove; the jolt of the train knocked it loose and it came down and knocked the cheese sauce over. We had quite a mess of cheese sauce all over the kitchen."

Back in 1994 when they were raising money to get the place back together, Bessie and crew built the largest blueberry cake. "It got in the Guinness Book of Records in '95," she smiles. "And then another time we got all the volunteers and members together and had a pancake breakfast, served about 300 that morning with baked beans and sausage."

And then there was the turkey incident.

Bessie's assistant Kim is, according to Art Clowes at the Salem and Hillsborough, a "tall drink of water that might weigh 98 pounds soaking wet. They were getting some 30-pound turkeys ready to start roasting. Kim, concerned about letting Bessie lift anything heavy, either tries herself, or gets one of the men — if they happen to be around — to do the heavy lifts.

"Anyway, this day no one was there except Bessie, so Kim started to lift this turkey that had been placed in a roaster ready for the oven. Kim apparently sort of got it off the counter and as she was turning towards the stove she lost her balance and down on the floor went Kim, with the roaster and its turkey still inside about on top of Kim.

"Kim has quite a laugh and it usually doesn't take much to get her laughing. As Bessie tells it, Kim started to lift the roaster and turkey up, and to get up, but got laughing, with the result that the two ladies spent almost half an hour in various attempts to get the turkey in the oven, most of it laughing." Bessie didn't have any recipes to pass along because she doesn't use them.

"My cooking is all old-fashioned cooking, down and out farm cooking — roast beef with onions and salt and pepper and gravy. For my dressing, which everyone loves, I cut potatoes in squares, mix them with homemade bread, onions, summer savory and butter. Put it all in and cook it. Don't mash potatoes or wet bread."

As for her famous rolls, she says she can't give away her recipes, but "you take a quart of milk, put it and margarine in the microwave and warm up. Add two teaspoons of yeast, with sugar, and let it raise. Add flour and work and work it. Let it raise once. Come out just as fluffy … I guess I've been making them so long."

Crabapple Catsup

Crabapples are all too often overlooked! Three pounds of fruit that has been cored, one and three–quarters pounds sugar, one quart vinegar, one tablespoonful each of cloves, cinnamon and pepper and one teaspoonful of salt. Scald the fruit, run it through the sieve, then mix all ingredients together and boil until it is almost as thick as jam.

We are all starting to think screens down, storms up, sealing the home for winter. Most of us forget to think in terms of sealing the home from insects and rodents seeking warmth. Add caulking compound to all cracks you can locate around windows, doors, pipes and wires. Stuff any larger holes with something nasty, like steel-wool pads with soap in them: keeps the four-leggers away. Oh, and the top of the chimney should be screened to keep out birds, and the dryer outlets should be screened. Mine manages to fall off many a summer — I always envision little mice going round and round with my clothes.

Flights of Fancy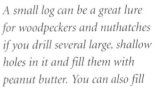

A small log can be a great lure for woodpeckers and nuthatches if you drill several large, shallow holes in it and fill them with peanut butter. You can also fill these holes with fat drained from cooking meat (chill and spread in with a knife), or shove pieces of suet into them.

RUMMY PEARS

Excellent as a dessert or served as a side with pork or chicken. This recipe makes one quart. Try others with a variety of flavours such as lemon, cinnamon sticks or orange. You can also substitute brandy for the rum.

2 lb	very firm pears	1 kg
2 cups	sugar	500 mL
2 cups	water	500 mL
¼ cup	lime juice	60 mL
	grated rind of 1 lime	
4	whole cloves	4
3	lime slices	3
	sprig thyme	
½ cup	white or dark rum, or more if necessary	125 mL

Peel, halve and core pears. Combine water and sugar in a saucepan, cook until sugar has dissolved. Stir in lime juice, rind and cloves. Gently add pear and simmer 2–3 minutes until just tender. Place carefully in a large sterilized glass jar with a few cloves, lime slices and a sprig of thyme. Fill 3/4 full with syrup, then top with rum to fill jar. Seal and process in boiling water bath for 15 minutes. To serve, chill well.

October

— *Savoury soups
and stews return as
temperatures fall.*

A nation cannot rise above the level of its homes; therefore women must work and study together to raise our homes to the highest possible level.

— Adelaide Hoodless, founder of the Women's Institute

A new breakfast sensation was discovered in Nova Scotia, hooking me on combining yogurt of choice, granola and fresh fruit or dried cranberries. The crunchy combination of whole grains and nuts is also great with milk. This basic granola mix is good as a snack, a topper or, with the addition of butter, as a crisp pie shell.

Preparing your own is a great way to get kids involved. They invent combinations and store them in zip bags with their names on. Amazing how easy it is to get kids to eat when it's their "own." My friends use this original recipe, from *Back to Basic*, a Nova Scotia government publication, as a guide. "You get to control the sugar and fat, unlike commercial mixes. We divide it before adding the nuts and let the kids choices start there."

— CBM

GRANOLA MIX

	6 cups	rolled oats	1.5 L
	1 cup	shredded coconut	250 mL
	1 cup	wheat germ	250 mL
	½ cup	sunflower seeds	125 mL
	¾ cup	cashews, halved	175 mL
or	½ cup	chopped almonds or sesame seeds	125 mL
	1 cup	soybeans, roasted and ground	250 mL

Combine in large bowl and set aside.

½ cup	safflower oil	125 mL
½ cup	liquid honey	125 mL
½ cup	water	125 mL
1 ½ tsp	salt	7.5 mL
1 ½ tsp	vanilla	7.5 mL

Simple Pleasures

Mix together in separate bowl, pour over dry ingredients. Stir well to coat all. Spread on 2 greased baking sheets, bake 25 minutes at 325°F, stirring frequently. Cool thoroughly.

1 cup raisins (or ½ cup chopped dried apricots)

Add raisins or apricots, mix well and store in airtight containers. One-third cup granola makes a good-size breakfast serving. Makes 11 cups.

Living History

In the village of Middle West Pubnico, in Yarmouth County on the south shore of Nova Scotia, lies a veritable treasure. Our introduction came on a dark and stormy night — really. It was blowing up a gale and raining buckets. The village, nestled on a peninsula between the waters of Pubnico Harbour and Lobster Bay, is exposed to the elements and let us know it. This is not a place you stumble across passing through. You have to go to the Pubnicos: West, Middle West and Lower West.

Pubnico, derived from the Mi'kmaq word "Pobomcoup," means "place where holes have been made in the ice to fish" — an occupation still carried on. To appreciate this area consider that Pubnico celebrates its 350th anniversary in 2003. Not far along the highway Port Royal, the oldest settlement, celebrates its 400th in 2004.

When Phillippe D'Entremont settled here, it was with the idea of starting anew. In 1653 there was nothing waiting for the Acadians.

Settlement took a fortitude that few of us today can imagine or identify with. "The people were close to starvation. Indians left meat on the rocks, they told them what to drink — spruce beer they called it. The vitamin C prevented scurvy. They knew how to grow corn," he said.

Newcomers learned to hunt wild game. They fished the seas. Women milked the cows, did the butter and the bread, ground grain, made soap from fat, prepared meals and nurtured families, while the men did the clearing. They survived invasion by the Dutch and deportation by the British.

…

Our first stop was the Red Cap Restaurant and Motel. Dashing through pelting rain, we practically fell through the door. Warmth, the comforting aroma of home cooking and a friendly smile greeted us. Ahhhhhh! We instantly agreed that we may just stay, to heck with braving the elements for a bed.

We had no idea that we had found one of the best places to sample authentic Acadian cooking in Nova Scotia. We had come for the Acadian museum — almost next door — and found a second treasure. The menu was a veritable feast of Acadian dishes. I couldn't resist trying the râpure, or Rappie Pie as we English-only speakers call it. This traditional dish is a combination of grated potato and meat seasoned with salt and pepper and onion, which is baked to gold brown. It is eaten as is, spread with butter or molasses — the blackstrap kind — or both. I tried both and would opt for butter. Luckily for travellers and locals alike,

October

the Red Cap is no summer place. It's open year-round.

RAPPIE PIE (RÂPURE)

Serves 10–12

Tradition has it that the potato, the main ingredient of râpure, reached Nova Scotia by the mid-1700s. It is also said that an Acadian returning to Nova Scotia after the deportation may have met a German soldier and acquired the idea of grating potatoes before cooking them.

In Germany grated potatoes are part of traditional cuisine, as are potato pancakes in Poland, poutines râpées in New Brunswick and even "la râpure" in some Acadian areas. Only in southwest Nova Scotia, however, is pâté a la râpure made using a recipe unique to the area.

Pâté a la râpure is made from potatoes, grated raw, before being cooked. What makes their râpure unique in taste and texture is the separating of grated pulp from the juice, then the adding of a special broth to replace the removed liquid.

The folks at the Red Cap and the museum say the name of the person who made this "breakthrough in taste" has been lost in the mists of râpure history.

A generous portion of either beef, chicken, clams or wild game mixed in with the other ingredients is perhaps the most important feature of the traditional recipe for la râpure. The most difficult choice which the connoisseur of râpure must face is precisely — which flavour this time?

1	5–6 lb roasting chicken or other fowl	1
2	onions, chopped	2
²/₃ pail	potatoes (peeled washed and grated)	²/₃ pail
2	slices salt pork, chopped and scalded	2
	season to taste (salt, pepper, chicken spice)	

Cut chicken into pieces. Place in large pot with onions and seasoning. Add water to cover, simmer until meat is cooked. Remove meat from bones, cut into small pieces. Reserve broth or cooking liquid, keeping hot. Have boiling water available in case you do not have enough broth.

Squeeze water out of grated potatoes by putting 2 to 3 cups at a time in a cotton bag, or use a juicer if you have one. Measure the water before discarding. Place pulp in a large bowl and cover.

Grease pans (two 9 x 13-inch or one 12 x 18-inch).

Mix the potato pulp to loosen, pour hot broth into pulp, stirring well. Add enough broth and boiling water to equal amount of water extracted from potatoes as measured previously, plus about 2 more cups.

Place 1 layer of scalded potatoes in pan and add the cut-up meat. Add remaining potatoes on top. Place layer of scalded pieces of pork on top.

Bake 2 hours in a hot (400°F) oven.

…

The good folks at Le Musée Acadien de Pubnico-Ouest gave us two more regional recipes that use grated potatoes.

DUMPLINGS

Combine 1 pound grated potatoes, $^1/_2$ teaspoon salt, $^1/_4$ teaspoon pepper, $^1/_8$ pound margarine and $^1/_2$ teaspoon salted chives*. Pour 1 $^1/_2$ cups boiling broth or water gradually over mixture. Mix well. Drop large spoonful of mixture over slow-boiling stew and cook for 30 to 45 minutes.

POTATO PANCAKES

"Delicious with minced clams mixed in."

Grate 2 pounds of potatoes. Pour 3 cups boiling broth or water gradually over mixture. Mix well with $^1/_2$ cup flour, salt and pepper to taste. In frying pan with very hot oil, fry on both sides till golden brown. Makes 20 pancakes.

*Salted Herbs— I used chives cut from my pot on the window and it worked great. But since then my friend Sherry Pelky, who lives near Woodstock, N.B., has introduced me to the salted herbs that were put down by the Acadians and are an important ingredient in their cuisine. Cut chives, shallots and onion shoots were layered with salt in crocks or glass containers, using about a half cup of coarse salt to four or five cups herbs. After several days a brine formed and preserved them. They were then used as a seasoning, particularly in meat dishes.

Musée Acadien

When visiting any historic dwelling I gravitate toward the kitchen, spending so much time there that the rest of our group has completed its tour before I'm ready to move on. Result is I often see only one room of these wonderful historic homes. Such was not the case at the Musée Acadien in Middle West Pubnico. They told me I should visit the attic, so I did and saw two rooms.

First the kitchen. Artifacts and a good guide, Bernice d'Entremont, provide a view to life in this kitchen years ago. The tools of ancestors are lovingly preserved: the necessaries for butter-making (a churn, butter pot and dish), a spinning wheel and candle-making equipment. Bernice tells us that when making butter from cream that was not rich, innovative housewives would colour it with a little dandelion. She reminded us that graters are used to make Rappie Pie; "To get early graters a hunter put up a tin and shot it.

"Sheep were kept on islands just offshore all year, as they are today. Once a year they were rounded up, brought ashore in boats for shearing. Today they are also vaccinated and the wool is sold in bulk, rather than spun and woven by women sitting beside the fire.

"Fresh eggs were put in brine in a crock. When time came to cook, they would not salt as much as usual because the eggs would absorb some of the salt through the shell. Eggs were a precious commodity used only for special things, because they could also be sold or bartered for other goods."

Canvas flooring (reminded me of old-style linoleum) was used during the winter to keep the drafts down, then put upstairs in the summer. Canvas was used because of the menfolk being fishermen: once a canvas sail ripped or tore it was no good for the boats. It would be spread out in the attic and painted with as many as five coats before a motif or design was added. "It was hot in the attic," says Bernice. "So hard. This was very hard work."

…

A most memorable story was revealed upstairs in the attic, where a tiny table is littered with what to the untrained eye appear to be dozens of useless chips of wood. To those in the know, these wooden slivers represent an occupation that had great importance and was the foundation of one of Atlantic Canada's major suppliers of gear for the fishing and aquaculture industries.

In the early 1900s live lobster was sold for a mere 5 to 10 cents per pound. Pegs used to prevent lobsters from using their claws in captivity were whittled by hand, of local pine. Working at home, villagers made and packaged pegs in bags of 1,000, receiving the equivalent of 30 to 50 cents per bag in goods bartered from the local general store. Acadians eager to find employment produced millions of lobster plugs to supply the entire East Coast lobster fishery. By the early 1930s the little village was known as the "Lobster Plug Capital of the World." Virtually every necessity of life was paid for by whittling the plugs.

Bernice pointed out that the kitchen was the largest and warmest room in the house. This was where the family lived. When weather prevented outdoor work, people spent their time by the fire whittling lobster plugs, knowing that 1,000 tiny wooden pieces (just a little bigger than a cribbage peg) would mean the family could go to the store to stock the cupboards. Whittlers made their own special knives and gloves with finger guards of heavy cloth or leather, for the work could be dangerous.

Gradually production became mechanized, but the importance to the local economy remained. In 1975 Vernon d'Eon sold his boat, gear and licence to buy the local lobster plug factory. Employees made more than 500 million lobster plugs in the nine years before the government decreed the plugs should be replaced with rubber bands. The company had grown from a one-man backyard operation to a large international operation.

Even though the lobster plug is no longer produced, Vernon d'Eon's pride in that heritage is reflected in the company's name, which did not change with the times. "I am very proud to be part of this valuable heritage and our history, very proud to be Acadian, and this is why our company is called Vernon d'Eon Lobster Plugs Ltd.," said Vernon.

Cranberries

Ruby red fresh cranberries are abundant in the fall. Just bag up and freeze and you'll have enough for months to come. Cranberries have nourished Canadians from the days of the earliest Native peoples, who not only used them fresh and dried as food but also as medicine and tonic. Recipes for their use abound in old cookbooks. Strong in its traditional role as sauce served with turkey dinners, it was overlooked for other uses for several decades before regaining favour in the kitchen. Today we recognize the nutritional value of the cranberry; rich in vitamins, minerals and beneficial antioxidants, it is also useful as a flavourful ingredient. However, we still fail to use this wonderful berry to its full potential. Consider these recipes, old and new, and enjoy!

WILD CRANBERRY PUDDING

Put 3 cups of cranberries into saucepan and cover with water. Add 1/2 cup sugar and boil until berries have all burst. Add enough custard to make it thick.

CAPE BRETON CRANBERRY PIE

3 1/2 cups	cranberries	875 mL
1 1/2 cups	white sugar	375 mL
1 1/2 tbsp	flour	22 mL
1/4 tsp	salt	1 mL
3 tbsp	water	45 mL
2 tbsp	melted butter	30 mL

Chop cranberries, mix with remaining ingredients. Fill unbaked pie shell with mixture and arrange strips of pie crust crisscrossed over top. Bake at 450°F for 10 minutes; reduce heat to 350°F and continue baking for 40 minutes.

CRANBERRY-RAISIN LATTICE PIE

1 cup	white sugar	250 mL
2 tbsp	flour	30 mL
1 cup	water	250 mL
3/4 cup	raisins	175 mL
1 1/4 cups	cranberries, cut in half	300 mL
	crust for a 9-inch pie	

Mix sugar and flour in saucepan. Stir in water. Cook, over moderate heat, until bubbling; stir constantly. When sauce thickens, stir in raisins and cranberries. Cook 5 minutes. Remove from heat and cool slightly. Line pie plate with crust and fill. Cover with lattice top. Bake 30 minutes at 400°F then for 30 minutes at 325°F.

October

STEAMED CRANBERRY PUDDING

½ cup	molasses	125 mL
2 tsp	soda	10 mL
½ cup	boiling water	125 mL
½ cup	butter or margerine	125 mL
1 ½ cup	flour	375 mL
1 tsp	baking powder	5 mL
½ tsp	salt	2.5 mL
1 cup	cranberries, cut in halves	250 mL
1 cup	seeded raisins, dusted with flour	250 mL

Mix in order given. Steam 2 hours. Serve with sauce.

SAUCE:

1 cup	brown sugar	250 mL
3 tbsp	flour	45 mL
½ tsp	salt	2.5 mL

Gradually pour over this:

2 cups	boiling water	500 mL
2 tbsp	butter	30 mL
1 tsp	vanilla	5 mL

Boil 5 minutes.

The Duke of York Cranberry Farm

Checking my morning e-mail I saw a message from my good friend and mentor, Silver Donald Cameron, a fine writer from Cape Breton who treats friends to copies of his newspaper columns. When I saw the subject, "The Duke of York Cranberry Meadow," I ran upstairs for a fresh cup of coffee. I knew this was going to be a good read.

Don was waxing lyrical about eating cranberry bread that he said resembled raisin bread but was "freckled with 'craisins' – dried cranberries instead of dried grapes." His neighbour, Claire Doyle, had made the bread using cranberries grown and dried by her and husband, Hubert, on their cranberry farm on Isle Madame, an island located at the southern-most tip of Cape Breton Island.

The Duke of York Cranberry Farm was homesteaded in 1892, when Dr. Eli Josslyn of Cape Cod, Massachusetts, advertised that he wanted peat fields with access to fresh water for growing cranberries. Jack Latimer, Hubert's grand uncle, of Arichat, responded and Dr. Eli established the first cranberry operation in Cape Breton, the third in Nova Scotia. Latimer became manager and eventual owner.

The operation remained in full produc-tion until the late 1950s, but by1997, only five acres of the original plants survived. The Doyles have been working for more than half a decade to slowly restore the operation, renewing dikes, planting new vines and open-ing the old farmhouse to vacationing tourists.

They have taken the cranberry business one step farther, producing juices, jams, jellies, fruit leathers, those "craisins" Silver Don likes so well, and cereal flakes. Duke of York cran-berries are sold through healthfood stores and by the Doyles who drive to Halifax's Brewery Market on Saturdays. Claire collects recipes old and new and shared this one.

CLAIRE DOYLE'S CRANBERRY CHUTNEY

16 cups	cranberries	3.5 L
3 tsp	salt	15 mL
2 cups	cold water	500 mL
3	large chopped onions	3
3 cups	white sugar	750 mL
½ cup	flour	125 mL
3 tsp	mustard	15 mL
1 tsp	ginger	15 mL
½ tsp	turmeric	2.5 mL
3 cups	white vinegar	750 mL
	water	

Prepare cranberries the night before: cut lengthways, add 3 teaspoons salt and 2 cups of cold water. Strain before adding to the following: Sift together flour, mustard, ginger, turmeric and sugar. Set aside. In a large pot add vinegar and water. Set aside 1 ¼ cups to mix flour paste. Bring water and vinegar to slow boil and precook onions for approximately 3 minutes. Add cranberries, mix flour paste and gradually add to 3 mix.

Keep chutney cooking on a slow boil for an additional 15 minutes, stirring to prevent the paste from sticking to the bottom. When berries are tender (still whole), remove from stove and place in sterilized jars. This recipe makes 12 250-mL jars.

COOKED JERUSALEM ARTICHOKES

Serves 6

Jerusalem artichokes, native to the Maritimes, are ready for digging now and can be enjoyed until the ground is too hard to work, especially if you spread straw over your bed to extend the digging season. The large bumpy roots store well for a few weeks in a cold cellar. Do remember to leave a few in the ground (covered with soil to discourage mice); they will sprout a new crop for next year.

1 ½ lb	Jerusalem artichokes	700 g
¾ tsp	salt	3 mL
	boiling water	

Wash artichokes, scrape and place in cold water. Drain; add salt and boiling water to cover. Cover pan, cook about 30 minutes or until tender. Season with butter and pepper. Alternative: Dice artichokes and serve with Browned Onion Butter.

BROWNED ONION BUTTER

Serves 4

6 tbsp	butter	90 mL
1 tbsp	minced onion	15 mL

Heat butter and onion until both are browned.

JERUSALEM ARTICHOKES WITH PARSLEY SAUCE

Serves 6–8

4 cups	cooked Jerusalem artichokes	1 L
	parsley sauce — recipe follows	
	paprika	

Combine artichokes and sauce, heat thoroughly. Sprinkle with paprika to serve.

PARSLEY SAUCE

Basically a white sauce with parsley added, this can be made with cream for a creamier presentation, or with $1/2$ cup of grated cheese added for a cheese sauce, or with the chopped whites and mashed yolks of 2 hard-cooked eggs stirred in for a real old-fashioned treat.

3 tbsp	butter	45 mL
3 tbsp	flour	45 mL
2 cups	milk	500 mL
$1/2$ tsp	salt	2.5 mL
$1/8$ tsp	pepper	.5 mL
2 tbsp	minced parsley	30 mL

Melt butter, stir in flour to form a roux, add milk gradually, cook slowly until thickened. Add salt, pepper and parsley. Makes 2 cups.

Spaghetti Squash

Late in the winter I finally admitted that I would probably never cook the spaghetti squash that had been residing in a basket in my kitchen for more than a year. Grown by a friend, it had been one of many contributed to our larder, but for some reason was never cooked. Our good friends Beth and David came to visit and went home bearing that one last squash. They not only had a meal from it, they dried the seeds and planted them the next spring in a new section of their country garden.

The seeds grew. And grew. And grew. Those seeds, obviously from a hybrid, resulted in a crop that included spaghetti squash, the old-fashioned round squash, vegetable marrow and pumpkins. All were harvested and several families enjoyed the bounty well into the winter. I saved some seeds and this spring tossed them into a planter just outside our kitchen door, certain it was a lesson in futility. But no, just days later the earth started to rise — literally. Those seeds erupted into life. Transplanted to our friends' garden they are thriving and we are anxiously waiting to see what we get this fall.

We love spaghetti squash, baked or "nuked," smothered with a vegetarian spaghetti sauce. In fact I sometimes plan it for the day after pasta to use up leftover sauce.

The most daunting aspect of this veggie is splitting it in half lengthwise. Frankly, this is one place where I believe men should show their superior strength. It needs a large, strong knife because the skin is leathery and tough. That's why it keeps so well. Don't try to cut through the circle marking the stem end; cut beside it. Once cut, scoop out the seeds — setting aside a few for next year's garden, of course.

To serve plain, dot a few pats of butter inside, cover the cut side with foil and place in a cake pan or dish, cut side up, with a little water in the pan. Place in oven preheated to 375°F and bake 40 to 60 minutes, depending on size. Test by poking with a fork. Strands should be slightly crunchy.

To serve with a sauce, turn upside down in a baking pan or shallow dish, add 1/4 cup of water and bake as above.

Microwaving depends on the size of the squash half. I start at five minutes on high and test.

To serve: Remove from oven, carefully remove any liquid. Use forks to separate flesh into strands resembling spaghetti. If very juicy you might want to place in a colander briefly to drain. Serve as in next recipe or with a small pat of butter. Leftover spaghetti squash is also a nice salad garnish, as long as it's not overcooked.

BUTTERY GARLIC AND PARMESAN

2 tbsp	butter	30 mL
1	clove garlic, minced	1
1/4 cup	Parmesan, freshly grated if possible	50 mL
1/4 cup	finely chopped parsley salt and pepper to taste	50 mL

Melt butter, add garlic and gently sauté 5–6 minutes, without browning. Sprinkle with pepper and salt if desired. Toss with spaghetti squash, Parmesan and parsley and serve hot.

VEGGIE TOMATO TOPPER FOR PASTA OR SPAGHETTI SQUASH

When making for company I add a chopped tomato at the last minute and sprinkle with chopped chives or another fresh herb.

1–2 tbsp	olive oil	15–30 mL
1	clove garlic, minced	1
2 cups	diced vegetables (onion, carrot, mushrooms, peppers, broccoli, etc.)	500 mL
25–oz	700-mL jar pasta sauce grated Parmesan	700 mL

Heat saucepan to medium heat. Add oil, heat, then add garlic. After 2–3 minutes remove garlic to prevent it from browning too much, stir in veggies to brown slightly. Remove veggies. Wipe out any excess oil. Return vegetables, garlic and pasta sauce. Stir and heat through. Serve over pasta or spaghetti squash with grated Parmesan.

Browned Mashed Potatoes

Mash Yukon Gold potatoes, cook in a little salted water, add egg yolks (for colour and taste), mix well. Put in a piping bag and pipe out rosettes or other shapes, or mix in a little corn and shape, coat with bread crumbs. Roll into a little log and roll in almonds. Place on cookie sheet and bake or broil till browned.

Pumpkin Season

I realized this year why the tradition of carving pumpkins at Halloween flourishes from year to year. It's because the plants are so prolific! Imagine the poor cook, overwhelmed with pumpkin after pumpkin. She'd already made pumpkin pie, pumpkin loaf, stored a bunch in the cold cellar. It's no wonder the big orange globes were turned over for carving!

SALISBURY PUMPKIN SPICE CAKE

2 cups	flour	500 mL
1 tsp	salt	5 mL
2 tsp	baking powder	10 mL
1/4 tsp	baking soda	1 mL
1 tsp	ginger	5 mL
1/2 tsp	nutmeg	2.5 mL
1/2 tsp	cinnamon	2.5 mL
1/4 tsp	ground cloves	1 mL
1 1/2 cups	brown sugar	375 mL
1/2 cup	soft margarine	125 mL
3/4 cup	cooked pumpkin	175 mL
1/4 cup	milk	50 mL
2	eggs	2

Mix ingredients. Turn batter into a greased 13 x 9 x 2-inch pan. Bake at 350°F for 35–40 minutes. Cool in pan and ice.

NEW GLASGOW PUMPKIN CUPCAKES

1/2 cup	butter or margarine	125 mL
1 1/3 cups	sugar	325 mL
2	eggs, beaten until frothy	2
1 cup	pumpkin or winter squash, mashed, cooked, unseasoned	250 mL
2 1/4 cups	all-purpose flour, sifted	550 mL
3 tsp	baking powder	15 mL
1/2 tsp	baking soda	2.5 mL
1/2 tsp	salt	2.5 mL
3/4 tsp	ground ginger	3 mL
1/2 tsp	ground cinnamon	2.5 mL
1/2 tsp	ground nutmeg	2.5 mL
3/4 cup	milk	175 mL
3/4 cup	coarsely chopped pecans or walnuts	175 mL

Cream butter and sugar until light, beat in eggs; mix in pumpkin. Sift flour with baking powder, baking soda, salt and spices; add to creamed mixture alternately with milk, beginning and ending with dry ingredients. Mix in nuts.

Spoon into well-greased muffin tins, filling each about 3/4 full. Bake at 375°F for 25 to 30 minutes or until cupcakes begin to pull from sides of tins and tops are springy to touch. Cool cakes upright in their pans on wire racks for 5 minutes, then remove and cool to room temperature before serving. Frost or not, as you wish.

CRUSTLESS PUMPKIN PIE

3	eggs	3
1/3 cup	honey	80 mL
1/2 tsp	ginger	2.5 mL

½ tsp	nutmeg	2.5 mL
½ tsp	cinnamon	2.5 mL
½ tsp	salt	2.5 mL
1 ½ cups	cooked pumpkin	375 mL
1 cup	evaporated milk, undiluted	250 mL

Preheat oven to 325°F. Beat eggs slightly. Add honey, spices, salt and pumpkin. Mix well, add evaporated milk. Pour mixture into deep, buttered 9-inch pie pan. Bake 50–60 minutes, or until set in centre. Chill thoroughly before cutting. To serve, cut like pie and add whipped cream or ice cream if desired.

Spiced Pumpkin

This is a tempting novelty, sure to become a favourite in every household where it is tried. Peel a pumpkin and cut it in halves, removing all seeds and the soft inside portion, then cut in neat pieces, not too large. Mix equal parts of good vinegar and water, put the pumpkin in this and let remain overnight. In the morning, make a syrup in the proportion of two pounds of sugar to a pint of water, boiling until about as thick as good maple syrup. Add two or three pieces of ginger root, tied in a little muslin bag with a half dozen cloves and three or four pieces of stick cinnamon, then put in the pumpkin, well drained; simmer gently until pumpkin is clear and very tender, but not long enough to break into pieces or get mushy. Arrange in jars or crocks, boil the syrup down a little, pour it over the pumpkin, seal when cold.

PUMPKIN PRESERVE

Mom made jams and jellies. That's all we had on our bread in the winter: jams and jellies. When we ran out she made pumpkin jam, cut it up in little pieces and put in a little lemon.

1	medium-size pumpkin	1
1 lb	sugar	450 g
½ cup	lemon juice	125 mL

Cut pumpkin in half, remove seeds, peel off rind. Slice in ³/₈-inch pieces. Pack slices in a crock, alternating layers of pumpkin with layers of sugar. Pour the lemon juice over it. Let stand for 2 days. Drain. Make a syrup of sugar and 1 pint of water. Boil pumpkin in this until pieces are very soft. Pour off syrup; boil syrup until thick. Then pour syrup over pumpkin and seal in jars. If desired, boil with the syrup a little ginger root and fine lemon peel. Makes about 4 quart jars.

Thankgiving

There is evidence that the custom of giving thanks has been celebrated in Canada for more than four centuries. In fact, English explorer Martin Frobisher held the first formal North American "thanksgiving" in Newfoundland in 1576, 15 years before the pilgrims in Plymouth.

Anyone who has been outside in the fall will understand why goose dinners are traditional celebratory fare in the Maritimes. Canada geese are so plentiful and carry on so many honking conversations as they fly over head that it can seem deafening. Even our dog casts annoyed glances upward. Accompanied by carrots, turnips, potatoes and, at times, parsnips, goose stuffed with a delicious potato or cranberry stuffing and served with rich gravy is as popular today as long ago. One given: the vegetables were almost always mashed. Sometimes together.

POTATO STUFFING

In Pictou County it was common practice to use mashed potatoes in poultry stuffing rather than bread. Originally the mashed potatoes were mixed with raw oatmeal and seasoned with locally grown summer savory. Later, this became a Nova Scotia-wide practice but bread replaced the raw oatmeal.

1 dozen	potatoes, cooked and mashed	1 dozen
8	slices of dry bread	8
½ tsp	parsley	2.5 mL
1	medium-size onion, chopped	1
½ tbsp	sage or savory	7.5 mL
	salt and pepper to taste	

Soften bread with cold water. Fry onion until soft, add salt, pepper, parsley, sage or savory. Mix together with bread, heat until it dries out, then add the potato. Stuff the bird.

Cranberry stuffing is made by mixing a handful in before stuffing the bird.

BAKED TURKEY SANDWICHES WITH CHEESE

Leftover turkey? Try this baked sandwich for a change of pace. I like to make a cheese sauce as you would for Welsh rarebit (see index). All you need: toast; sliced cooked turkey; sliced tomato; cheese sauce; cooked or canned asparagus; grated cheddar cheese.

In a baking dish arrange slices of toast in a single layer so that they just fill the bottom of the dish. Top each with turkey and tomato slices. Top with another layer of toast. Pour hot cheese sauce over all. Arrange asparagus on each sandwich, sprinkle with a generous heaping of cheddar cheese. Bake at 400°F until heated through.

PICKLED EGGS

We are so fortunate to always have eggs available. In days past eggs were highly valued, both to barter or sell and to eat. In times of plenty, when the hens were laying, the surplus would be preserved for those times when they were not. Some eggs were kept for baking, but others were pickled to enjoy as a cold complement to a meal.

12	eggs, hard-cooked and peeled	12
1 ½ cups	vinegar	375 mL
½ cup	water	125 mL
1 tsp	salt	5 mL
1 tsp	pickling spice	5 mL

Place eggs in large jar. Put remaining ingredients in saucepan, boil 5 minutes. Strain over eggs. Cover and refrigerate. Let eggs stand at least 3 days before using.

Periwinkles

I was sipping my morning coffee when the phone rang. It was CBC Television, calling to see if we could do a story … on periwinkles. "Ooooooookaaaay," says I, knowing that any publicity an author can get is good. "Just what are we going to do here?" Turns out that a reporter had observed a couple out on the beaches gathering up a container full of the tiny black sea snails. When he asked what they were going to do with them, they said they would be eating them. "So," says he, "could you gather some, then we'll come to your house and film you cooking and eating them?" "Sure," says I. "When?" "This afternoon," says he.

Well, that started a flurry of activity. First I had to clean the kitchen — TV cameras pick up everything! Then I had to go find periwinkles — of course the tide was in. Rushing back home I changed my clothes, brought some semblance of order to my wind-tossled hair and rushed to set the scene. Next step was to figure out how to cook and eat periwinkles. Didn't seem that there was enough meat in there for a sparrow, let alone a TV crew.

Just because I have written a number of cookbooks they expect me to know everything. I even got a call one day from a woman who had collected a pail full of moon snails and wanted them for supper. They cook up like rubber; I told her to whiz them in the blender for a chowder, hoping that they are actually edible!

Back to the periwinkles. Here is what I finally found for a recipe, thanks to an old Canadian Fish Recipes booklet, circa 1950. As when harvesting anything from the wild, make sure your location is safe for shellfish picking.

STEAMED PERIWINKLES

Wash periwinkles thoroughly, place in steamer or sieve over rapidly boiling water. Steam 10 minutes. The meat is easily removed with a nut pick. Serve with melted butter, salt and pepper. Allow 1 cup periwinkles in the shell for each serving.

My periwinkles were small, so we used a pin. Took a lot to get a taste.

From My Kitchen Window

I make several trips a year across Northumberland Strait to Nova Scotia and east down the "shore road," aka Sunrise Trail. It's a lovely drive, and Tipsy and I always take time for walks en route. One golden fall day, while walking across a field, I was lured up a hill by a stand of full-growth hardwood trees. Stately oak, planted in a line; another row of poplars, seeming to be in the throes of old age — unlike the oaks, which were in their prime.

The trees drew me to a depression marking the location of a homestead long gone. A crumbling stone fireplace and chimney stand at one end, a monument to the individuals who had loved their home enough to plant trees that would probably not mature in their lifetime.

Flights of Fancy ◄━

Sunflowers have changed from beautiful sun-yellow flowers bobbing in the wind to heavy heads, so laden with seed they tip closer to the ground each day. Judging by the interest of the chickadees it's time to harvest now or leave the seeds to the birds. Armed with our trusty shears we lob off the flower heads. The stem is cut so close to the head that we have just enough to poke through it with wire to hang the head from the rafters until ready to use.

The best heads, well shaped with no missing seeds, will be wrapped for Christmas gifts. The rest we will hang outside close to the kitchen window, so that we can watch the antics as birds dig out the seeds.

Millet, wheat and other grains harvested and dried this way can be fashioned into swags or bundles tied with a ribbon or coloured raffia — great gifts, or decorations for your own backyard.

As I stood there my mind recreated the home. The massive fireplace marked the kitchen. For a moment I dwelt on the hearth: a solid slab of stone, worn by many feet, and the trappings required to cook in a fireplace. I wished, briefly, that I could lift it up and take it home. But no, its place is here, part of the mute testimony to our forebears.

Standing where I envisioned the kitchen I pictured a window; there to the east, so that the morning sun would warm the heart of the house. From my kitchen window, I saw an apple orchard, trees gnarled now in testimony to their long life of bearing fruit, planted down the hillside, closer to the stream where moisture would always keep them healthy. This being fall the leaves were almost gone and fruit covered the ground. Yellow, deep red, crimson and green; obviously an orchard planned to provide fruit for many uses.

I pictured the lady of the house, stirring the porridge in a cauldron hung over the fire as she awaited her family's arrival for breakfast. The day, shorter now as winter draws near, holds forth the promise of crisp air, redolent with the earthy smell of fall; of fallen leaves, of damp earth and of apples.

I could feel happiness in this place and hated to leave. I wanted to stay — to build on this wonderful spot that had obviously been chosen with love, to recreate the kitchen of my visions and to cook in the fireplace.

It was this walk, and this "visit" to a kitchen of yesteryear, that nurtured my interest in kitchen memories and my determination to write this book.

Today we see "kitchen witches," cute little characters riding brooms, hanging in kitchens to bring luck. In Victorian times, ivy was the big thing. They thought it scared away witches!

November

— the garden is put to bed, the stew
pot on the stove and the magic of
Yule season is awakening.

ook what you love, for those you love, and you will be a great cook. Good food is simple food; fresh quality ingredients prepared simply, properly and with care. If you take the best ingredients, prepare them the way you want, and use recipes as a guideline, you will get perfection on the plate.

— Chef Stefan Czapalay, Halifax, N.S.

Back in the 1980s three cookbook authors, Angela Clubb, Kasey Wilson and myself, had a grand time giving cooking classes at Stanhope Beach Lodge in Prince Edward Island. Those classes and food shows we attended were some of the "most fun" days of my life. We shared experiences, laughs and recipes. I had just discovered regionally produced Belgian endive, so Angie gave me this recipe from her cookbook, *Mad about Cheddar*. It's been in my recipe box ever since, a breakfast favourite. We pull it out when leeks and endive appear at the market. I've modified it, leaving out the half-teaspoon of sugar she puts in with the salt and substituting low-fat sour cream. And, if it's just Jack and I at home, I use old cheddar! If you don't have Belgian endive, substitute celery, cut thin on the diagonal.

ANGELA'S ENDIVE AND LEEK QUICHE

Line a 10-inch quiche or pie pan with pastry. Prick bottom with fork and prebake in a 400°F oven for 10 minutes.

4 cups	chopped Belgian endive	1000 ml
2 cups	chopped leek (white parts only)	500 ml
1/4 cup	butter	50 ml
1/2 tsp	salt (optional)	2.5 ml
2	eggs	2
1	egg yolk	1
1 cup	sour cream (low-fat works fine)	250 ml
1/8 tsp	pepper	.5 ml
1/8 tsp	nutmeg	.5 ml
1 1/2 cups	grated mild or medium cheddar	375 ml

Simple Pleasures

In a pan with a cover, melt butter. Add endive, leek, salt and, if you are using it, sugar. Cook covered, over moderate heat, for 10 minutes. Uncover and cook over high heat until liquid has evaporated. Cool. Combine remaining ingredients. Beat lightly, then stir in vegetables. Pour all into prebaked pastry shell, bake at 350°F for 40 minutes or until centre is set. Cool 10 minutes and serve.

Witloof Chicory

Witloof chicory is an exciting vegetable because its tender, bullet-shaped shoots can be harvested in the dead of winter. Planted in May or June, it matures into plants with rich green leaves by fall. Just before the ground freezes hard, but after several good frosts, they are dug up, the tops cut off to leave a stub, and the roots trimmed to an 8- to10-inch clump. These are stored in the root cellar in boxes of sawdust or sand. When the snow is on the ground, a fresh vegetable can be had by taking the steps to transform these ugly brown roots into crisp white salad greens known as Belgian endive.

In my experience growers of this yummy vegetable are old-style European gardeners or farmers, or descended from them. They've told me of two methods of sprouting. A commercial farmer in Nova Scotia places the roots on racks and harvests sprouts as they come. Others plant roots in containers in their basements or root cellars, harvesting when white shoots poke through the soil.

Living History

Lunenburg's Fisheries Museum of the Atlantic is not a place that first comes to mind when thinking culinary history, yet this is one of the few sites where you can get a feel for the life of those who cooked (and ate) at sea. As well as gaining knowledge about household goods and seafoods, you can actually brave gangplanks to visit shipboard kitchens or galleys. The good folks at the museum welcomed us, not only guiding us through the many exhibits but also providing the culinary information that follows.

Day 2 (yes, you need two days to really take it all in) of our visit was stormy. Rain blew in from the Atlantic in ferocious gusts. I, in my intrepid reporter mode, boarded the variety of fishing vessels that form part of the museum complex. Even tied at the wharf they rocked and bobbed, forcing us to hold on as we made our way below decks. In vessel after vessel we tried to imagine cooking for a hungry crew in such conditions.

The *Teresa E. Connor* presents a vivid image of life at sea.

The forecastle, or "fo'c'sle," was home for most of the fishermen on the Lunenburg schooner. Smaller than my living room, the area was where the crew ate and slept. Bunks rimmed the hull. In the centre the galley table was surrounded by chests containing the crew's worldly goods and used for seats. A stove at one end projects the dual role of this space: rails around its surface kept pots and pans from tumbling off as the vessel pitched and rolled. Iron bars held mitts to dry. Cozy and warm, the fo'c'sle was the centre of activity.

I'm sure I would have found the life deplorable. A tried and true landlubber, I got seasick with the vessel tied to the wharf! However, the truth is that Lunenburg Saltbank fishermen ate hearty after working long hours on the open sea. The cook had a very important role in life away from home, serving four squares a day.

The following was a typical day's menu, according to a poster provided by the Fisheries Museum of the Atlantic and obtained from Clarence Allen (1882–1970), a Lunenburg Saltbank cook.

Breakfast 4–7 a.m.:
Scouse — a type of stew made from potatoes, cubed salt beef, onions, pepper and salt
Baked beans
Potato hash
Hot biscuits, bread and butter
Tea, coffee

Dinner 10 a.m.–noon:
Salt plate beef stew
Dough boys
Pea soup
Pumpkin pie, cakes, cookies
Tea, coffee

Supper 4–5 p.m.:
Baked beans
Potato hash

Fish chowder
Loaf cake
Bread, butter
Cakes, cookies
Tea, coffee

"Mug-up," served between 9 p.m. and midnight — only when on the banks, when the day's work was done:
Blood ends — ends cut off the large backbones of codfish, broiled, served with pork scraps and onions
Bread cookies
Tea, coffee

Other staples:
Kartoffelsuppe — a soup made from cooked flour, potatoes, onions, seasonings, eaten with sauerkraut

Hurrican souple — made from whole dried peas

House Banking — cooked salt cod pieces covered with fried onions and salt pork scraps

Hagdown Pot Pie — a type of seabird found on the Grand Banks.

The high-calorie, high-protein diet was especially suited to their strenuous and often cold, wet work. For those who felt hungry between meals, the shack locker, a cupboard in the forecastle, was always well stocked with pastries, bread and butter, and sugar; the coffee and tea pots remained hot on the stove 24 hours a day.

Here we also found the following accounting

of "the baker of the first loaf of bread aboard a Lunenburg Schooner," Captain Martin Mason (1843–1940), who went to sea at age 10 and became master of his first ship at age 21:

"I went to cook on a Labradourman when I was only 10 years old, and cooked for a crew of 14 men. In those days, bread baking aboard fishing schooners was unknown; a biscuit called hardtack being used for bread, and many times it was so hard it had to be broken with a hammer. Among the ships, there was only one barrel of flour, which was used mostly for making plum duff, a delicacy served to the crew on Sundays.

"Accustomed to eating Mother's good home made bread, I didn't relish the hardtack, so on my third trip out as cook, a bottle of yeast from Mother's larder was smuggled aboard into the forecastle, and dreams of bread-making began to take shape.

"When the barrel of flour came aboard, I said to the Captain, I'm going to make bread.

" 'Tut, tut! Boy', said he, 'you can't make bread.' "

"In spite of this discouraging reply, the young cook, who many times had watched his mother at the task, knocked in the head of the barrel and proceeded to make his first batch. 'My, my, and what bread it was!' said Captain Mason. 'It raised so high in the oven that I couldn't get it out without upsetting the loaves from the pans, and how the crew enjoyed it!!' As a result of this first experiment, the Captain of the schooner ordered a quantity of the hardtack be returned to the outfitters, and in its place more flour came on board.

"Thus, the name of the precocious lad goes down in the annals of history as the pioneer breadmaker in connection with the Lunenburg fisheries."

Sauerkraut

One can't possibly speak about Lunenburg without mentioning sauerkraut, for it is a part of the heritage of the region that remains a "strong" favourite. Sorry, I couldn't resist. Our family's little bit of kraut tradition involves some rather smelly concoctions that my husband and our friend Russell Rogers cooked up on gals' nights out. Sausages and kraut, boiled up together — their idea of heaven.

They are, however, amateurs compared with Joe Levy of East Tannetcook. This mussel farmer is a legend in the world of sauerkraut makers, so when I got the chance to sit with his family at an aquaculture conference I was thrilled.

"Dad made the best sauerkraut in Atlantic Canada. He had a cutter made with two knives — made thin, long shreds. He only used sea salt, got from Turks Island — about one sailor's mug (about 2 cups) to a half barrel (100-pound barrel) cabbage. Dad used to like to use oak barrels beef came in. I used to get them in Halifax." Another at the table recalled sauerkraut made in molasses puncheons.

"When we were young he had a pole press, would set my brother and I on the pole and we would go up and down till we got the juice out.

"We took sauerkraut to the Halifax market. People knew his sauerkraut. Once he ran out, so he got some from someone else. A fellow came back the next week and railed at me — 'This is not your father's!'"

They also had a couple of tips for sauerkraut makers. "Dad gave his sauerkraut recipe to a guy from Covehead (P.E.I.). It went mouldy on him. That's 'cause he used early cabbage. You need late winter cabbage for good sauerkraut."

Joe happily shared two of his recipes with us, adding, "I make the best Solomon Grundy there is. They come from everywhere for it." Well, thinks I, Sauerkraut Salad, Solomon Grundy and mussels from his Perrang Cove Cultivated Mussels in Seabright, N.S. — what better regional menu than that!

JOE LEVY'S SAUERKRAUT SALAD

1 qt	sauerkraut, save juice	950 mL
1	green pepper, cut up small	1
3	small onions, cut up small	3
3	medium-large carrots, shredded	3
1 cup	sugar	250 mL
1/2 cup	vegetable oil	125 mL
1/2 cup	vinegar	125 mL

Mix all together. After about 30 minutes it's ready to eat. Joe says use Heinz — the only true cider vinegar, "Don't use vinegar with cider flavouring."

JOE'S SOLOMON GRUNDY

Soak the herring overnight. Take skin off and bone out. If doing 1/2 dozen herring, use 3 onions.

	herring	
1 cup	sugar	250 mL
3 cups	Heinz cider vinegar	750 mL
1 cup	water	250 mL
	onions, sliced	

Use true cider vinegar, never white — it makes the herring soft. Mix vinegar, water and sugar together. Pour over fish. Never boil the vinegar or put spices in, because that makes it soft and kills the flavour of the herring. This is also good made with mackerel. Store in cool place until ready to use.

Sauerkraut is bully
Sauerkraut is fine.
We out to know it
For we eat it all the time.

Put the cabbage in a "barl."
Stamp it with your feet,
When the juice begins to rise
The kraut is fit to eat.

Put it in a pot
Set it on to "bile."
Be sure to keep the cover on,
Or you'll smell it half a mile.

—copied from a restaurant wall in Lunenburg
and said to be a very old rhyme

Pickled Cabbage

This pickled cabbage is made by shredding cabbage finely (there are special cutting boards for this purpose), then packing it solidly in a tight container (half barrels are commonly used). The cabbage is sprinkled with coarse salt, layer by layer, as it is placed in the container. It makes its own pickle. A weight is placed on top, so that the sauerkraut is kept pressed and under the pickle. (Strangely enough, some say the pickle in the barrel rises on the full of the moon and recedes as the moon wanes.) This method came with advice to use the juice to make a cocktail. Mix two parts tomato juice with one part sauerkraut juice and add a pinch of horseradish, or serve as clear juice slightly diluted with lemon juice added to taste, and a dash of paprika. Pucker up and enjoy!

Sauerkraut or Salted Cabbage

Take as many firm heads of cabbage as you wish, remove the outer leaves; cut cabbages in halves and quarters; trim away the cores and cut cabbage into finest shreds possible. Line the bottom of a crock, tub or half barrel (if you wish to make so much) with fresh green cabbage leaves, covering them evenly with salt; then pack the shredded cabbage in layers, sprinkling each with salt. The rule is 1 ounce of salt to 2 pounds of cabbage. Pound the latter down vigorously after placing each layer so that the juice will begin to flow and, mixing with the salt, form the necessary brine. When container is full, press cabbage down firmly and cover with a clean white cloth, placing a wooden cover or large plate on top of this and putting on a heavy weight. Fermentation will begin almost at once if the weather is warm and will continue for 2 to 4 weeks, during which time the surface of the brine should be skimmed every day or so to keep a scum from forming. The cloth, cover and weight should be occasionally washed and scalded. As soon as no more bubbles appear on the surface, the sauerkraut is ready to store or for immediate use. To make sure that fermentation has ceased, the following test is good: drop in a bit of blue litmus paper, which you can get at any drugstore; if it turns red, you may seal the container at once; if it remains blue, more time must be allowed for fermentation. Sauerkraut may be eaten cooked or raw; we like it served in different ways, and I shall be pleased to learn of new ones.

—Mrs. C.W.B., from a recipe scrapbook bought from an auction

Bird's Nest

This recipe came from a member of the Ladies Auxiliary to the Royal Canadian Legion in Mahone Bay, Nova Scotia. The amount of sauerkraut and eggs varies with the number at the table. All you need: eggs; sauerkraut (scald if very salty and pour off the water).

Fry sauerkraut until tender, stirring occasionally. Make indentations and put in eggs (without shell). Cook until done. Serve with bread or potatoes.

CORNED BEEF AND SAUERKRAUT

"Years ago, people were not regarded as good providers unless they had in the cellar at least a half barrel of sauerkraut, and pickled beef."

— FMH

| 3 lb | corned beef | 1.4 kg |
| 4 lb | sauerkraut | 1.8 kg |

Put meat in pot with enough water to cover. Bring to boil, then reduce heat and simmer for 1 1/2 hours. Add sauerkraut and continue to cook for 1 1/2 hours. Drain kraut and serve with the meat and mashed potatoes. Fresh beef, loin of pork or spareribs may be used in preference to corned beef.

Boiled Dinner

It's almost worth cooking a boiled dinner just for the aroma. Perfect on a cold winter day. There is no question that the menfolk in my family would go for sauerkraut with sausages, but my palate prefers the old-fashioned boiled dinner made with a piece of ham or corned beef, cabbage and loads of root vegetables. If using ham I add a bay leaf or two. If using corned beef — the kind you buy at the meat counter that looks like pickled raw meat, not canned … I don't.

Quantities for this one-pot supper are simple enough — enough of everything to feed however many you need to feed. Left overs are great fried up the next day: just drain and chop everything, then place in a skillet and allow to brown before turning or stirring. Traditionally one would have used bacon drippings in the skillet, but today we tend to opt for oil.

"Boiled dinner" meant different things in different areas. We were offered a boiled dinner in a fisherman's home after my husband had finished trimming the feet of the family's mossing horses; it was similar to the following, but prepared with salt cod in place of the meat. (Mossing horses are big sturdy steeds, used to pull rakes through the surf to gather Irish moss, the seaweed that is part of our Maritime food tradition.)

All you need: 1 piece of corned beef or ham (I prefer smoked ham with no or little fat); potatoes; turnip or parsnips; cabbage, remove core and cut into quarters or eighths; carrots; onions; bay leaf, optional.

Place meat in pot, cover with water and cook at a low boil for 1 to 2 hours depending on size. Add vegetables and cook another hour, or until tender. Remove from broth, serve with butter for vegetables and mustard for meat.

CORN BEEF

Corning beef was a method of preservation which virtually none of us do today. But just in case you want to try this method here is a very old recipe. Doesn't say how long it keeps!! But I don't imagine that was a problem.

1 gal	water	3.8 L
½ lb	brown sugar	250 g
1 ½ lb	fine salt	700 g
½ oz	saltpetre	12.5 g

Prepare beef by removing bones and excess fat; lean meat corns best. Boil all ingredients except meat for 15 minutes. Skim and allow to cool. When cold, pour liquid over the beef in a crock. The meat must be completely submerged, so place heavy weight on a plate over it to keep it under water. Store in a cold place.

Peas Pudding

Old documents sometimes refer to a pudding boiled up with salt beef or pork rations. Later, those of Yorkshire descent would prepare this pudding with a version of the boiled dinner. Salt meat was set to boil for the day. A bag of split peas, which had been soaked in cold water for a couple of hours, would be boiled along with the meat for two more hours. I suspect that constituted dinner long ago.

A more modern recipe, from Lee and Barbara Lowerison of Sackville, New Brunswick, appears in *Tastes of the Tantramar: Recipes & Remedies from Our Yorkshire Roots*, a book written to honour the pioneering spirit and quiet influence of more than 1,000 immigrants who left Yorkshire between 1772 and 1775 to purchase and work their own farms in the Chignecto Isthmus region — the stretch of land that joins New Brunswick and Nova Scotia. They suggest that the peas be removed from the bag, placed in a bowl and mixed with butter, covered and kept warm in the oven. Meanwhile, add veggies to the meat and water, and cook up until done.

Around the Kitchen Table

Every family has its traditions. One of ours was list-making. In the early days of our life in our new country, my family would get together on a regular basis with an aunt and uncle and cousins, along with our grandparents.

Gathered around the kitchen table, which was festooned with catalogues, pads of papers, pencils and scissors my cousins and I would begin one of the most enjoyable experiences of the year … the making of the Christmas lists. It was an effort that went on for several days, even weeks as we revised and added to our lists, but it began sitting at the kitchen table. Catalogues from Simpsons and Eatons were clutched close; the Christmas one was the most sought-after and, I'm sure, the focus of some squabbles for possession, although I don't remember them.

There was one rule for list-making: you had to include as many things as would fit on a sheet

"Coming up to my 72nd birthday, two things I remember from when I was growing up give me warm thoughts.

"Once the fall set in, my father put a large pan of oats in the oven and there they stayed through the winter and cold spring. When we took our gum-rubbers off when our day was through he filled them with oats, and sat around the stove. When the oats were poured back in the pan in the morning, the boots were lovely to put on. We were five children. Now the other thing was, and this I'm sure you have heard of, once the winter set in my father made a large pot of oatmeal porridge which sat overnight on the back of the stove. In the morning it was moved over and warmed up for us, so nice and thick and a nice nutty flavour. Eating it after it's made fresh is not the same — no way.

"Gum-rubbers! Winter boots for the less moneyed of us, terrible, heavy black rubber which after you wore them for a while caused you to have a dark ring around your leg."

— Winnie Stewart,
Summerside, P.E.I.

of foolscap paper and they had to range from inexpensive through to dream items. It had to be fun and everyone knew they would not get everything — or even a significant percentage of what they listed. They did know that what they got would be something they wanted, that it would be the colour and size they requested and that it would not be duplicated.

This was the beginning of the Christmas season for us. The act of getting the family together for list making drew us all into the spirit of things. We wrote down all manner of items. I remember my Aunt Jean always listed a fur coat. She was the most sophisticated in the family and dreamed of such things. We all laughed over it every year.

The lists were a practical thing to do. We children knew that this was our wardrobe for the next few months; we also knew that requests for school supplies were more likely to be met than those for expensive toys. Times were tough as the families worked to establish themselves in a new country. That didn't take any joy from list-making, it just ensured that what we did get was right.

The only family members who deviated from our lists were our grandparents. Nanny and Nampy always made everyone's gifts, sometimes supplementing them with a few store-bought things, but not often. For us kids it varied. One year we girls got cradles (made from six-quart baskets) complete with blankets, pillows and sleepwear for our dolls, all hand-sewn by Nanny. Over the years she made us mittens, sweaters, all sorts of clothes, pencil cases, doll clothes … Nampy made sets of trays, jewellery boxes, cabinets, toys — I treasure many of them to this day.

CHERRY ALMOND MACAROONS

A perfect treat for list-making day could be these delightful macaroons made by my friend Gloria Matheson. Festive, they bring a little touch of Christmas, especially if served up with a hot cider. We share many memories of the days when we both worked in the kitchens of Stanhope Beach Lodge. An all-you-can-eat lobster buffet and two restaurants kept the staff hopping, but we still managed to have fun. After years of the occasional howdy-do in the mall, Gloria called one day, upset because her bread just wasn't up to snuff. We decided it was the outside temperature and humidity. Sure enough, months later Gloria called again — this time in November — to say her bread was back to its delicious self. Phew! I'm no bread expert so I was glad to have guessed right! But then Gloria always did have a magic touch and man, does she love to bake.

4	eggs, separated	4
¼ tsp	salt	1 mL
1 ½ cups	granulated sugar	375 mL
3 cups	coconut	750 mL
1 ½ cups	flour	375 mL
1 ½ cups	red and/or green cherries, chopped	375 mL
1 ½ tsp	almond extract	7.5 mL

Beat egg whites and salt in small mixer bowl until foamy. Gradually add sugar, beating until very stiff, about 4 minutes. Beat egg yolks in large mixing bowl. Stir in coconut. Add flour, cherries and extract, mix well. Stir in egg-white mixture, thoroughly; mixture will be very stiff. Drop by tablespoons onto greased baking sheets. Bake at 350°F for 10–15 minutes or until set and edges are very light golden.

Kate's Nettie

On November 27th, 1892, a young lady from a well-to-do family in Halifax by the name of Kate Shannon wrote in her diary: "We were by no means inclined for an early tea, so shortly before 8 we had a sort of pick-up affair which was much more fun. We didn't go to church because Nettie was so very tired. We held a council of war as to what we should eat, for Wallace forgot to bring out any bread yesterday and there wasn't much of anything to be had. There was only a

My good friend Debbie Gamble-Arsenault remembers when she would go to stay overnight at the home of the family's housekeeper in Alexandra, P.E.I. "She would heat bricks on the open oven door. At bedtime they were wrapped in newspapers, then towels, and taken to bed to keep our feet warm."

I remember my mom used to heat towels on the oven door. As a child I suffered from earaches, so my mom would lay a warm towel on my pillow for me to lie my ear on. She would pull the covers up so that only my nose and eyes were exposed to the cold night air. The towels almost made it worth having an earache! I still, to this day, put a fluffy towel over my pillow when I have a miserable cold.

Storing Potatoes

"For most us, storing potatoes isn't a big deal. We have a dry, cool spot away from the light. Besides, usually they don't stay around long. Well, one senior said her spuds were always sprouting on her because she only eats one small one at a meal, so even five pounds last a long time. I found her solution when I was putting away the broom after a wee spill. She had hung her potatoes, in old pantyhose, from a hook in the broom closet. Located near the back door it was cool and dry. She tied one leg into a loop to hang by, and dropped potatoes into the other."

— CBM

Medicinal Receipts

Homemade Liniment

3	eggs, broken in, shells and all	3
1 pt	vinegar	500 mL
1 pt	turpentine	500 mL
1	cake camphor	1

Let set for 12 days; shake daily. Then strain through muslin and use as liniment.

small piece of the last loaf left which Wallace said would be enough with some jam for him. There was a bit of apple cake which Nettie said was plenty for her, and two tea-rolls which I said were plenty for me. So we made Nettie sit still while we got the tea, which we ate promiscuous like, without substituting the tea cloth for the cretonne one. Wallace went off after his jam and found some cold potatoes; inquired of Nettie if they were wanted or if he could have them. Nettie said yes, and asked if he wouldn't like them fried, whereat I volunteered to fry them. So he assented and I cut them up, and he got the pan and the cooking butter which was also nearly exhausted (we finished it between us), and while I was getting the potatoes underway Wallace was seized with the brilliant idea to scramble some eggs, which he did in fine style when I had removed my chef d'oeuvre. So with milk for me, coffee for Nettie, and tea for Wallace, the crust, the pie, the rolls, the taters, and the eggs, we made quite an affair of our picnic tea and it was great fun — only it wasn't much like any Sunday I ever spent before!"

A Baking Tradition

As I write this I sit in the kitchen of my friend Helen Grant. She's making cookies for her church's annual Christmas tea and pantry sale. Her famous oat cookies are in high demand with the ladies of the town and my creativity is nourished by the decadent smells coming from the oven. The dogs — her Barney, a great white standard poodle who is tall enough to lean in and eat from the table along with the humans if he was allowed, and my Tipsy, a lovely black mini schnauzer princess who has to stand on her back legs to give her buddy a doggie kiss — and I are salivating over what Helen calls "the burnt ones." A little darker brown than her standard, these leftovers are up for grabs and grab we three do. We share. Of course, I as the human am in charge of the sharing and might get a few more nibbles than my canine troops. Might — they watch me pretty closely.

Helen lives near Three Brooks, Nova Scotia, between Pictou and Toney River; that's just east of River John, south of Caribou River. She grew up on Caribou Island, a descendant of early settlers who arrived in the area on the *Hector* in 1773. Helen's mom, Hazel McCabe (who married a Falconer), was a master at cooking many of the traditional dishes and introduced me to them many years ago. The oat cookies that follow were her recipe, but be warned: to make them like the masters you must practise and practise to get them thin enough, and cook to just the right pale golden brown.

FALCONER'S SCOTTISH OATMEAL COOKIES

This old Scottish recipe makes a crunchy oat bar that is excellent for dipping in tea or coffee, delicious served with raspberry jam and lovely on its own. Use a very large bowl for mixing.

Combine together dry ingredients:

2 cups	sugar	500 mL
5 cups	flour	1.25 L
5 cups	oatmeal	1.25 L
2 ½ tsp	salt	12.5 mL
1 tsp	baking powder	5 mL

Rub in (as for pie crust):

| 1 lb | Maple Leaf Tenderflake Lard | 450 g |

This takes perseverance. Keep rubbing until there is no evidence of fat having been added, no lumps, and all is a fine, even texture.

Mix together:

| ⅛ cup | water | 30 mL |
| 1 tsp | baking soda | 5 mL |

Keep mixing so that the soda doesn't settle, sprinkle over dry mixture, blend in.

Push most of dry ingredients to one side of mixing bowl. Add 1 tablespoon water and work into part of the dry ingredients to form a ball of dough the right consistency to roll. Remove that ball; roll on a board lightly dusted with flour, using rolling pin that has also been lightly dusted. Roll until even and less than 1/4 inch thick. Trim off broken sides; cut into squares. Using a lifter, place on ungreased baking sheets, pop into hot oven. Watch them carefully: being so thin, they can easily burn. Cook 10–12 minutes at 425°F until golden brown. Remove from pan immediately when taken from oven. Repeat procedure until all dough is used. This makes a large tinful of bar cookies that keep extremely well.

Oh, weary mothers mixing dough,
Don't you wish that food would grow?
Your lips would smile I know to see
A cookie bush or a pancake tree.

—The People's Home Recipe Book, 1910

November

177

Nampy and Nanny

My grandparent's marriage spanned two world wars and Nampy served in both, but still managed to sire a passel of children. Between wars he was a cabinet-maker, and I remember him having a huge garden and chickens. Nanny's lot was not an easy one; nor was his, for that matter. Money was not to be wasted on frivolities such as butter.

Once a week, on Sundays, Nampy would put the saved-up cream in a bottle and shake and shake and shake it until he made enough butter for his wife's breakfast. I can remember his walking around the kitchen, shake, shake, shake. Funny, I don't remember Nanny spreading that butter or eating it and now wonder if we grandchildren were shooed from the room to let her enjoy it in peace.

Maritime women of yore were expert butter-makers. Cream was saved and stored until it had a slightly sour taste. Then it was churned into butter. Once butter formed it had to be washed, and washed, in cold water to remove all of the buttermilk. Salt was added and the butter formed into blocks. In some cases fancy moulds were used. Butter could often be bartered, or sold for pin money. Interestingly, winter butter was pale, often almost white. When the cows were put back to pasture it would yellow up again.

Make Your Own Butter

Pour 1 cup cold whipping cream (35%) into an airtight jar and cover with a lid. Shake the jar vigorously for a few minutes until the cream yellows and thickens. There, you've just made butter. It's easy and natural.

You can make butter, as well. Made from a natural ingredient, milk, it is simply a matter of separating the cream from the milk, agitating it vigorously until it thickens, then washing and forming into blocks. Folks have been doing it this way for about 4,500 years and savour the flavour as much today as back when it was used in religious ceremonies! Many, many old books and accountings talk about making butter.

Darby's Mother's Kitchen

Darby sat in a traditional rocker beside the wood stove in Indian River, P.E.I. Twinkling eyes and a ready grin let us know that this is a true storyteller. Just get him started and the tales will flow for hours.

We spoke of winter in the traditional-style farmhouse he grew up in near Indian River.

It was so cold that the water would freeze, even in the bedroom above the kitchen. "We had a hole cut in the floor to allow the heat from the kitchen to rise so it was fine to go to bed, but in the mornings, when the fire in the stove had died down, our glass held ice, not water.

"We had a back kitchen where Mother did a lot of the work. After she had finished she would wash down the table. Well, on cold days it would freeze before it dried. The floor was sloped in that back kitchen, so on very cold days anything you put on the table would slide off because of the ice that formed on the table."

Living History

Gail Larter has worked in the Rose Bank Cottage kitchen for more than 10 years. To get ready for work she dons an authentic 1817-costume and takes a step back in time, assuming the role of part of the household at Ross Farm Museum in New Ross, N.S.

The cottage kitchen is a hub of activity at Ross Farm. Often visitors are met with all the bustle and delectable smells of food preparation in a 19th-century kitchen. At other times the atmosphere is quieter, with perhaps only a solitary woman working at her carding or spinning. Whatever activity is happening you will be met with a smile and, if you take the time, an opportunity to learn the work of the women of the house in pioneer days.

Like others who work in historic kitchens, Gail had to learn the old ways. For her it meant cooking on an open hearth, using a wood stove and much more. She has totally enjoyed the experience. Sometimes they cook full meals, which are served to staff. Stews are a favourite as they were in days past.

"We have fun with stews and they have a beautiful flavour. People who taste it think it is so good! It's because it is cooked over an open fire for such a long time, in an iron pot." Unfortunately, government regulations (which I think are really dumb and go too far in regulating our lives) prohibit their serving meals or selling baked goods. But you can sample. You might not find stew the day you drop by. For us there were cookies, several kinds, still warm and absolutely delicious. Or you might find chicken and dumplings, or a fruit and custard pie, two of Gail's favourites.

CHICKEN AND DUMPLINGS — 1817 STYLE

This would have been made in a large cast iron pot that was suspended in the open hearth. Just make sure that you have a heavy-bottomed pot with a tight-fitting lid.

Simmer chicken, onion, salt and pepper in enough water to cover chicken, for $1 \frac{1}{2}$ to 2 hours. Remove chicken from broth. Cool enough to handle and remove skin and bones. Dice meat.

Add water to stock, add potatoes, carrots, turnip and summer savory. Cook 1 hour, then return the deboned chicken. Simmer 15 minutes. Before serving, add dumplings.

DUMPLINGS:

2 cups	flour	500 mL
1 tsp	salt	5 mL
4 tsp	baking powder	20 mL
1 tbsp	shortening	15 mL
3/4 cup	milk	175 mL

Combine first 4 ingredients, add milk and mix. Spoon on top of hot stew. Cover. Cook 15 minutes without lifting the lid. Serve at once.

RHUBARB CUSTARD PIE

In the 1800s this would have been served with clotted cream. Today ice cream is a little easier to come by.

2 cups	sliced rhubarb	500 mL
1 cup	sugar	250 mL
2 tbsp	flour	30 mL
1	egg, beaten	1
	unbaked pie shell	

Mix flour and sugar, add beaten egg. Stir in rhubarb. Turn into unbaked pie shell. Bake at 375–400°F 45–50 minutes, or until done.

APPLE CUSTARD PIE

"We had this very old Rhubarb Custard Pie recipe, which was good, so we reduced the sugar, replaced the rhubarb with apples and put a lattice on top. It is delicious and is an original to Ross Farm."

—Gail Larter

2 cups	sliced apple	500 mL
3/4 cup	sugar	175 mL
1 tbsp	flour	15 mL

1	egg, beaten	1
	pinch each of cinnamon and nutmeg	
	pastry for 1 pie	

Mix flour, sugar and spices. Add beaten egg. Stir in apples. Turn into unbaked pie shell. Do pastry lattice on top. Bake at 375–400°F for 50–60 minutes. The filling will bubble up through the lattice. Serve warm with clotted cream.

Herbs

Like many Maritime homes of days past, Rose Bank Cottage had a back kitchen. The main kitchen is a fairly large room, with the open hearth dominating one inside wall and lots of room for storage cabinets and a table and chairs. The back kitchen was smaller, with a wood stove, the seats on benches raised to reveal storage for firewood. In the winter, coats and boots would be left here to dry. In the summer the hearth would not have a fire unless it was a cold day. Cooking was done in the back kitchen to keep the house as cool as possible. In the fall both kitchens were often used, especially if putting food by. During our late-fall visit we noticed paper bags hanging above the stove. "We gather summer savory, wash and drip-dry it," said Gail. "Then it is put into bags. It keeps the flies and dust away. When done (dried) we can just crumble it in the bag and put into containers to store."

December

— Good food and the joy found in its preparation are the essence of this season.

We spent this winter very pleasantly, and had good fare by means of the Order of Good Cheer which I established, and which everybody found beneficial to his health, and more profitable than all sorts of medicine we might have used. This Order consisted of a chain which we used to place with certain little ceremonies about the neck of one of our people, commissioning him for that day to go hunting. The next day it was conferred upon another, and so on in order. All vied with each other to see who could do the best, and bring back the finest game. We did not come off badly, nor did the Indians who were with us.

— Samuel de Champlain, The Voyages, written in 1613 and referring to 1606, when Champlain and his men prepared gourmet meals in their wilderness outpost at Port Royal, Nova Scotia. The spirit of good food and fellowship of "L'Ordre du Bon Temps" social club lives on today and is reflected in Yule and Thanksgiving celebrations around the Maritimes.

ANNAPOLIS VALLEY APPLE SPICE BRAN MUFFINS

There is something absolutely wonderful about the scent of muffins baking in the oven and coffee perking on the stove. A warm muffin served with a quartered crisp apple from Nova Scotia's Annapolis Valley is a favourite breakfast.

3 cups	wheat bran	750 mL
3 cups	all-purpose flour	750 mL
1 ½ cups	dried cranberries (substitute raisins or chopped dates, if desired)	375 mL
1 tbsp	cinnamon	15 mL
1 ½ tsp	baking powder	7.5 mL
1 ½ tsp	baking soda	7.5 mL
1 tsp	salt	5 mL
1 tsp	ground ginger	5 mL
1 tsp	nutmeg	5 mL
	grated rind of 1 lemon or orange	

1 cup	applesauce	250 mL
¾ cup	granulated sugar	175 mL
½ cup	vegetable oil	125 mL
3	eggs	3
2 ¼ cups	milk	560 mL
½ cup	fancy molasses	125 mL

Preheat oven to 400°F. Lightly grease nonstick muffin pans. Combine bran, flour, cranberries, cinnamon, baking powder, baking soda, salt, ginger, nutmeg and rind. In separate bowl, beat together applesauce, sugar, oil and eggs until well mixed. Stir in milk and molasses. Add to dry ingredients, stirring just enough to moisten; be careful not to overmix. Spoon into muffin pans. Bake for 20 minutes or until tops are firm to touch.

GERMAN WINTER DELIGHT

For those who need a heartier breakfast we cross lower Nova Scotia to the Lunenburg area for a quick, satisfying breakfast (or supper) that the housewife took to the table in the iron pan to keep it hot, presumably a cast iron fry pan. A Nova Scotian culinary tradition was brought to Lunenburg more than two centuries ago by a group of Germans who became subjects of the British Crown after the accession of George I, Elector of Hanover. Throughout the years a distinctive dialect and culture, as well as many fine culinary traditions, have been maintained.

6	slices bacon, fried crisp and crumbled	6
2 tbsp	chopped onion	30 mL
3	large potatoes, cubed and boiled	3
	salt and pepper to taste	
6	eggs	6

Brown onions and potatoes in bacon fat, stirring frequently. Sprinkle with salt and pepper. Break eggs into pan, over potatoes; do not beat before hand. Cover and cook over low heat until eggs are set. Grated cheese may be sprinkled over potatoes before eggs are added, if desired.

Sausages are a part of Maritime life and not just the German-style version served up in Lunenburg. "Gut pudding" refers to a "poor man's sausage stuffed with cornmeal and suet," according to food guru Marie Nightingale. As she says, you won't find those in the grocery store of today.

December

LUNENBURG SAUSAGE

While it is unlikely that you own a sausage mill or sausage casings, this is such a famous and delicious recipe that it is worth making for use in meat pies, or fried in patties or as poultry stuffing or any other way that sausage meat is used. In Lunenburg, it is often eaten with sauerkraut. This is a fairly large batch, so freeze in small amounts what is not needed. (Make sure your ground pork and beef are not made with previously frozen meats if you plan to freeze your sausages.)

10 lb	ground pork	4.5 kg
2 oz	pepper	50 g
1 tbsp	allspice	15 mL
¼ cup	coriander	60 mL
7 ½ lb	ground beef	3.5 kg
2 tbsp	salt	30 mL
½ tbsp	savory	7.5 mL

Mix all together.

…

"Grandmother had several old wooden trunks in her kitchen. One for us kids held board games as well as old magazines and catalogues to cut up for scrapbooks, crafts and accessories for our paper dolls. Another held kindling and old papers for the wood stove, the third held boots and shoes. They all had padded tops so were ideal as extra seating. Everyone always seemed to end up in the kitchen."

'Tis the Season

'Tis the season for entertaining and special treats. Whether for invited guests or a significant other, we all want to do something a little extra for those special people in our lives. However, there is a little "but" that comes into play: We just don't have the time, or often the energy, to do the elaborate preparations that Grandma used to do. Today's host simply does not want to be shut in the kitchen, separated from the celebrations by time-consuming food preparation.

Fortunately, with today's ready supply of quality foods and the ease of preparation that many offer, entertaining can become as much a pleasure for the hostess as for the guest. The secret is to think ahead, have ingredients on hand and to plan something sinfully simple. Maritime seafood works wonderfully well.

If you have a larger crowd and want to prepare ahead, try lobster, either by removing meat from the shell yourself or buying it frozen. Both methods have advantages. You can usually avoid the cooking phase by ordering it precooked from your seafood retailer. Frozen lobster meat has been removed from the shell and is precooked, ready to use. Since it has already been cooked it should be added at the last minute and cooked just long enough to warm it. The addition of such a special ingredient can turn party fare from mundane to magnificent.

LOBSTER CROUSTADES

Perfectly wonderful appetizers, these fantastic finger foods come to us from West Coast food maven Kasey Wilson. When she visits P.E.I. she's amazed that Maritimers can buy lobster at McDonald's and they treat it as a bit of a can't-go-wrong dish, especially during the holidays. She says, "I never can brush the insides of the darn cups with butter; so I always butter the bread (both sides) before I push it into the muffin cups." Make them ahead and pop them in the oven when you need them.

18	thin slices white bread, cut in 3-inch rounds	18
2 tbsp	butter, softened	30 mL
1/2 lb	lobster meat, cooked, cut into small pieces	225 g
1 tbsp	red, green or yellow peppers, chopped finely	15 mL
1 1/2 tbsp	mayonnaise (to bind)	20 mL
1 tsp	lemon juice	5 mL
4	drops Tabasco sauce	4
	pepper to taste	

Preheat oven to 350°F. Brush muffin tins with butter. Fit bread rounds into each mould to form a cup. Brush inside with butter. Combine lobster, peppers, lemon juice, Tabasco and pepper with enough mayonnaise to bind. Spoon into cups and bake 10 minutes. Serve immediately.

NOVA SCOTIA LOBSTER POT

There is no more social way of entertaining than with finger food that gets everyone involved. Dip bread cubes, then when the filling is gone break up the bread bowl and enjoy! Janice Raymond of the Nova Scotia Department of Fisheries once told me this was a favourite recipe:

2 cups	cooked lobster meat	500 mL
or		
1	11-oz can frozen lobster meat, thawed	1
1	loaf round, unsliced pumpernickel bread	1
8-oz	package light cream cheese	227 g
1 cup	light sour cream	250 mL
1 tsp	Worcestershire sauce	5 mL
1/2 tsp	Tabasco sauce	2.5 mL
1/2 tsp	minced garlic	2.5 mL
2 cups	grated cheddar cheese	500 mL
1/2 cup	chopped green onion	125 mL
	dash salt and pepper	

Drain lobster, cut into bite-size pieces. Hold in refrigerator. Slice top off loaf of bread. Scoop out the inside of the bread, leaving a 1-inch/2.5-cm layer around outside and bottom. Reserve bread, cut into cubes, for dipping. Preheat oven to 350°F. In a large bowl, cream the cream cheese. Add sour cream, Worcestershire sauce, Tabasco sauce and garlic; mix well. Fold in grated cheddar cheese, green onion, and spices. Fold in lobster. Fill bread shell with lobster mixture. Place top on bread loaf and wrap in foil. Place on cookie sheet and bake for 70 minutes, until mixture is thoroughly heated. Serve with bread cubes, crackers or cut-up fresh vegetables to dip. Makes 10–12 appetizer servings.

CREAMY LOBSTER FILLING OR DIP

A wonderful filling for mushroom caps or celery, topper for crackers or cucumber slices, or great for use as a dip with crunchy vegetables. An excellent use for broken lobster meat or that taken from legs and knuckles.

1 cup	cooked lobster meat, chopped quite finely	250 mL
8 oz	cream cheese, softened	227 g
1 tbsp	Worcestershire sauce	15 mL
2	drops Tabasco or hot pepper sauce	2
1 tbsp	lemon juice	15 mL
¼ cup	chopped parsley	60 mL
½ tsp	salt (optional)	2 mL

Combine all ingredients thoroughly. Chill before serving.

SMOKED TROUT SPREAD

A modern version of a very old-fashioned and very good, full-flavoured spread. Delicious served with bread that has been rubbed with garlic and brushed with olive oil before grilling, or as the star attraction with a colourful plate of crudités. Also very nice as a gift for a host or hostess. This makes 6 ramekins. Covering each with a thin layer of melted butter will allow the paté to keep for 2-3 days in the refrigerator.

12 oz	smoked trout fillets, skin removed	325 g
½ cup	sour cream	125 mL
½ cup	farmer's cheese or dry cottage cheese	125 mL
2 tbsp	lemon juice	30 mL

pinch cayenne
salt and freshly ground black pepper, to taste

Purée fish (a food processor works great). Blend in sour cream and cheese until smooth, adding in other ingredients. Don't overprocess — you just want to combine it. Pour mixture into small crocks or ramekins, cover with plastic wrap or melted butter and chill.

The Lightkeeper's Wife

Just for a minute or two let your mind take you back in time. Imagine a storm, waves — huge waves, pounding into shore to break over the rocks at the base of a cliff with thunderous power. Now imagine a lighthouse, on a small peninsula butting out into the tempest. The rain is pelting down, the wind is howling, those waves are breaking right up against the lighthouse itself. Inside, the lightkeeper keeps watch, tends his lamp and prays that this storm will pass without tragedy striking those at sea.

Downstairs, perhaps in an attached home, the "Mrs." listens to the storm as she tends her kitchen stove, preparing meals for those on watch. All too aware of the perils that could befall her loved ones, and strangers not yet met.

Storms, for all their ferocity, were just one challenge facing the lightkeeper's wife. The isolation was certainly another. But the biggest day-to-day challenge had to be feeding the family. Most of these early lights did not have power. Groceries were delivered infrequently and contained little in the line of convenience food.

Soups, chowders and stews would definitely have been on their menus, as would dishes "of the sea," for the hook and line or a forage for clams were often the only means they had of supplementing supplies brought in by boat. Dry goods that stored well, along with root vegetables for the cold cellar, were their staples.

Gifts of Giving

Mama was the last and 14th child, born in rural Quebec in 1911. Although her father was a well-to-do landowner, he expended very little on his family. To put things in perspective, he was one of the first in the community to have a motor vehicle. He housed it in the barn, polished it daily and covered it every night. He took it out once a week on Sunday mornings and drove to church. His wife and children walked. He was as miserly with food, and there never seemed to be enough to really fill the children's bellies.

Growing up, I remember how Mama made sure that food was plentiful in our house. Not only for us, however, but for every visitor and friend who came to our home. After introductions, Mama would take all newcomers straight to the kitchen and show them the fridge and cupboards with exhortations to not go hungry, to be sure to help themselves and to make themselves "at home."

Once, when Mama went to work at Papa's office, we had a housekeeper. I remember how mortified Mrs. Ferguson was to see a rather raggedy neighbourhood child gobble up bananas and apples day after day after day. Finally, with great indignation, she complained to my mother about "that child" who was stealing food and Mama looked her straight in the eye and said, "No, he's not stealing. That's what the food is there for. He's simply doing what I asked ... not to go hungry."

— Sandra Phinney of Yarmouth, Nova Scotia, who says lots of her kitchen memories have to do with growing up and lots of THOSE memories have to do with her mother, Marguerite Phinney.

Parsnip Patties

The lady who gave me this recipe said she made sure she had leftover parsnips from one meal to make these for noon the next day.

Boil parsnips until tender, mash with butter, salt and pepper and form into flat cakes. Lightly coat with flour. Fry to golden brown.

Sandra also wrote the following:

Remembering the Angel

The nuns didn't believe in Santa or his elves
but their faith in angels doubled
when the good doctor's wife
delivered a basket of presents to the convent
that crystal clear Christmas Eve.

Merciful goodness!
nine wee boxes blazoned with red satin ribbons
and a name tag for each sister signed with
discreetly scripted words
"for medicinal purposes."

She had often thought about these dear souls
they worked so diligently
to teach, to pray, to care for the poor, and
she'd yearned to be able to lighten their load
but wondered what to give these nuns
who had taken vows of poverty
and shied away from things material.

The day before Christmas she awoke
with a smile.

A visit to the bishop suggesting
the nuns should have a tonic
after all, she was the good doctor's wife
what better person to make arrangements
of course he agreed.

As each nun opened her box
eyes grew bigger and brighter
as first they took out vials of honey
then wonderful plump lemons followed by
tiny sacs of cloves
then they burst out with glee
as miniature bottles of brandy were discovered
at the very bottom of each box.

It became a tradition all those years ago
and lasted until the convent closed its doors
now it's part of our family folklore.

The angel's name was Marguerite.

SANDY'S EGGNOG PIE

We've known Sandy since she was a wee nipper from Alexandra, P.E.I., raptly watching my farrier husband shoe horses. Today Sandy is a busy veterinarian based in Yarmouth, N.S., with a family of her own. A woman who loves her kitchen, she presents us with a basket of homemade goodies each Christmas that we really enjoy. This year she gave us a recipe for a brand-new dessert in her repertoire.

| 1 ¼ cup | crumbs | 310 mL |
| 3 tbsp | square of margarine | 45 mL |

Mix together and pat into a spring form pan to form the base. Prepare filling

1 cup	eggnog	250 mL
1	package vanilla instant pudding	1
1–2 tbsp	rum	15–30 mL
1	large container of Cool Whip	1
	nutmeg	

Mix pudding mix with eggnog, rum and sprinkle of nutmeg. Beat 1 minute. Let stand 5 minutes, then fold in 2 cups of Cool Whip. Spoon over base. Chill 2–3 hours, then top with remaining Cool Whip, sprinkle with nutmeg. May be frozen.

SPIRIT OF THE SEASON PUNCH

This recipe was passed around at our motorcycle touring club meeting. Everyone raves about it and we all take pride in the fact that it uses Red Rose tea, a Maritime tradition.

4 cups	water	1 L
10	Red Rose tea bags	10
15 cups	apple juice or cider	3.5 L
1 cup	lemon juice	250 mL
2 cups	brown sugar	500 mL
12	whole allspice	12
12	whole cloves	12
4	cinnamon sticks, broken	4
2 ½ cups	red wine	625 mL

In a large saucepan, bring water to boil. Add tea bags, cover and brew 5 minutes. Remove tea bags. Stir in juices, sugar and spices. Simmer, stirring occasionally, 10 minutes. Remove spices; stir in wine and heat through. Serve warm, garnished with apple slices.

DECEMBER 14 — Called my mom and dad tonight, to see how they are. Ontario got hit by a major storm, and even though bad weather usually misses their "close to Niagara" town I always have to check. Dad, said Mom, is busy making pork pies. Now in my family the old-fashioned English pork pie is as much a part of Christmas as turkey is in most Maritime households. It is the one thing that Dad held over from his days operating a bakery.

Another thing that was different at our table was the stuffing in the bird. My mom never, ever used sage. She says it used to make my great-grandfather ill, so it was always drummed into the family not to use it. Today I find sage overpowering and unsettling to my tummy.

Years ago Mom would stuff the bird with a sausage stuffing made with stale bread, chopped onion, a little thyme or marjoram, salt and pepper and, of course, well-cooked, crumbled sausage meat. These days, at 80-something, if she is doing a chicken or a turkey breast she pops an apple and onion inside and cooks the stuffing on the side. But not at Christmas. Joan, a family friend, makes up stuffing and sends it, along with a chicken from their farm and all of the Christmas dinner fixin's, to my parents. Everything is frozen and comes with instructions on how to get it ready. What a wonderful, considerate gift to give to seniors!

Christmas Cheer Cake

When we first moved to Sherwood, P.E.I., we rented an apartment across the road from Jean Kimpinski. She was a great friend to me in those early days in a new neighbour-hood. We spent hours in her kitchen, many of them taken up with Jean trying to teach me how to make bread. Became fairly proficient, but I have to honestly say it always seems too much work for something that the menfolk would scoff down in one sitting, so I don't do it often. These days I opt for my breadmaker.

Our first Christmas as buddies we decided to make a big batch of fruitcake for our own use and to give to friends as Christmas gifts. On the appointed day, we began. The recipe called for the candied fruit and nuts to soak in a little rum for a short time. In they went, into a huge pot, along with the liquor. Not much later the power went out! Oh well, we shrugged, the fruit will be okay.

The power was out for several days, due to a severe winter storm. Not only could we not cook, we were faced with keeping warm and occupying the kids. Besides, the roads were impassa-ble and getting to Jean's house would have been a foolhardy thing to attempt. Jean, being a thrifty soul, kept her eye on the fruit. No way she was going to waste it. This was a very significant invest-ment of cash for both of us! As time went by the fruit began to look a bit "dried out" so Jean decided to moisten it with a little more rum. Then a little more. And a little more after that.

As soon as the power came on I rushed right over and we set to completing our cake-making marathon. Ended up with more cakes than anticipated — that darn fruit had swelled up far more than usual! It was okay, though; we felt justly rewarded for our efforts. Each loaf was lovingly wrapped; Jean said it was best if left to cure for a week or two before slicing. And we mailed it off to family and friends, rather proud of our homemade Christmas gifts.

Finally the day came when we sliced into the cake ourselves, ready to sample our masterpiece. I swear, an hour later I was as drunk as a skunk. There was so much rum (and I later found out, brandy, because she ran out of rum) that one slice could give you a buzz, two the giggles and three … well, that cake gave many people a very happy Christmas feeling, at least for a few hours. The downside was the cost — two bottles of rum and a half bottle of brandy, compared with the planned cup or so of rum and the reportings of severe headaches among recipients who had overindulged in what my grandmother called, "that lovely moist cake." The recipe for that cake has been lost but the following, which I made with my friend Helen for many years, can be made with a "touch of the rum."

TRADITIONAL FRUITCAKE

This delicious recipe for fruitcake comes from friends in Pictou County. If you like a little touch of the "good stuff" drain the juice from the pineapple, measure it and replace it with the same amount of rum or brandy. Or you can sprinkle your choice over the fruit the day before you begin. Makes the cake moister, and delicious.

½ lb	mixed peel	225 g
3 lbs	sultana	1.5 kg
2 lbs	seeded raisins	900 g
1 lb	dates	450 g
1 lb	butter	450 g
3 cups	brown sugar	750 mL
1 tsp	soda	5 mL
1 lb + 1 cup	flour	450 g + 250 mL
2 tsp	vanilla extract	10 mL
1 dozen	eggs	1 dozen
½ lb	walnuts	225 g
2 lbs	cherries (red and green)	900 g
½ lb	citron peel	225 g
1 cup	crushed pineapple	250 mL
3	packages, cut candied pineapple	3
2 tsp	lemon extract	10 mL
2 tsp	almond extract	10 mL

Tip

To prevent dried fruits in cake batter from sinking to the bottom of the pan dust them with flour, or shake fruit and flour together in a bag until coated. If prunes or apricots are too dry, soak them in strong tea to plump.

Put 1 pound of flour on fruit. To the 1 cup flour add soda and 2 tablespoon salt. Add to creamed butter, sugar and eggs, mix with floured fruit. Grease tins and line with heavy brown paper, greased. Bake in slow oven for 3 hours.

SUGARPLUM BREAD

With all of the sweets and rich foods around this season, I always like to have a fruit bread as a lighter offering. For Christmas I spread with a vanilla glaze and decorate with candied red and green cherries and almonds or pine nuts. The rest of the year I dust the loaves with icing sugar.

— JK. A delicious from-scratch treat from New Brunswick.

1 tsp	sugar	5 mL
1 cup	warm water	250 mL
2	packages active dry yeast	2
½ cup	sugar	125 mL
½ cup	butter or margarine, melted	125 mL
2 tsp	salt	10 mL
1 tsp	grated lemon rind	5 mL
6 cups	all-purpose flour	1.5 L
4	eggs	4
1 cup	raisins	250 mL
¾ cup	chopped mixed candied fruit	175 mL
⅓ cup	pine nuts or slivered almonds	80 mL
	vanilla glaze or icing sugar (optional)	

Dissolve 1 teaspoon sugar in warm water in large mixing bowl. Sprinkle in yeast. Let stand 10 minutes, then stir well. Add ½ cup sugar, melted butter, salt, lemon rind and 2 cups flour. Beat for 2 minutes at medium speed of electric mixer. Add 2 cups more flour and eggs; beat 3 minutes. Stir in almost all remaining flour, using enough to make soft dough; knead dough on floured board until smooth and elastic, about 8 minutes. Place in lightly greased bowl. Cover with greased waxed paper and tea towel. Let rise in warm place (75–85°F) until doubled in volume, about 2 hours.

Punch down. Turn out on lightly floured board and knead in raisins, candied fruit and nuts. Shape into 2 round loaves. Place each in a well-greased 9-inch round cake pan. Cover with tea towel and let rise in warm place until doubled, 1–1 ½ hours. Bake at 350°F for 45–55 minutes. Remove from pans immediately. Cool on wire racks. To serve: spread with vanilla glaze or dust with icing sugar if desired. Makes 2 loaves.

BANBURY TEAS

Since I was born near Banbury in England (yes, from the old nursery rhyme "Ride a cock horse to Banbury Cross") and went to school near the famous monument, and since my mom and dad operated a bakery, it is natural that these filled pastries are part of my repertoire. One change I often make is to Canadianize them by replacing the traditional raisins with dried cranberries. You can make them as covered tarts, or as follows:

1 cup	raisins or dried cranberries or a combination	250 mL
1 cup	sugar	250 mL
1	egg, beaten	1
1 tbsp	butter, melted	15 mL
3 tbsp	fine bread crumbs	45 mL

juice and grated rind of one lemon

pastry (equivalent to amount for a one-crust pie)

Combine all but pastry. Roll out thin pastry (¹/8 inch) and cut into 10 3-inch squares. Divide filling among squares. Fold each in half to make a triangle, sealing edges by brushing with water and crimping. Cut a small "X" in top of each. Bake at 350°F until browned, about 20 minutes. If using puff pastry, follow recommended cooking method.

BANGBELLY

Bangbelly is actually a traditional Christmas Eve dish in Newfoundland, but so many "Capers" come from "The Rock" that it has migrated to Cape Breton.

3 cups	cooked rice	750 mL
1 cup	flour	250 mL
1 cup	molasses	250 mL
2 cups	raisins	500 mL
1 ¼ cups	salt pork, cubed	300 mL
1 ½ tsp	baking soda	7.5 mL
1 tsp	baking powder	5 mL
1 tsp	cinnamon	5 mL
½ tsp	allspice	2.5 mL
¼ tsp	cloves	1 mL
¼ tsp	mixed spice	1 mL

Allow rice to cool, add salt pork and molasses. Sift together flour and spices. Add raisins, mix all ingredients together. Pour into 9 x 9-inch greased pans. Bake at 350°F for 1 ¼ hours.

OYSTER STEW

Serves 4

1 pt	oysters (with liquor)	475 mL
¼ cup	butter	50 mL
1 cup	light cream, scalded	250 mL
3 cups	milk, scalded	750 mL
	pepper	
½ tsp	salt	2.5 mL
½ tsp	paprika	2.5 mL

Pick over oysters; cook in butter and oyster liquor until edges curl. Add cream and milk. Heat to boiling and season. Serve at once with crackers.

"Ho, Ho, Ho!"

One Christmas Eve I, an only child, was playing in a room that combined kitchen and living room — at least in my mind. There was a fire roaring in the big open stone fireplace and the grown-ups were sitting at the table, playing cards. The stockings were hanging from the mantel, a small table-top tree graced a sideboard and the scent of Christmas was in the air. I was supposed to be in bed, but as usual had cajoled another few minutes to play.

Suddenly there was a clatter outside and a loud "Ho, ho, ho!"

"Oh," my mother cried from the pantry. "He's early!"

"Quick," called another adult, probably my dad, "he mustn't see Julie or he'll pass by."

Hands gathered me up and popped me under the table, with the admonition to stay silent and to hide. The tablecloth was long and feet and knees surrounded me on all sides. A meek little child, I sat on the cold stone floor, knees pulled up to my chin, and scarcely dared breath.

Clomp, clomp, clomp, footsteps came in the door. "Ho! Ho! With that fire roaring in the hearth I had to come in the hard way," I heard a booming, laughter-filled voice say. "The weather isn't the best, so we had to get a good start."

There was much rustling, an offer of refreshments, then clomp, clomp, the door closed and he was gone.

I was hustled off to bed, but not without a glance at the mantel, which confirmed that the stockings had been filled and a few gifts added to those on the sideboard. I had glimpsed black leather boots, high, with red trouser legs tucked inside. Those stockings, filled to the brim, confirmed it: I had seen him!

I've heard it said that a bowl of pipin' hot oyster stew formed a traditional Christmas Eve supper, a tradition carried to the Maritimes by English settlers. In my experience, those oysters were just as likely to be brought up from a keg in the cellar and enjoyed on the half shell. Regardless, oysters are a part of Maritime tradition.

CHRISTMAS FRUIT SALAD WITH KIRSCH

Serves 6–8

"This is a standby for dinner, a must have in your repertoire."

— Karen Murray, Prince Edward Island

KIRSCH SYRUP:

¼ cup	water	50 mL
¼ cup	sugar	50 mL
¼ cup	Kirsch (white cherry liqueur)	50 mL
1 tbsp	lemon juice	15 mL
1 tsp	grated lemon rind	5 mL

In a saucepan, combine water and sugar; bring to a boil and boil uncovered for 3 minutes. Remove from heat. Stir in kirsch, lemon juice and rind. Cool.

FRUIT SALAD:

1 cup	mandarin orange segments	250 mL
1 cup	pineapple chunks (fresh is best, canned will do)	250 mL

1	Delicious apple, peeled and diced	1
1	banana, sliced	1
1 cup	red grapes, seeded and halved	250 mL
2	kiwi fruit, peeled and sliced	2
6	maraschino cherries, quartered	6

Combine fruit, pour syrup over. Chill an hour before serving. Nice served in stemmed glasses, with buttery cookies or white Christmas cake.

Julie's Trifle

Christmas is not Christmas in our household unless there is a trifle on the table. There are as many variations as people; I remember my Aunt Jean made a rich, flavourful masterpiece topped with whipped cream, shaved chocolate and cherries — totally decadent. My trifle is much lighter, actually a lovely Boxing Day dessert after the overeating that seems to be a mandatory part of Christmas dinner. Since my husband is diabetic, but loves trifle, I make this version especially for him. Just drop the sugar-free versions of ingredients if you don't have those concerns.

Very showy when made in a straight-sided glass bowl. Quantities depend on the size of the bowl and the number to be served. Use any combination of fruit and flavours of Jell-O. We like the red and green for Christmas. Plan at least a day to make this dessert, to allow for setting times for layers.

All you need: ladyfingers, pound cake or sponge cake left out to go stale; sugar-free strawberry jam; 1 can orange segments packed in their own juice, no sugar added, drained; sliced strawberries (if frozen thaw and drain well); 1 package sugar-free lime Jell-O; 1 package sugar-free strawberry Jell-O; custard made with Bird's Custard Powder (I cut the sugar in half); cake decorations.

Spread jam on stale cake, place pieces in bottom of glass bowl. Sprinkle orange segments over cake. Make lime Jell-O, cool, gently pour over cake and orange segments. Place in refrigerator. When set repeat with strawberries and strawberry Jell-O. When firmly set, make up custard, cool and add for final layer. Decorate with sliced almonds, red sparkles and silver balls. Serve cold.

HOT SPICED CRANBERRY PUNCH

Cranberries are our merry berries, always available at happy holiday times. I first had this at a Christmas party where it simmered on a wood stove. It's a modern version of an old favourite. This is a little sweet for my taste, so I cut the sugar back. Judge by your taste whether you prefer sweet or tart.

4 cups	cranberry juice	1 L
4 cups	apple cider	1 L
1/4 cup	brown sugar	50 mL
2	cinnamon sticks	2
1 tsp	whole allspice	5 mL
1/2 tsp	whole cloves	2.5 mL
1	lemon thinly sliced (optional)	1
	a few whole cranberries (optional)	

Combine all ingredients in a large saucepan. Simmer 15 to 20 minutes. Strain. Serve hot in punch cups. Float fresh lemon slices and cranberries on top, if desired.

LUNENBURG DUFF

"This Christmas pudding utilizes the ingredients that were available in early days, but has been revamped a little for today. In days past, spices would have been ground in the kitchen."

—Helen Grant

1 ½ cups	brown sugar, packed	375 mL
2 tbsp	shortening	30 mL
3	eggs	3
1 cup	sour cream	250 mL
1 cup	milk	250 mL
½ cup	molasses	125 mL
4 cups	flour	1 L
2 tsp	baking soda	10 mL
1 tsp	cream of tartar	5 mL
1 tsp	cinnamon	5 mL
1 tsp	nutmeg	5 mL
¼ tsp	ground cloves	1 mL
	raisins, candied peel and nuts to suit your taste	

Combine all ingredients, steam 3 hours. Serve warm with a lemon or brandy sauce, and whipped cream.

PICKLED HERRING

Serves 6

When immigrants from Europe came to this country they brought many traditions with them. One, still observed, is the eating of herring on New Year's Eve — believed to bring good luck in the coming year. Our family made a large crock in the old days, because the family was larger. I've reduced the amounts.

— CBM

8	medium-sized herring, cleaned	8
¼ cup	salt	50 mL
1 qt	water	950 mL
1	sliced onion	1
¼	sliced lemon	¼
1 tsp	peppercorns	5 mL
¼ tsp	allspice	1 mL
1 pt	vinegar	500 mL
1 pt	water	500 mL
6	whole cloves	6

Make a brine with 1 quart water and the salt. Soak herring in this solution for half an hour, then remove and wipe dry. Place single layer of herring in a crock, top with layer of onion, lemon and spices. Repeat. Cover with vinegar and water, set crock in kettle of cold water. Bring water to boil, let mixture cook until meat comes away from bone. The herring is ready to use when cold. Keep in cool place.

Holiday Leftovers

Okay, so after the holidays you have all those leftovers to contend with. The following recipes are just a few suggestions for what to do.

CLEANUP DAY POTATOES

Serves 4

2 cups	leftover mashed potatoes	500 mL
1	egg, separated	1
1 cup	leftover cooked vegetables	250 mL
4	eggs	4
4 tbsp	milk or cream	60 mL
4 tbsp	grated cheese	60 mL

Thoroughly mix potatoes with yolk of 1 egg. Form into 4 "nests" on greased pie plate or baking sheet; brush each with slightly beaten egg white, place 1/4 cup vegetables in each. Place in preheated 375°F oven for 15 minutes; remove and add 1 tbsp milk to each. Break 1 egg into each, top with 1 tbsp grated cheese and return to oven for 10–15 minutes until eggs are set and cheese melted.

Turkey

Sitting in the kitchen, pickin' at the chicken …" Well, in this case, the turkey. After a fine traditional turkey dinner, with the dishes "done up," the lady of the house finally sat herself down at the table, turkey carcass in front of her. Weary feet glad of a respite. It was relaxing work. The pleasant hum of the menfolk talking and the children laughing form a backdrop that emphasizes the feeling of satisfaction that comes from nurturing one's family with a good home-cooked meal.

The turkey platter is flanked by a big soup pot to one side and a china bowl on the other. Bones and scraps go in the pot, meat into the bowl.

At my friend Helen's home, the soup ranks high in importance. Her daughter Anita, away at school on the other side of the nation, had already called: "Make me some soup, Mom. I'll be home in six weeks."

Anita's Turkey Soup

"Make so it's thick. It has to be thick. I hate thin soup. Cook until it's cooked, and that's all," mutters Helen when I ask her formula. "I find the biggest mistake people make is they try to water soup down too much. Need the flavour in the broth to have a decent soup and must have a bit of fat in it. Make sure to cook cabbage long enough. If refrigerated, when you spoon it out it's thick — almost congeals. Then it's done right."

All you need: juice from the turkey (gel in fridge, remove fat); stock, made by boiling carcass (bones), draining and skimming off fat; 1/2 cup rice; soup mix (the mix of dried pasta and grains or 1 cup of barley or split peas); carrots; onion; turnip; red cabbage (small head, cut finely); turkey meat, picked off bone; potatoes; salt and pepper to taste.

Chop all vegetables. Combine all in large soup pot and simmer for several hours. All Potatoes and meat go in last. Cook until it's thick.

Mrs. Mac

Her name was Martha MacFarlane. Since it wasn't proper to call adults, except for relatives, by their first name, we kids called her "Mrs. Mac."

Whenever it's cold outside and the wind is blowing snow against my window I think of Mrs. Mac. She didn't like winter, either. Often when I cuddled on her knee, she told me about crossing the ocean in January, from England; how the ship would heave with every wave that hit the deck and turned to ice.

Mrs. Mac was a war bride. I didn't know what a warbride was, but I knew that if Mrs. Mac was one it had to be something good. Mrs. Mac was a midwife too. I didn't know what a midwife was either, but again, if Mrs. Mac was one … I knew she was some kind of very special wife.

The only complaint Mrs. Mac ever had was about the weather — the cold. But there was nothing cold about her. She had the warmest heart of any person I have ever known. Mrs. Mac brought warm knitted mittens and socks at Christmas, and whenever a baby was born, Mrs. Mac was there.

On a bitter cold night in January 1930, Mrs. Mac and the doctor hovered by the mother's bedside. The labour was long and difficult. When the child was born, both mother and infant were very weak. It was exactly 6 a.m. Mrs. Mac went to the window while the doctor examined the baby. She blew a peephole in the frosty pane with her warm breath.

"It's the dawning of a new year," she smiled as she looked out of the window. "A new decade. What a wonderful day for a child to be born."

The doctor muttered, "It's not a good day for anyone to be born, with economic depression all around us and rumours of war."

The mother didn't hear, but Mrs. Mac did. She took the infant from the doctor, wrapped it tightly in a blanket and laid it gently beside its sleeping mother. "I'll take over now," Mrs. Mac told the doctor, and there was no mistaking the annoyance in her voice as she ushered him out into the hall and opened the front door so he could leave.

A gush of cold air filled the house. "It's not likely the child will live through the night," the doctor told her. "Better to get her to a hospital. Her heartbeat is weak and she has pneumonia."

"Will they save her in the hospital?" Mrs. Mac asked. "No!" the doctor said. "But it would be easier on the parents."

"If the child is going to die, then she'll die at home," said Mrs. Mac.

She walked into the bedroom, lifted the infant from the bed and took her into the kitchen, while the father followed behind. "Stoke up the stove with some coal!" Mrs. Mac ordered. Then she placed the infant in a basket and put it near the open oven door, fashioning a tent over it with some blankets. All night Mrs. Mac sat inside the tent with the child, putting plasters of mustard on the infant's chest.

Around dawn the next morning, the phlegm that was congesting the baby's lungs expelled itself — Mrs. Mac told me it come out of the infant's mouth by the yard. When the doctor arrived later that morning, the infant's heartbeat was stronger, its lungs clear. And on this New Year's Day that child will be celebrating her 64th birthday.

So, Mrs. Mac, wherever you are, I want to thank you once again for saving my life. And I want you to know that you were right: no matter what's going on in the world — depressions, wars or rumours of war — it is a wonderful day when a child is born. Happy New Year, everyone."

—Evie Davidson, broadcast on "Island Morning," December 29, 1993

...

That memory of a dear friend who departed this life far too early stirred another for me. A memory of my husband's grandfather telling us of the tiny babies his daughter bore, so tiny that he bundled them up, put them in shoeboxes and placed them on the open door of the wood stove in their farm kitchen, nurturing them, keeping them warm.

Is it any wonder that I firmly believe the kitchen is the most important room in the house?

Sources

Periodicals:

Chatelaine, Toronto, Ontario, August 1978
Farmer's Magazine: devoted to the interests of
Agriculture in Ontario, Quebec and the Maritimes,
published in Toronto, Ontario, January 1940
The Moncton Times & Transcript
Yarmouth Herald
Yarmouth Telegram
Yarmouth Tribune

Books:

A Treasury of Nova Scotia Heirloom Recipes, Florence
M. Hilchey, Nova Scotia Department of Agriculture
and Marketing, 1967
The Atlantic Advocate's Holiday Book, Brunswick
Press Ltd., Fredericton, N.B., 1961
Back to Basics, Nova Scotia Department of
Agriculture and Marketing, undated
Domestic Life in Nineteenth Century Canada, Una
Abrahamson, Burns and MacEachern Limited,
Toronto, 1966
Down Memory Lane, Maplewood Manor Residents
and Senior Citizens of West Prince, P.E.I.
Favourite Recipes from Old New Brunswick Kitchens,
Mildred Trueman, published by Nimbus
Publishing, Halifax
Four Dozen Low Cost High Protein Egg Dishes,
Canadian Egg Marketing Agency
Four Years with the Demon Rum by Clifford Rose,
Acadiensis Press, Fredericton, N.B., 1980
From the Kitchens of Kings Landing, Kings Landing
Historical Settlement, Prince William, N.B.
*God Bless Our Home: Domestic Life in Nineteenth
Century Canada,* Una Abrahamson
*High Crest Enterprises Ltd. —10th Anniversary
Cookbook,* Nova Scotia, 1991
Home Management, unknown, approximately 1935
In New Brunswick We'll Find It, Lowell Thomas and
Rex Barton, D. Appleton-Century Company,
New York-London, 1939

*Ladies Auxiliary to the Royal Canadian Legion
Cookbook,* Helen Grant Collection
Mad About Cheddar, Angela Clubb, Clarke Irwin
(1983) Inc., Toronto, 1983
My Grandfather's Cape Breton, by Clive Doucet,
McGraw-Hill Ryerson Limited,
*Off Shore Islands of Nova Scotia and New
Brunswick,* Allison Mitcham, Lancelot Press,
Hantsport, N.S., 1984
Old Times Town and Country by "Bessie," Murray
River, P.E.I.
Perkins' Hearth Cookbook, Zion Guild, Zion United
Church, Liverpool, N.S.
People and Stuff, R.C. Montgomery, P.E.I.
Recipes From Cape Breton, First United Church
Afternoon Guild, Sydney, N.S., undated
Solidarity Cookbook Atlantic Women's Committee,
undated
*Tastes of the Tantramar: Recipes & Remedies from our
Yorkshire Roots,* Yorkshire, Tantramar Heritage Trust,
2000
*The History of the Lowbush Blueberry Industry in
Nova Scotia 1880–1950,* Nova Scotia Department of
Agriculture and Marketing, Gordon Kinsman,
Oct. 1986
Tide's Table Maritime Cooking from Inn on the Cove,
Goose Lane Editions, Fredericton, N.B.
The Modern Cookbook for New Brunswick, various
Women's Hospital Aids of New Brunswick and
L'Assomption Society of Moncton, 1920
The New Cook Book, by The Ladies of Toronto and
Other Cities and Towns, The Montreal News
Company, 1905
The New Household Manual, R. Morrow, Saint John,
N. B., 1901
*Whispers from the Past: Selections from the Writings
of New Brunswick Women,* Elizabeth W. McGaran,
Goose Lane Editions, Fredericton, N.B.

Papers, Pamphlets and etc:
Blue Ribbon Mayonnaise leaflet
Canadian Cuisine, 1966
Canadian Fish Recipes, Canada Department of
    Fisheries
Harrison Papers, Manuscript, Public Archives of
    Nova Scotia
Hilda Robinson Collection, Debbie Gamble-
    Arsenault
Maple Leaf Country Kitchen Cookbook
Robin Hood Baking Festival Recipe Book
The Butter Book, Dairy Farmers of Canada
To Potatoes with Love, P.E.I. Potato Marketing Board

Special thanks to:
Lisa Arsenault, Tignish, P.E.I.
Michelle Breker-Klassen, Bedford, N.S.
Sandi Clark, Yarmouth, N.S.
Stefan and Sharlene Czapalay, Halifax, N.S.
Debbie Gamble-Arsenault, Alexandra, P.E.I.
Helen Grant, Three Brooks, N.S.
Valerie Kidney, New Brunswick Tourism
Susan MacDonald-Boyce, Moncton, N.B.
Percy Mallet, New Brunswick Tourism
Gloria Matheson, Winsloe RR, P.E.I.
Sandra Phinney, Yarmouth, N.S.
Beth Smith, Indian River, P.E.I.

The staff and volunteers at:
Department of Education, Nova Scotia
Fisheries Museum of the Atlantic, Lunenburg, N.S.
Harris' Quick-n'-Tasty, Yarmouth, N.S.
Nova Scotia Dept of Fisheries and Aquaculture
Nova Scotia Museums
Public Archives of Nova Scotia
Public Archives of Prince Edward Island
Red Cap Restaurant and Motel, Middle West
Pubnico, Yarmouth Co., N.S.
Ross Farm Museum, New Ross, N.S.
Ross-Thomson House, Shelburn, N.S.
Shelburne Historical Society
The Acadian Museum, Middle West Pubnico,
    Yarmouth Co., N.S.
Tourism New Brunswick

Index

About the Author

*A*uthor of 16 books — many of them focusing on the Maritimes, their people, traditions, places and cuisine — Julie Watson has also published hundreds of articles in magazines around the globe. Her primary focus is food, travel, and entrepreneurship. In that vein she also acts as a consultant for the culinary, hospitality and seafood industries. Julie lives in Winsloe, Prince Edward Island with her husband Jack and their dog Tipsy. She frequently teams with her son John, a photographer, to capture the best of the Island in both visual and written mediums.

Simple Pleasures